Property, Women and Politics

Property, Women and Politics

Subjects or Objects?

Donna Dickenson

RUTGERS UNIVERSITY PRESS
NEW BRUNSWICK, NEW JERSEY

First published in Great Britain 1997
by Polity Press in association with Blackwell Publishers Ltd.

First published in the United States 1997
by Rutgers University Press, New Brunswick, New Jersey

Library of Congress Cataloging-in-Publication Data

Dickenson, Donna.
    Property, women, and politics : subjects or objects? / Donna Dickenson.
        p.   cm.
    Includes bibliographical references (p.   ) and index.
    ISBN 0-8135-2457-1 (cloth). — ISBN 0-8135-2458-X (paper).
    1. Women—Social conditions.   2. Women—Legal status, laws, etc.
3. Women—Economic conditions.   4. Women's rights.   I. Title.
HO1206.D5   1997
305.42—dc21   97-21504
                                                                                CIP

Printed in Great Britain

Contents

Acknowledgements

Time is a commodity which few women possess in great quantity, and I am particularly grateful to colleagues and friends who gave me so much of theirs. Fiona Williams, Professor of Social Policy at Leeds University, provided detailed comments and cheering support on my introduction and first chapter. I am indebted to Inez Sutton of Ruskin College, Oxford, for suggesting the model of the *ketuba*, which I draw on in chapter 7. Renée Hirschon, Jackie Waldron and Shirley Ardener of the Centre for Cross-Cultural Research on Women, Queen Elizabeth House, Oxford, all helped to flesh out my skeletal knowledge of anthropology. Morwenna Griffiths of the University of Nottingham provided invaluable assistance with chapter 1, introducing it to two anonymous critical readers who helped to sharpen the argument. Susan Easton, Senior Lecturer in Law at Brunel University, was a great help in discussing Hegel in connection with chapter 4. Dr Susan Bewley, Director of Obstetrics at St Thomas's Hospital, London, was instrumental in helping me to formulate key ideas about property in labour and childbirth, used in chapter 7. The members of the Oxford seminar on feminist theory which met in spring 1995 under the leadership of Miranda Fricker and Sabina Lovibond introduced me to new areas of thought, particularly in the area of female subjectivity. Frances Kamm, Gillian Lockwood, and other attenders at the Oxford–Mt Sinai conferences of 1994 and 1996 helped to sharpen my interest in and arguments about gamete donation and abortion. And my friend of thirty years' standing, Mary Katzenstein of the Department of Government at Cornell University, first put questions about women, divorce and property into my mind ten years ago.

Not to succumb to male–female dualism, I also want to thank Martin

Bernal of Cornell for his clear insights into women in Athens, and Tony
McGrew of the Department of Politics at the Open University for many
helpful citations on women and development which I found greatly
beneficial for chapter 5. My thanks also to Alan Ryan, who first awakened
my interest in property during our doctoral supervision sessions, which
coincided with the publication of his own two books on the subject. And
of course I could say that I owe it all to Professor David Held, of the Open
University, who is also my editor at Polity Press. Despite my two-year
delay in replying to his invitation to write this book – his letter had got
lost in the post when I moved house – he persisted in assuring me that the
project remained relevant and worthwhile. The comments by Susan
James, acting as a anonymous reader at Polity, were also very encouraging during some of the many doubt-inducing stages of the writing.

Finally, my thanks and love to Chris, Anders, Kate, Pip and Rob – those
'close to home', in Christine Delphy's phrase.

An earlier, abridged version of chapter 1 appears as 'Property,
particularism and moral persons' in Morwenna Griffiths and Margaret
Whitford (eds), *Women Review Philosophy: New Writing by Women in
Philosophy* (Nottingham: University of Nottingham Education Press,
1996). The brief discussion about citizenship and military participation in
chapter 2 is abridged from my chapter on 'Counting women in: redefining democratic politics' in Anthony McGrew (ed.), *The Transformation of
Democracy? Globalization and the Post-Westphalian World Order* (Cambridge: Polity Press, 1997). Parts of chapter 3 appeared in a reading guide
to Carole Pateman's *The Sexual Contract*; the guide was published by the
Open University in 1988 as block 7 of course D308, 'Democratic government and politics'. Extracts from Hegel's *Philosophy of Right* appear in
chapter 4. These are taken from the translation by T. M. Knox, first
published by Clarendon Press, 1952, then as an Oxford University Press
paperback 1967. These are reprinted by kind permission of Oxford
University Press. The section of chapter 7 on gamete donation and
ownership of body parts was published in the *Journal of Medical Ethics*
23:2 (April 1997) under the title 'Procuring gametes for research and
therapy: the argument for unisex altruism'.

Introduction

Why the title *Property, Women and Politics: Subjects or Objects?* The subtitle clearly harkens back to one of Simone de Beauvoir's dualisms, the one which I think has best withstood the test of time and the interrogation of contemporary feminist writers who justifiably suspect all dualisms.[1] In *The Second Sex* Beauvoir writes,

> Now what marks the specificity of woman's situation is that while she, like any other human being, is an autonomous freedom, she discovers and chooses herself in a world where men force her to assume herself as the Other: they claim to fix her as an object and to doom her to immanence, since her transcendence is to be perpetually transcended by another essential and sovereign consciousness.[2]

The notion of woman as object has worked its way into popular thought: the outcry against women as mere sexual objects in advertising, for example, uses Beauvoir's terminology. But in this book I want to do something different from what prevails in popular speech at the end of the century, something more akin to what Beauvoir originally had in mind, I think.

In *The Second Sex* Beauvoir offers three uses of the subject/object distinction. First, there is the 'despotic subject', who views others as an object: the position corresponding to what Beauvoir calls 'male sovereignty'. In this dualistic formulation, the sovereign existence of a subject requires the presence of an object. To apply this split to property-holding, men's status as property-holders would require the objectification or commodification of women: as sexual objects in pornography, for example, or as wives who could be 'owned' (communally or privately).

As the legal theorist Carol Rose points out, there has been far more feminist interest in women as objects of property than as its subjects.[3] Yet this is implicitly to accept the sovereignty of the male despotic subject, I think. Why should feminists be content to accept that women can have no other relation to property than as its *objects*? In political theory and jurisprudence, property is generally linked to being a *subject*. Through gaining property, or more often through developing the sorts of virtues associated with careful husbandry – and I use the gendered term advisedly – individuals are frequently said to become moral and political agents.

Both nineteenth-century and second-wave feminists made good polemical use of the notion of women as objects, and it was strategically important that they did. But ultimately, I think, viewing women's relationship to property purely in the passive leads down a political and theoretical cul-de-sac. If we are to regard women as anything other than eternal victims, and property as something which can help women as well as harm them, we need to go beyond the simplistic categorization of women as mere objects of property-holding. And we *will* want to view property-holding as something which can help as well as harm women if we are interested in enhancing women's status as subjects, I shall argue. This is not to say that cases in which women really *are* objects will be ignored in this book; only that I do not want to prejudge the case by assuming that the relationship will necessarily be that simple. This is where we as feminists have gone wrong: in assuming too readily that women *are* objects of property, and that this is the only sort of relationship to property which we *can* have. Although most canonical theories of property are guilty of excluding the experience and condition of women, thereby ruling out full subjecthood for them, I will argue that the relationship between holding property and becoming a subject is not sex-specific.

However, I do not deny that women and their services *have* sometimes been regarded as (at least potentially) men's property. Honoré's classic list of entitlements and duties generated by ownership suggests so, when applied to women.[4] The owner of object X has (1) a right to its possession; (2) a right to its use; (3) a right to its management, that is, determining the way in which others can use it; (4) a right to the income that can be derived from its use by others; (5) a right to its capital value; (6) a right to security against its being taken by others; (7) a right to transmit it to others by gift or bequest; (8) a permanent right to these other rights, without any limit or term; (9) a duty to refrain from using X in a way that harms others, or liability for harm caused by X. All these terms have been satisfied in one legal system or another by men's rights in marriage. Right 1 entails a right to the wife's company and right 2 to conjugal rights; these, along with rights 3, 4, 6, 8, and 9, were all afforded to husbands under the doctrine of coverture, which will be detailed in chapter 3. Right 5 implies wife sale, not part of coverture, but formerly an established folk custom in rural England.[5] Right 7 is well known in many African cultures, which expect a widow to marry a husband's brother, and was also extant in ancient Athens. Women can certainly be property by Honoré's criteria, I agree, although I am also sympathetic to Catharine MacKinnon's cynicism:

> Women's sexuality is, socially, a thing to be stolen, sold, bought, bartered, or exchanged by others. But women never own or possess it, and men never treat it, in law or in life, with the solicitude with which they treat property. To be property would be an improvement.[6]

Clearly being an object excludes being a subject, an active agent, a full person. As the contemporary French feminist philosopher Michèle le Dœuff writes, 'To be only when one belongs to someone is not to be, but to have the status of a perceptible quality, like sweetness according to Plato: "To be sweet, but sweet to no one, is impossible." '[7] But if women are not always mere objects, yet are not full subjects either, what sort of subjects can they be? Beauvoir's second type of subject, the 'extinguished' subject, offers a grim answer. Women who are extinguished subjects are completely lost in identification with men; when they speak of women, it is as 'they' rather than 'we'. Despite my long fascination with George Sand, for example, I would class her as one of these when she writes,

> With very few exceptions, I do not long endure the company of women. Not that I feel them inferior to me in intelligence: I consume so few of them in the habitual commerce of my life, that everyone has more of them around than I. But women, generally speaking, are nervous, anxious beings who, my resistance notwithstanding, communicate their eternal disquiet to me apropos of everything. I begin by listening to them with regret, then I let myself be caught up in a natural interest for what they are saying, only to perceive that there was really nothing to get worked up about in their puerile agitations . . . I thus like men better than women, and I say so without malice.[8]

One reason why women might become 'extinguished subjects' again has to do with property. As Beauvoir writes, 'Woman does not claim the status of subject because she lacks the concrete means to do so.'[9] By 'concrete means' Beauvoir intends property, but not just property: she means all sorts of specific disabilities and barriers – of political or civil rights, of sufficient training, even of the right kind of clothes for activity rather than passive decorum.

To 'claim the status of subject' might entail developing the sort of mutual consciousness which typifies Beauvoir's third class of subjects, 'minority subjects'. Regarded as 'other' by dominant subjects of the first type, minority subjects none the less have enough sense of common identity to say 'we' of themselves rather than 'they', as extinguished subjects do. But can women be 'minority subjects'? After all, we are not a minority. If so, how can we claim this third sort of subjecthood, which relies neither on oppressing others nor on extinguishing the sense of self?

Beauvoir famously asserts that one *becomes* either a woman or a subject, rather than being *born* one. Successors to Beauvoir have problematized the entire category of subject, as does Catharine MacKinnon when she writes: 'Having been objectified as sexual beings while stigmatized as ruled by subjective passions, women reject the distinction between knowing subject and known object.'[10] Other sources of feminist disquiet with the notion of a unified subject have included postmodernist and deconstructionist writing, together with critique from black and lesbian feminists. While acknowledging the theoretical productivity and importance of this critique in chapter 6, I nevertheless maintain the practical value and philosophical possibility of being a subject, together with the epistemological openness of woman as subject: 'feminism . . . looks to the woman as the object of study in order to become the subject of herself.'[11]

In *Property, Women and Politics: Subjects or Objects?* I want to suggest that property is not peripheral but central to women's subjectivity. I shall be using property in a broad sense in making this argument, to include income as well as wealth, and what is commonly termed 'property in the body', as well as in material goods. But I shall also contest some common discourses about property, including 'property in the body' – although that might seem the one concept about property which *is* congenial to feminism. Instead, I will argue that property in the *person* is the more useful notion, and the more correct interpretation of the original usage in Locke. But my interpretation will still have a great deal to say about women and their bodies: I apply my reconstructed model of contract and property to case studies on gamete donation, contract motherhood, and sale of fetal tissue in chapter 7.

The first claim in this book, to recapitulate the argument thus far, concerns property and the status of subject. I argue that women's subjectivity is rightly a principal concern in feminist theory, but that we have ignored the important connections made in much 'malestream' political theory between becoming a subject and the developmental aspects of property. Where property is seen as a positive *good* – a view which predates Thatcherism, having its roots in Aristotle – it is a double deprivation if women are propertyless. When women are blocked from controlling their own income, holding property, or gaining custody of their children,[12] and these things are not merely permitted to men but extolled, women are not just being denied something neutral, but something of active benefit. More strictly, it is not *having* goods that conduces towards the virtues in Aristotle and towards self-sufficient autonomy in the liberal theorists; it is *being* the sort of person who has them.[13] That person is active, rational, full of foresight, responsible, free – and fully human. We may or may not want to accept that view of personhood, but it is older and richer than Thatcherism.

Socialist feminisms, which *could* have something to say about property, have often tended to be atheoretical or even antitheoretical, in so far as they conceive of feminist theory as an impractical and implicitly conservative theory of difference.[14] 'Although the significance of property is a commonplace in class analysis, and basic to a materialist interpretation of social phenomena, little systematic attention has been directed to this factor in the analysis of women's position.'[15] On the other hand, masculinist socialism is notorious for leaving women out. In chapter 5, however, I argue that the Marxist concept of alienation and the domestic mode of production, a concept developed by the Marxist feminist Christine Delphy, *do* have something specific to say about women's propertylessness in both rich and poor countries.

Standpoint feminist philosophy has gone some distance towards claiming the status of subject as knower for woman, but it has been more interested in the *epistemological* ramifications of man as subject/knower, woman as object/categorized. Feminist political theory has dealt more extensively with concepts such as political participation, citizenship and authority than with property, as if that idea had been tainted by triumphalist right-wing politics.[16] But why should the devil get all the good tunes?

As a particularly concrete concept in applied political theory, property has also been of little interest to psychoanalytical feminisms of the French sort or to psychological feminisms of the American variety. The dominance in Europe of linguistic or psychoanalytical feminists, such as Luce Irigaray and Hélène Cixous, has coincided with the influence in America of object relations, psychological and maternal feminisms, leaving little space for practical legal and political concepts.[17] (Second-wave feminism did focus on women's property and poverty in its early stages, but this concern is now much more pronounced in economic development and social policy literature than in feminist theory.) When French linguistic feminism does deal with property, it tends to be simultaneously hostile and utopian – assuming that women have been merely the objects of exchange, and that there can be nothing in production or exchange for them. For example, Luce Irigaray writes:

> But what if these 'commodities' refused to go to 'market'? What if they maintained another kind of commerce, among themselves? Exchanges without identifiable terms, without accounts, without ends ... Use and exchange would be indistinguishable. The greatest value would be at the same time the least kept in reserve. Nature's resources would be expended without depletion, exchanged without labour, freely given, exempt from masculine transactions: enjoyment without a fee, well-being without pain, pleasure without possessions. As for all the strategies and savings, the appropriations tantamount to theft and rape, the laborious accumulation of capital, how ironic all that would be.[18]

Of course it is entirely credible that feminist theory should find property an alien concept, given canonical political theory's exclusion of women from the nexus between self-development, political rights and property-holding. That women *have* been excluded is my second claim in this introduction, and I explore it further in close analysis of Aristotle, Locke, Hegel, Marx and Engels in chapters 2 through 5. If women have at times been construed as property, men are indisputably 'the lords and owners of their faces'.[19] Hence, particularly in liberal thought, it is only men who, having a property in their own persons, can contract to form civil society and government. Feminist theorists such as Carole Pateman have astutely remarked on the deliberate subordination of women in liberal theory, whose resurgence in politics must make us particularly alert to how, as Pateman says, 'the whole package is marketed under the name of freedom.'[20]

On the other hand, property has been less contentious than the political participation to which, in the liberal tradition, it gives rise. Gains in economic rights have often been achieved more easily than claims for equal political participation. The nineteenth-century women's movement, particularly in the United States, deliberately prioritized property reform over suffrage. In Europe the various married and divorced women's property acts precede the vote by periods of up to a hundred years. Historically, both some of the greatest abuses *of* women and the greatest initial progress *for* women have been in the arena of property law. Generations of feminists, and even not-so-feminists, like Sand, have regarded property reform as *the* crucial reform for women. Before we rest on our laurels, having finally achieved equal rights under the tax laws at the late date of 1990 in Britain, we should think very hard about whether property questions are any less pressing at the end of the twentieth century than at the century's start, when Virginia Woolf asked in *A Room of One's Own*, 'Why are women so poor?'

This brings us to the third claim introduced here, at the start of *Property, Women and Politics*, that there is a dialectical relationship between women's propertylessness and their lesser status as subjects. Women, now and in the past, have typically held less property than men, and sometimes no property at all. *It is because they are propertyless that they are not construed as political subjects; it is because they are not accorded the status of subject that they hold little or no property.*

Women are still poor. Feminist theory's neglect of property flies in the face of economic and political reality for a great number of women. Property remains as important as ever, if not more so, to those increasingly deprived of it, and those in turn are disproportionately female; for example, the worsening situation for divorced women in the West has been documented by Lenore Weitzman,[21] Mavis MacLean[22] and Jan Pahl.[23] Just as the Church rejected the right to profits made from non-productive labour through usury, so have courts and legislatures been loath to recognize women's rights to wages for the allegedly non-productive labour of housework, to divorce settlements giving the non-working wife a share in the husband's pension entitlements, or to 'palimony' based on an unmarried female partner's contribution to the maintenance of a household or business. The feminization of poverty in the West and in the Third World alike radically undermines women's political participation and contrasts with the dominance of contractual, market-orientated models of ethics, social life and economics. There is now a hollow ring to those few left-of-centre perspectives which did try to provide alternative formulations of property – for example, Charles Reich's blithely 1960s-style contention that government benefits can be interpreted as a new type of property to which we all have a rightful and enduring claim.[24] New forms of common male property rights in women – pornography in particular – also continue to trouble the relationship between women and property.

As Alan Ryan puts it, 'Moderate property leads to moderate ambitions leads to moderate politics.'[25] Ryan believes that when we assert property rights, we are really after security rather than property itself. There is a theoretical basis for this claim not only in Locke, but also in the rather modern (though also classical) view that job security and moderate property enhance autonomy, create fulfilment, give interest in civic life and produce freedom. In a property-minded age dominated by rights rhetoric in politics and the reality of job insecurity, will women's relationship with property become even more troubled?

In the face of these practical urgencies, many theoretical feminisms have too readily accepted – rather than challenged – the truism in 'malestream' theory that property is an idea whose time has passed. On the one hand, property has been reduced by mainstream jurisprudence to the notion of a series of obligations between persons, rather than a thing in itself; on the other, property rights have long been presented in more left-wing perspectives as artificial constructs.[26] Carol Rose rightly points out that this theoretical neglect in mainstream theory sits oddly with the political resurgence of neoliberal models of property, for good or ill: the break-up of the old command economies, interest in tradable environmental rights as a possible solution for pollution, and the apparent demise of Keynesianism.[27]

The troubled relationship between women and property is explored at greater length in the practical sections of this book. The third claim introduced here – that women have held and continue to hold less property than men – is considered through *praxis* pertaining at the time of each of the grand theories whose exclusion of women is the subject of my second claim. At the end of each chapter on a canonical theorist, I set forth evidence of the particular property regime obtaining when he wrote – showing that women tended to hold less property, or to hold it in ways that did not threaten male subjectivity. *Property, Women and Politics* thus considers the difficult relationship between women and property from a novel viewpoint: synthesizing 'malestream' political theory from liberal and non-liberal traditions, feminist theory, history, anthropology and practical social policy.

My view about property rights parallels that of Catharine MacKinnon on free speech. When either is used as a defence of privilege, it is suspect. This was the way property rights *were* presented in the US under Ronald Reagan and in Britain under Margaret Thatcher, and the way the First Amendment to the US Constitution was used by the pornography industry in the Indianapolis regulation case brought by MacKinnon and Andrea Dworkin.[28] But when rights in free speech or property are an agenda for the dispossessed,[29] it is a very different matter. As Le Dœuff says, the notion of rights, whether in speech or property, 'can be effective when used polemically, in so far as it protests against limitations or privileges. When this intention is lost, the notion may become vague and prove incapable of challenging scandalous phenomena. It loses its critical power.'[30] It is not rights theory itself which is necessarily to blame, but the political use to which it is put. Liberal theory is not the unmitigated evil for women which some feminist theorists have accused it of being; but neither is it anything like a sufficient analysis in itself. We can extract something of benefit from liberalism, I think, but somewhat against its will. And it is important that we do so. My fourth and final claim in this introduction is that we *can* and *should* develop a theory of property which is liberating for women. That new understanding will build on canonical theory, but it will also be crucially different. In a project as large as this, some business will inevitably remain unfinished. I do not claim to provide a fully mature feminist theory of property, although in chapter 7 I try to give as precise a prediction as possible of what such a theory would look like, and how it would bear on practical ethics.

Feminists have asked, 'Are there some philosophies which are more appropriate than others to thinking about women's liberation?'[31] Existentialism, for example, rests on a voluntarism which says little of women's embeddedness in relationships.[32] Rights theories have come in for the same critique. Although Aristotelian virtue ethics is having a revival,[33] I have argued elsewhere that feminists must condemn a system in which the ill-chance of being born female limited women to a single, confining virtue: *sophrosyne* or self-restraint.[34]

In asking '*Are there some theories of property which are more appropriate than others to thinking about women's liberation?*' I proceed from a prior question, '*To what extent are the various canonical theories involving property particularist in ignoring women's property situation?*' To explore these two central questions, in each of the first five chapters I follow the strategy which is writ large in chapter 1. There I measure an avowedly universalist, gender-neutral contemporary theory of property against its own standards. Has the theory attained 'universality' only by omitting the experience of half of humanity? If women counted, would the theory still work? How does the theory measure up to the anthropological reality of women's actual property rights? The first chapter sets the scene by showing that gender blindness in relation to women and property is not merely historical; but it does have historical roots, which the next four chapters will trace. Chapters 2 through 5 do not give an uninterrupted linear history of women and property, but a series of snapshots at particularly crucial stages of development, so to speak.

In chapter 1, 'Property, particularism and moral persons', I examine an influential recent general theory of property, by the legal theorist Stephen Munzer, which relies on crucial psychological assumptions about motivation and agency in the acquisition of property. I test the empirical basis of these presuppositions against women's experience in other cultures and other periods in our own culture. Feminist anthropological, psychological and historical accounts allow us to begin piecing together a theory of property which is more genuinely general than Munzer's. Chapter 1 ends with three conclusions: (1) a general theory of property need not be incompatible with a feminist emphasis on lived experience; (2) the construction of property as sets of relations rather than things, which is the accepted model in most jurisprudence and political theory, may also be compatible with a feminist emphasis on relatedness; (3) a motivational, developmental account of property as intertwined with personhood and agency could also be attractive to feminist theory.

The next four chapters use the same method of comparing a key theory of property against women's experience, but with a more specific focus. Each opens with the treatment of a crucial concept about property in a canonical male theorist; identifies crucially gender-blind rather than gender-neutral anomalies in the theory when measured against the reality for women; and examines alternative formulations by contemporary feminist theorists. Again, I do not claim to give a linear history of canonical or feminist political theory, any more than I can tell the entire story of women and property in a book of this length. What I have tried to do is to select canonical theorists – Aristotle, Locke, Hegel, Marx and Engels – who privilege *praxis*, who view property not as an adjunct or addendum, but as central to what it means to be human. If women have lesser property entitlements in those theories, it implies that they cannot be fully human.

In chapter 2, 'Origins, narratives and households', I begin with the grandfather of universalist theories, Aristotle, whose exhaustive works include all human knowledge and yet somehow exclude half of humanity. I argue that while Aristotle did not conceive of women merely as objects of property, he did deny them full subjecthood. To put the matter in more modern terms, women's labour is not seen as adding value; but why not? Here my focus is on household economic production in a preindustrial society, and the practice against which I compare the theory is that of Greek property and marriage laws. The Athenian property regime was harsher for women than that of other Greek states, it will emerge. It is unfortunate for women than the classical political theory developed in Athens reflects a particularly misogynist property system. Perhaps this helps to explain why classical and subsequent accounts have considered that women had nothing to do with property – and those subsequent models have included feminist ones. The connection between virtue, subjectivity, civic membership and property is clearly elucidated by the example of Aristotle and Athens. This chapter demonstrates the need to distrust ahistorical essentialism and the corresponding need for narrative, drawing on the linkages between property, societal constructions and narratives suggested by Carol Rose.

Chapter 3, 'Contract, marriage and property in the person', moves on from Aristotle to Locke, and from the preindustrial household to early capitalist marriage. In an extensive critical discussion of Carole Pateman's *The Sexual Contract* – which carries over into other chapters but is primarily concentrated here – I examine the relationship between property in the person, humanity and political participation. I conclude that what is wrong with the 'sexual contract' is not that it is a contract, but that it is sexual. Jeremy Waldron's distinction between property in the body and property in the person turns out to be crucial here, and I return to it when I attempt in chapter 7 to sketch a reconstructed theory of property. My aim in this chapter is to strengthen the feminist challenge by making it more sophisticated, not to give further ammunition to already well-munitioned neoliberals. But I shall also be arguing that feminists have been too quick to dismiss two concepts central to liberal thought on property: contract and property in the person. Women *can* use both, I assert, to claim the status of subject.

This chapter also tells the particular story about marriage and contract that we have inherited from the Anglo-American legal doctrine of coverture, which applied to married women with particular ferocity in Locke's time. Once again, our prevailing narratives about women and property turn out to reflect a property regime which was unusually punitive for women. I argue that even feminist accounts of contract and property under liberalism, especially Pateman's, need to break free from that historical conditioning.

In chapter 3 I will be content to prove the *negative* claim that contract is *not* itself inimical to women's interests, in the context of liberal contractarianism. Contractual relations do not have to be unequal and oppressive, although many feminists have thought them so. Chapter 4, 'Property and moral self-development', advances the argument further by positing *positive* benefits in contract for women, developing a style of thinking suggested by a feminist analysis of Hegel. The justification offered for contract by Hegel turns out to centre on self-development and agency, also crucial to Hegel's broader justification of property. Although Hegel does not extend the full benefits of either contract or property to *women's* self-development, I shall begin to formulate ways of doing so in chapter 4, and chapter 7 will take that analysis further, when I come to reconstruct property.

The Lockean view of property as a special right is contrasted in chapter 4 with the general, developmental right to property found in Hegel. Hegel's model of property might be attractive to many feminists: it is consistent with an emphasis on forging a new subjectivity, with property not as instrumental to other goods but as a part of identity formation. But Hegel does not site women within developing modernity; they remain confined to their archaic role, when all else in modernity is change. Nor does Hegel see that the problem of poverty in early capitalist society, and in particular the massive rise in prostitution which I detail, makes women's confinement to the traditional private sphere deeply problematic.

In addition, this formulation incorporates a view of *contract* as a moral experience, a bond between myself and other owners – which, I argue, radically challenges Pateman's critique, suggesting that contract can be enabling and empowering. In chapter 3 I asserted that property and contract are not necessarily oppressive for women. Chapter 4 advances a stronger argument: that property and contract are actually *liberating* when construed as *developmental* rather than instrumental, and in terms of *general* rather than special rights.

Hegel can be interpreted as deepening the meaning of contract, to encompass mutual recognition, but restricting the breadth of its application. His attack on the notion of marriage as a contract, which he terms a 'shameful' idea, is consistent with a non-liberal view that society is not contract all the way down. This notion is particularist in Hegel, and the inadequacy of his understanding of women and modernity is illustrated by my discussion of prostitution and industrialization. Chapter 4 thus contributes several important building blocks to my reconstructed model of property:

1 The vision that 'everyone must have property' as a general right because property is instrumental to identity development, as a first stage;
2 The insistence that contract, the second stage of identity development, *is* only a stage, and not the template for all social relations (not for marriage, for example);

3 The recognition of experiential and relational ethical models which is
   implicit in Hegel's thought;
4 The importance of embodiment in self-development;
5 The possibility of respecting the agency of the propertylessness which is
   afforded by the master–servant parallel. A Hegelian analysis helps us see
   how women make sense of their 'no-property' worlds.

In examining the Hegelian developmental model of property-holding,
chapter 4 asks whether only *private* property can satisfy the needs of an
active moral agent. If not, it appears that what we require is not property
in itself, but that which produces property: labour, of which property is
merely the congealed remains, in a Marxist view. Is it labour or property
which makes the subject something other than object? Marx answers that
it is labour, *praxis*, productive work which transforms the material world
to fit human needs; but he none the less relies crucially on the Lockean
assumption of property in the person. Feminists have contested this
assumption: is it salvageable for women? And are other relevant Marxist
notions, particularly alienation and reproduction, helpful in understanding how women have made sense of their 'no-property worlds'? Chapter
5, 'Labour, alienation and reproduction', draws on the work of Marx,
Engels, Catharine MacKinnon and Christine Delphy in examining these
and related questions.

Women are neither simple *objects* of property-holding, nor are they
unqualified *subjects* whose property-holding may suffer under rectifiable
practical handicaps. A materialist analysis might offer a less static and more
activist possibility, if it could categorize different sites of oppression, rather
than a simple dichotomy of victims and oppressors; and a materialist
feminist position might also avoid the relativistic multiple essentialisms of
cultural feminism.[35] In particular, it seems possible that the Marxist
concept of alienation gets at some of this strangeness, allowing women to
be agents rather than mere objects, but impaired subjects. I ask whether we
can transform the notion of alienation to fit women's typical *propertylessness
in their labour*, even though the Marxist interpretation of the concept relies
crucially on *ownership* of property in one's labour, and even though it is
applied strictly to 'productive' rather than reproductive labour in Marx.
Women's propertylessness in their labour is illustrated in empirical material
from sub-Saharan Africa.

These first five chapters primarily *deconstruct* and contest the concept of
property, by drawing out the inadequacies of canonical treatments of it.
Because much mainstream theory continues to move resolutely away from
feminisms and to ignore the insights of feminist deconstruction of the
canon, we need to go on insisting that the basic concepts of political theory
should count women in. (This is never the same as adding them on.)

Property, I have argued throughout, is an extremely suitable case for the deconstructionist treatment in both mainstream and feminist theory, although the related concepts of contract, rationality and subjectivity have been better explored.

The first five chapters, together with this introduction, lay the foundations for a *reconstructed* theory of property.[36] This they do by salvaging neglected insights and concepts in canonical theorists which could, if sensitively reconstituted, elucidate women's property situation. Although property and contract have been almost entirely the province of mainstream rather than feminist theorists, it is none the less inadequate to concentrate solely on the canon. We want a view of property which will also allow women to figure as something *other than objects*, but we have not yet fully established what kinds of *subjects* they will be. That is the concern of chapter 6, 'Another sort of subject?' Here is where feminist analyses of subjectivity play their part, in questioning the notion of the unified subject, as do Judith Butler and Luce Irigaray. In an extended discussion of Irigaray's work, I ask whether a theory of property needs a more polymorphous notion of the subject than mainstream theory generally assumes. This pluralistic notion of property is actually rather similar to the notion of the subject as a profusion of past experiences and events. What is actually the mainstream legal notion of property, as bundles of relations, is far more compatible with recent feminisms' deconstruction of the subject than most feminist theory realizes. The chapter also examines recent feminist deconstruction and reconstruction of practical reason, concluding in favour of a non-instrumental model of rationality.

However, I have not chosen to accept Irigaray's doubts about the impossibility of any woman ever becoming a subject, since she is either 'subjecting herself to objectivization in discourse – by being "female"' or else 're-objectivizing her own self whenever she claims to identify herself "as" a masculine subject'.[37] Nor do I accept that the category 'woman' is unusable – despite the arguments to the contrary of some deconstructionist feminists such as Christine Sylvester[38], who will only use the word 'woman' in inverted commas. In Jane Smiley's novel *Moo*, an African-American woman professor of English muses on how the category of 'literature' has been deconstructed out of existence, just at the time when it was about to be taken over by formerly subservient groups such as women and African-Americans. That, she reckons, is no coincidence.

Chapter 7, 'Reconstructing property', extends and yet transcends the first five, attempting a reconstruction of property in a way that will work for women. The characteristics of a woman-friendly model developed in chapters 1 through 6 do not constitute a full-fledged theory of property; I have never pretended that they would. At best they are the foundations of the edifice. But even in the absence of a fully gestated theory, they may lead to some compelling and unexpected applications. The purpose of this chapter is to explore four such possible applications, drawn from medical ethics and family policy:

1 The sale and/or donation of gametes in *in vitro* fertilization (IVF) and other reproductive technologies;
2 Contract motherhood, frequently known as paid surrogacy;
3 The sale and use of fetal tissue (which also entails a brief discussion of abortion);
4 The marriage 'contract'.

My guiding hypothesis throughout the book is so simple as to be open to accusations of cliché: that the relationship between women and property is always different from that which holds for men. Yet obvious though it is, this difference has been ignored in conventional theory. This means that supposedly general and universalist conventional theories are nothing of the kind. They are particularist and, specifically, masculinist. It takes a feminist analysis to get the other half of humanity noticed, and to make the theories whole. It is therefore feminist theory which is genuinely universal.[39]

This has further important implications. If conventional masculinist theory is not universal, it cannot be made so merely by adding the odd mention of women's situation, or by kowtowing at the end of an introduction, 'Everything that is said applies to men *and* women'.[40] The bedrock notions of what it means to hold property, and of why holding private property is part of being a public person, are undermined by asking what it means for women's labour not to be considered as producing wealth, and for women not to be admitted to public life. There is something gravely wrong with the fundamental categories and modes of masculinist thought about property, I argue. But it is only by starting with the conventional theory that we can see why an unconventional one is necessary.

In beginning each of chapters 2 through 5 in the apparently conventional way, by looking at the 'great men' associated with each topic, I might lay myself open to criticism. Can the relationship between women and property be examined through the lens of received theories and canonical philosophers? As Michèle le Dœuff writes,

> when I feel the difficulty of grasping, and then of conceptualizing the 'woman question', the question of women both in general and in philosophy, I have to conclude that this question cannot be integrated into our received frameworks of thinking, be it everyday thinking or that developed by philosophy. Such considerations lead me to wonder if all thinking might not be built on the rejection of a certain number of realities, of which that is one.[41]

Yet Le Dœuff perseveres. With any degree of sensitivity to the Woman Question at all, it is easy to be put off by what she calls 'stupid utterances made about women by people who, in principle, have no right to stupidity'[42] – canonical philosophers. But she urges her readers to transcend their righteous annoyance: what a philosopher has to say about women unlocks the key to his entire enterprise. 'Far from giving way to disgust, women should know that the sexism of philosophical discourse offers them a hold on that discourse and that they can re-examine it in a way which has never been done before.'[43]

Besides, I would argue, what philosophers have to say about women and property underlies jurisprudence and law about property rights, and everyday beliefs about why women's rights are less than genuine. It is only by problematizing property theories, through asking whether they count women, that we can, as Le Dœuff says, 'bring to light what is at stake in these utterances, by showing that they are pertinent at a level different from the one at which they appear to have meaning'.[44]

Although this is the sort of claim which brings the pillars of the academic temple crashing down on one's head, my project tries to do for gender what Marx attempted for class. I aim at a historical as well as a philosophical inquiry into the division between those who own property, particularly in the body, and those who sell body-rights and the fruits of their labour. In this book I will try to link materialist and idealist feminisms, anthropology and jurisprudence, empirical social science and political theory. I realize that there is a fair amount of hubris involved in all this. I can only hope that my readers will be as deeply challenged and fascinated by these large questions as I am, and that they will be charitable towards loose ends and unfinished business.

1

Property, Particularism and Moral Persons

This chapter opens with two crucial questions articulated in the introduction:

1 To what extent are the various canonical theories of property particularist in ignoring women's property situation?

and its corollary:

2 Are some theories of property more appropriate than others to thinking about women's liberation?

These two queries relate to my fourth and final claim in the introduction: that in order to develop a model of property which is liberating for women, we must begin by deconstructing and analysing how women figure in canonical theories of property. This is so despite my second claim: that much canonical theory has implicitly or explicitly excluded the experience of women. My intention is similar to Le Dœuff's: 'to bring to light what is at stake in these utterances, by showing that they are pertinent at a level different from the one at which they have meaning.' It is 'what is at stake' for women, property and politics that is pertinent to my project, not the canonical discourse *per se*. But at the same time there *is* more that is pertinent in the canonical discourse, I argue, than feminist theory has so far recognized.

Clearly, however, the first question needs narrowing down. It is beyond the scope of even an ambitious book like this one – and beyond the bounds of possibility – to evaluate *all* existing theories of property. Instead, in this chapter I shall concentrate on an emblematic and original modern theory of property set out by Stephen R. Munzer in 1990.[1] It is vital to start with a modern theory – to show that gender particularism is not merely historical but is still dominant even in the most widely accepted and carefully constructed present writing. What makes Munzer's theory particularly relevant is that it stands in the developmental, psychological tradition which links property to enhanced subjectivity. Munzer relies very heavily, by his own admission, on what he presents as universally applicable motivational background factors. He is therefore vulnerable to evidence showing that these psychological arguments are *not* generic, but are applicable only to men's experience of property-holding. Anthropological evidence at both the specific and the general level will be introduced to support this contention.

However, I have no intention of setting Munzer up as a straw man, or even as a straw person. Munzer's mode of operation in *A Theory of Property* is careful and synergistic, bringing together insights from jurisprudence and political theory. His book is intended as an original theory of property, not a survey,[2] and thus it is comparable to the canonical normative works of political theory which I shall examine in chapters 2 through 5. This is especially true because Munzer means his theory to carry implications for politics and social policy,[3] as the canonical works have done. The last three chapters of *A Theory of Property* measure ownership and control of business corporations, gifts and bequests, and government 'takings' of private property against the normative theory developed earlier, relying heavily on constitutional law and political science. This is similar to what I attempt in chapter 7: applying my own normative reconstruction of property – admittedly less of a 'grand theory' than Munzer's – to concrete examples such as payment for gamete donation. So Munzer's ambitions and procedures are similar to my own: he tries to unite apparently disparate areas of scholarship and to make good use of practical examples.

Yet I shall be arguing that despite its apparently prudent methodology and painstaking argumentation, its avowedly gender-neutral language and its genuinely broad focus, Munzer's theory ignores women's experience of property. The theory has attained 'universality' only by excluding half of humanity. If this is so, it emphasizes the ongoing relevance of the first question above. Particularism is by no means dead and buried with the canonical theorists. I shall argue that testing 'universal' pronouncements against feminist anthropological and historical accounts might help us to outline the requirements for a theory of property which is more genuinely general than Munzer's, and in the process to begin answering the second question. I realize that I might myself be vulnerable to a charge of having drawn up a shopping list of societies which illustrate my own interpretation of women's relationship with property. At this point in my argument, however, I am concerned mainly to refute Munzer's supposedly universal statements about motivations and psychology in property-holding, so that I have indeed largely chosen my examples with a purpose. By the end of the book, a fuller discussion will emerge.

Yet the answer to the second question will turn out to be more favourable to Munzer than to some recent feminist theories of agency and morality. I shall suggest that Munzer is correct to link moral agency and even some types of virtue to an active relationship with property. The relationship which Munzer posits between agency and property is more conducive than an 'ethic of care' to women's liberation, I assert. Munzer's model of property presents, in modern dress, many of the justifications of property which link it to becoming an active moral and political agent, in fact to self-liberation.

Throughout this book, but particularly in this chapter, I am concerned to bridge the increasingly canyon-like divide between 'mainstream' political theory and feminist discourse. My purpose in beginning with Munzer's theory of property is not to widen that gulf by dismissing Munzer as sexist and naive, but to pave the way for a reconstructed theory of property which avoids the particular sorts of overgeneralizations endemic to both sides, and which incorporates the best insights of both masculinist and feminist theories. Thus chapter 1, which deconstructs a supposedly universal theory of property as particularist, is balanced by chapter 7, which attempts to outline a genuinely universal theory.

Munzer: a propertyless world?

Munzer offers a 'pluralist' theory of property balancing three principles usually taken to be competitive: utility and efficiency; justice and equality; and desert based on labour. Much of his book is taken up with working out when and how each of the principles can override the others, with consistent implications for challenging a purely laissez-faire model of property distribution. In their introductory formulation, the three principles are presented as follows.

Utility and efficiency Property rights should be allocated so as to maximize utility and efficiency regarding the use, possession and transfer of things; but utility has priority over efficiency when the two conflict. The principle of utility emphasizes maximizing preference-satisfaction for *all* individuals, but does not tell us how to make interpersonal comparisons *among* individuals. Efficiency invokes individual preference-satisfaction; but there are some property preferences which we will not want to satisfy, no matter how strongly individuals hold them, since they threaten general utility.

Justice and equality Unequal holdings are justifiable if everyone has a minimum amount of property and if inequalities do not undermine a 'fully human life in society'.[4] In contrast to the principle of utility and efficiency, which deals with preferences, the principle of justice and equality is concerned with 'basic needs and basic capabilities'.[5] The first condition of the principle of justice and equality is what Munzer terms the 'Floor Thesis': that everyone should have a minimum of property. Rather than taking precedence over the second component if there is a conflict, as utility does over efficiency, the Floor Thesis is the basic requirement of the justice and equality combination. The second component, which Munzer calls the 'Gap Thesis' – that inequalities should not be too great – is simply a side constraint. Nor does it limit absolutely the amount of wealth which the richest may possess; it is not a 'ceiling' thesis.

Labour and desert Private property rights are justified by labour input, but not absolutely: rather in a form which is qualified by the rights of others, limitations on acquisition and inheritance, general scarcity, and the nature of work as a social activity. This is a merit-based principle, in contrast to the other two, which were based on worth: the equal worth of all individuals' preferences, in the principle of utility and efficiency, or of all individuals' needs, in the principle of justice and equality. The principle of labour and desert relies crucially (in its original formulation by Locke, as Munzer interprets him) on a conception of the labourer as having an exclusive liberty to use his body to produce things of value, and a corresponding right to possess the profits of that labour.

Note, in passing, how the last principle in particular emphasizes property's relation to *persons and bodies*. This will be an ongoing theme of my book as well. In chapter 3 I shall distinguish between property in the person and property in the body; in chapter 7 I shall use that distinction in reconstructing a preliminary but genuinely universal model of property.

Now in themselves Munzer's principles and conclusions do not look particularly radical. Carol Rose argues that they are all essentially reducible to the standard wealth-enhancing or preference-satisfying conception, and are thus neither radical nor competing.[6] Indeed Munzer does not intend them to be particularly new, although he notes that the principle of . utility and efficiency, which is not avowedly concerned with social justice, can be an argument 'for disrupting even rational and institutionally legitimate expectations about property'.[7] Still, a 'pluralist' theory – which is what Munzer intends, even though Rose doubts that he lives up to his own expectations – necessarily borrows from many sources, and needs to make itself widely acceptable. That the Floor Thesis, in particular, *is* conventionally acceptable has been demonstrated on an empirical basis in the time since Munzer's book appeared.[8]

The interest of Munzer's work is not so much in its conclusions as in its presuppositions, I think. Specifically, Munzer's theory is rooted in a particular psychological view of what makes people work for gain, and what it means to flourish as a human being. It is a conception which justifies private property as meeting a universal human *need* for having one's expectations mean something, for the stability which Munzer presents as vital to the well-being of people and society. Although Munzer describes his approach as intuitionist[9], it appears to me a form of moral realism or naturalism in so far as it relies on certain morally relevant and empirically verifiable facts about human motivation and nature.[10] It is therefore important to find out whether these psychological truths really are universal. As Munzer himself stresses,

> it is not enough to present only abstract arguments for these principles. Rather, it is essential to be keenly aware of the psychological, social and economic context to which the arguments apply. And to develop that awareness it is vital to understand how persons and their bodies relate to the world of things. Only if the groundwork is laid well will arguments for the theory itself be convincing.[11]

Munzer realizes that his account of people's motivations about property may not be cross-cultural – that it may not apply to non-Western societies, although he claims that 'it reveals a great deal at any rate about developed Western societies'[12] – but he shows little or no awareness that it does not apply across *genders*. Further, his account is profoundly ahistorical; it does not apply to many earlier periods in liberal Western societies, and, I would suggest, it is still not fully true of our own period. This raises serious questions of how limited a 'general' theory can be and still call itself general. A truly universal theory of property will be a feminist one, as I argued in the introduction; like most 'mainstream' theories, Munzer's model is actually particularist.

Munzer follows a conventional masculinist epistemological strategy of deliberately distancing his theory from history by the use of hypotheticals.[13] Now perhaps it might seem unfair to charge him with ignoring *anyone's* particular historical situation, women's or men's, when he has purposely chosen to count history out. But the result of this thought experiment *is* meant to apply to our 'real world', and to have something to say about the very specific practical applications with which Munzer's book ends. Throughout this book I am concerned to situate canonical discourse in women's actual condition – what Seyla Benhabib calls the 'doubled' vision of feminist theory:

In practicing this doubled vision we do not remain satisfied with analyzing textual discourses about women, but we ask where the women themselves were at any given period in which a thinker lived. With one eye we see what stands in the text, and with the other, what the text conceals in footnotes and in the margins. What then emerges is a 'discursive space' of competing power claims.[14]

A Theory of Property begins, then, with a thought experiment: we are asked to imagine a 'no-property world'. This is not an environment which lacks the *objects* of property, such as personal possessions or capital in the form of machinery and factories; rather, the *relations* of property-holding and property transfer are absent. Artefacts exist, but there are no rights of excluding others from their use, or means of transferring them through inheritance, gift or sale. Munzer intends this picture to startle the reader, to reveal just how central property is to human society and motivation. Without exclusive property rights, the technological level of production would remain simple, even primitive, he asserts. 'People would probably not make the necessary sacrifices unless they could be confident of substantial control over the use and disposition of these things – which would require property rights.'[15] To rephrase Munzer in Hobbes's glorious language, without security there would be

> no place for Industry; because the fruit thereof is uncertain: and consequently no Culture of the Earth, no Navigation, or use of the commodities that may be imported by Sea; no commodious Building; no Instruments of moving, and removing such things as require much force; no Knowledge of the face of the Earth; no account of Time; no Arts; no Letters.[16]

Besides this instrumental account of property, Munzer also uses arguments more commonly associated with Kant, Hegel and Aristotle. Not only are 'stable possession and use . . . necessary to achieve some abiding ends'[17] important to moral agency, but property-holding is also conducive, within limitations, to virtue. So in the no-property world we would have much to lose: our most cherished projects and a portion of our moral identity.

Yet what is *really* startling is not Munzer's picture of a propertyless world; it is his failure to realize how very *ordinary* this world is, how many women have lived and still live in such a world. The Athenian wife of Aristotle's time, as chapter 2 will show, had no 'control over the use and disposition' of any personal property, or custody of her children. Yet she was expected to manage and fructify the household's wealth, including wealth in the labour of children, for whom she was expected to make 'the necessary sacrifices'. In this propertylessness she was in much the same position as married women under the Anglo-American law of coverture, detailed in chapter 3. Munzer makes what he calls an 'empirical assumption' that 'people prefer to have intimate articles as a basis for personality'.[18] Yet this account by Elizabeth Cady Stanton reveals that, although early nineteenth-century American women lived in a particularly individualistic, property-minded society, they had no more right to own intimate property than did Athenian wives.

> As my father's office joined the house, I spent there much of my time when out of school, listening to the clients stating their cases, talking with the students, and reading the laws in regard to women . . . Fathers, at their death, would will the bulk of their property to the eldest son, with the proviso that the mother was to have a home with him. Hence it was not unusual for the mother, who had brought all the property into the family, to be made an unhappy dependent on the bounty of an uncongenial daughter-in-law and a dissipated son. The tears and complaints of the women who came to my father for legal advice touched my heart and early drew my attention to the injustice and cruelty of the laws. As the practice of the law was my father's business, I could not exactly understand why he could not alleviate the sufferings of these women. So, in order to enlighten me, he would take down his books and show me the inexorable statutes. The students, observing my interest, would amuse themselves by reading to me all the worst laws they could find, over which I would laugh and cry by turns. One Christmas morning I went into the office to show them, among my other presents, a new coral necklace and bracelets. They all admired the jewelry and then began to tease me with hypothetical cases of future ownership. 'Now,' said Henry Bayard, 'if in due time you should be my wife, these ornaments would be mine; I could take them and lock them up, and you could never wear them except with my permission. I could even exchange them for a box of cigars, and you could watch them evaporate in smoke.'[19]

This excerpt suggests an interesting brief digression. In later life Stanton could have chosen to campaign for women's suffrage without property rights, although this passage indicates how central property was to her. But why didn't nineteenth-century liberal feminists simply assert that women could also participate in politics even if they lacked property, as could ex-slaves of the male sex? One possibility is that American feminists, in particular, were confined by the republican tradition, which associates possessing a minimum of property with a robust independence which enables the voter to make up his own mind.[20] Another explanation might centre on Anglo-American law's general disinterest in the nature of the owner. Whereas Roman law encouraged the question, 'What is it to be the owner of something?', English and American law and political theory tend to stop short at the empirical fact of possession, foreclosing metaphysical or psychological speculation.[21] The relationship between the subjectivity of the owner and the fact of ownership is more natural to Continental thought and law outside the liberal tradition: for example, Hegel and Marx, considered in chapters 4 and 5 respectively.

Sub-Saharan African codes, also explored further in chapter 5, typically require women to labour without control, security or expectation of gain on lands which belong to their husbands. Customary law in South Africa, for example, returns a husband's lands to his own kin after his death; during his lifetime he controls the product of his wife's labour.[22] Although some East African Muslim societies trace property rights in land through both the father's and the mother's lines,[23] and although Islamic law does give women the right to hold property, far more men than women in these cultures own coconut trees, cattle, donkeys, fishing boats, agricultural vehicles and implements. Africa may provide the greatest contrast between who does the work and who claims the proceeds, but the disparity between women's labour and what they are deemed to deserve is common. In Papua New Guinea, for example, women of the Hagen tribe raise pigs which are given away in ceremonial exchange by their husbands, who are under no obligation to consult their wives, although they may choose to make some compensation.[24] Yet Munzer doubts that people would engage in farming and animal husbandry unless they had property rights over the fruits of their labours.

We must be careful not to view women in patriarchal economic regimes purely as victims, and to avoid ethnocentrism. When wives are exchanged in cultures such as Papua New Guinea, for example, we tend to assume that they must be objects of wealth; the feminist anthropologist Marilyn Strathern reminds us that such exchange symbolizes the gift of aspects of the male person, not of the women as an object. Although women in wife exchange cannot be said to be full subjects, neither are they merely disposable property.[25] None the less, there is a question to be answered: if not for property rights, what do women in patriarchal economic regimes produce and reproduce *for*? Particularly in relation to physical reproduction, the very query jars. It sounds extremely odd to ask what a woman's intention is in giving birth, in the same way that Munzer can talk of a person's intention in interacting with the world being to gain property rights.[26] Is 'what for?' simply the wrong question to ask of women's lives? It assumes that there must be a conscious and voluntary motivation for economic activity, that women had a choice *not* to produce or reproduce. If a woman cannot withhold the use of her body from her husband, she cannot have an intention in giving birth.

Throughout the book I shall return to this profound enigma of what *does* motivate women's economic activity when they cannot profit in terms of property rights from the fruits of their labours. For the time being, I simply want to repeat that a feminist analysis, in which the central category has been said to be experience,[27] demonstrates vividly that Munzer's typology of motivations fails to take into account women's lived relationship to acquiring and maintaining property. People – mainly female people – *do* engage in productive and reproductive effort without the expectation of property rights in the fruits of their labours. Thus property and stability of expectation in it cannot be a universal human need, if indeed it is need that motivates action; and a naturalistic account of property as an objective need must fail. This is not to deny other, non-naturalistic accounts of why people *ought* to have property, even if they appear to act without needing it: for example, as a developmental force which enhances human agency – roughly, the account given by Hegel, which I develop at length in chapter 4. This suggests that a truly universal model of property – one that counts women in – will not be rooted in any allegedly general need, but in the link to subjectivity. Since feminist thought has been intensely concerned with the nature of the subject, we already have an encouraging indication that a feminist account of property will be a feasible project.

If women's motivation for productive activity is *not* control, it appears either that their needs are different from those which Munzer depicts as universal, or that Munzer's naturalistic approach is flawed. Within the late twentieth-century American or British household, there is still every indication that women do not exercise the same sorts of control over property that men do. Women may now have nominal rights to pooled resources within the household, but their needs often carry less weight.[28] Their entitlements do not increase with their earning power; wives are usually unable to purchase reduced work within the household through earning wages.[29] Wives are more likely to view their contribution to joint income as belonging to the household rather than as their own to control.[30] If what each sex looks for in productive labour depends on prevailing power relations and gender ideologies, rather than on some innate human need, then we cannot read any universal truth about motivations from people's economic activities. Still less can a theory of property be grounded in any such allegedly empirical facts.

Not only does anthropological and historical comparison demonstrate that the 'facts' about motivation are not so universal as Munzer makes them out to be – important though the evidence of history and anthropology will be throughout this book. There is also an argument in favour of reversing the direction of the argument, as Henrietta Moore asserts. Ideas determine the 'facts' about people's productive labour; the facts do not determine the ideas. Property, on this account, would be a *site of struggle*. As Moore writes,

> The outcome of bargaining and negotiation is never simply determined by economic factors, such as access to resources. Socially and historically specific views about the rights, responsibilities and needs of particular individuals are at least as important, and often more important, in determining the outcome of bargaining and negotiation.[31]

Again, this view is consistent with a feminist analysis. But conflict is largely missing from Munzer's version of property, as is any notion that control may be a two-edged sword for women. They are just as likely to be its objects as its subjects.

In his principle of labour according to desert, for example, Munzer presents incomes, salaries or wages primarily as belonging to the individuals who earn them, subject to rather vague strictures about the interdependent social nature of work. Yet even in Western marriages, and certainly in most non-Western cultures, the wife's income is not viewed as unequivocally *hers* in the same sense that the husband's is. She is under prior restraints or controls, from which earning an income does not free her; it may only tighten the bonds. Modernization can leave women with the burden of earning an income but no control over its disposition, particularly in virilocal systems where the wife lives with the husband's family. In India, for example, a bride who earns a wage will be expected to hand over her wage-packet to her parents-in-law. They will also control the wealth she brought into the marriage as dowry, with the father-in-law exercising control over any cash sums and his wife deciding on the disposition of movables.[32]

Rather than procuring her any financial independence, the Chinese peasant wife's earnings are again incorporated directly into the virilocal extended household. Agricultural wages from communal working, for example, are often given in one packet to the 'head of the household', who is almost inevitably male. The system of betrothal gifts which persists even in post-revolutionary China is predicated on very concrete calculations of the bride's expected earnings, as recompense for the expense entailed in procuring her.[33] When the private hiring of workers was prohibited by the communist regime, the only means of obtaining fresh labour for a peasant family was through the recruitment of women in marriage. Paradoxically, the effect of 'freeing' women for waged labour, coupled with the replacement of land by labour as the main source of a family's wealth, was to make them even more firmly objects of exchange in marriage than in pre-revolutionary China, even though the exchange of women in arranged marriage was abolished by the Marriage Law of 1950. Women alone contribute to all three sectors of the rural economy: waged labour, private sideline activities, and servicing of the household. But in none of these three areas are the products of their work regarded as belonging to them. The most basic notion of desert arising from labour does not apply to rural Chinese women, although the urban woman has somewhat more independence.

We have seen that Munzer's naturalistic account of property, need and control fails to capture the lived experience of many women. This is particularly threatening because Munzer has such high hopes for property-holding. In Munzer's view the possession of property is crucial not only to the frugal, enterprising motivation which builds a higher technological level in the economy – a utilitarian justification of property – but also to a Kantian emphasis on moral agency and personality. Is this to say that propertyless women cannot be full moral agents or virtuous persons? How have women who lived in a propertyless world reconciled their deprivation with making meaning in their lives? This is a grave problem if we do not wish to accept a realistic or naturalistic account of property as a universal need evidenced by human motivation across all cultures and both genders. Women have indisputably acted as agents in the absence of property rights; but have they been able to act as *moral* agents? Women, now and in the past, have tended to hold less property than men. Does that make them less than full subjects? Or, as I asked in the introduction, do they hold less property *because* they are not construed as full subjects?

Property, women and theory

The need to control property is taken as a given of human nature, then, in Munzer's theory. This carries with it the political implication that society *should* meet what is presented as a basic human need. Yet societal norms and rules have frequently forbidden half of humanity to satisfy this 'need'. This insight could lead us in one of four separate directions:

1 Rejecting a general theory about women and property altogether;
2 Accepting the need for a general theory, but basing it on separate female moral needs and motivations which predispose women to emphasize care and relationships rather than control and ownership;
3 Accepting the need for a general theory and basing it on a universal need for control and ownership, but demanding that women's need to control property be served equally along with men's;
4 Rejecting the objective notion of need altogether, and viewing property as a political arena of combat.

It is crucial at this stage of the book to establish which is the right direction to follow. If (1) is correct, my project is radically misguided. So let us begin with (1).

(1) *Rejecting a general theory about women and property altogether* Feminist epistemology distrusts abstraction as 'the first step down the road of androcentric ignorance'.[34] As Mari J. Matsuda puts it, 'The refusal to acknowledge context – to acknowledge the actual lives of human beings affected by a particular abstract principle – has meant time

and again that women's well-grounded, experiential knowledge is subordinated to someone else's false abstract presumptions.'[35] In property law, the abstract principle of female dependence on and protection by men has collided with the reality of dispossession and poverty for women who were *not* provided for by men, or who were indubitably property themselves. (Among the first to denounce this incongruity have been African-American feminists, such as Patricia J. Williams[36]: for them the experience of having been property is particularly tangible.) So the abstraction inherent in a general model of property and subjectivity might seem to clash with the experiential feminist distrust of false universalism. The attempt to draw up a set of overarching principles, as Munzer does, would be particularly suspect.[37]

However, I think this is to confuse *bad* principle formulation with principle formulation *per se*. It is not the attempt to establish general principles which is wrong, unless they are too abstractly deductive or faultily inductive. It is universalism which is not truly universal that we must distrust; but my project includes 'plugging the gaps' in canonical theory to make it *truly* universal, not particularist. By incorporating women's actual experience of property in the historical sections of chapters 2 through 5, I hope to fill in these rather substantial blanks. Furthermore – and this cannot be emphasized too often – there are many strands in canonical political theory, not all of them equally inhospitable to women. The task of the theoretical gloss in chapters 2 through 5 will be to isolate and carry forward any productive elements which we find in each theorist examined.

In setting up the three principles of his general theory of property, Munzer has abstracted too far from the lived experiences of women. This is not, of course, to say that there is one uniform category of 'women's experience'; to claim that would be to fall into the same trap of overgeneralization as Munzer does. We need what Kathy E. Ferguson terms the choice of 'some founding source for women's experience': sexuality, the gendered division of labour, the body, mothering, or 'the telos of nature'.[38] Is experience what women do, what women have done to them, or what women are? It has sometimes been said of nationality and democracy that before we can let the people decide, we have to decide who are the people. The same might be true of women and experience: before we can let women's experience count, we have to decide what counts as women's experience. None the less, if we rule out normative principles and unified categories of women's experience altogether, we wind up with relativism. And I agree with Virginia Held that if we accept postmodernist relativism, we risk undermining the entire feminist enterprise, which relies heavily on certain normative principles or notions as having genuine force: equality and justice among them.[39]

The task is to construct general theories which *do* acknowledge the variety of women's varied actual experience, and which reflect women's needs as well as men's. As Held puts it, 'Throughout most of the history of principles of equality, gender has been supposed to be a relevant difference permitting different treatment.'[40] In a sense, then, the aim is to *ignore* difference as a morally relevant excuse, but to *incorporate* difference in lived experience into general theory. It should then be possible to argue for both difference and equality, as Le Dœuff also insists, although the two so often seem to pull in opposite directions.

(2) *Accepting the need for a general theory, but basing it on separate female moral needs and motivations which predispose women to emphasize care and relationships rather than control and ownership* Secondly, we could allow Munzer his attempt to establish an objective basis for his theory of property in human needs, but deny that the need for stability in property relations is indeed universal. We might respect his naturalistic approach, which attempts to ground a normative theory of property in what people need in order to flourish; but we could deny that they need property as much as Munzer thinks they do. Munzer relies on a 'psychological presupposition that persons act to maximize preference-satisfaction, and that important among their preferences is a desire for property'.[41] But suppose that presupposition is masculinist?

This tactic might find support in feminist[42] moral theories which emphasize women's embeddedness in relationships – what I term an 'ethic of care' or 'maternal' feminism, a variant of 'cultural' or 'separate sphere' feminism[43]. This approach, influential in the 1980s but increasingly coming under attack,[44] relies on the notion of a different female 'moral voice'. That concept is generally traced to Carol Gilligan's *In a Different Voice* (1982), although Gilligan has explicitly repudiated the notion that women have a separate moral identity from men.[45] The common core of the ethic of care is that there is another model of moral agency than that of the rights-holding individual: one which emphasizes responsibility rather than rights, relationships rather than individualism, and caring rather than self-assertion. As Held says,

> Repeatedly, feminist approaches indicate to us that we ought to pay far more attention than most inquiry does to relationships among people, relationships that we cannot see but can experience nevertheless . . . They can be felt and understood, but, as experienced, are not reducible to the properties of individual entities that can be observed by an outsider and trapped into a causal scientific framework.[46]

In Munzer's world, the root of human motivation is 'to maximize preference satisfaction'. 'If persons' actions in satisfying their preferences benefit others, it is coincidental that they do so.'[47] Although Munzer later modifies the presupposition to make some room for benevolence, this is essentially Adam Smith's model of *homo oeconomicus*,[48] rational economic man. By contrast, if the psychological imperative for women *is* caring rather than controlling, to accept the premise of the ethic of care *in arguendo*, then perhaps women can live a fulfilled life without the particular security which property offers. In that case, women might conceivably be full moral agents without possessing property rights. Even more strongly, Jennifer Nedelsky claims that property rights are a will-o'-the-wisp of security: the image of a bounded self, secure within its wall of property rights, is not a self-image which fosters a healthy identity.[49] This would be a serious wound to Munzer's theory, but it would still accept his basic methodology: establishing empirically verifiable needs which a normative theory of property must satisfy.

However, women's proficiency at caring may not be natural but the product of their economic dependence: 'the survival skills of an oppressed group that lives in close contact with its oppressors'.[50] If so, it would be because they lack property that they are not subjects in the conventional sense, that they are primarily other-directed rather than autonomous. Maternal feminism then actually *reinforces* oppression by shifting the desired locus of change to personal relationships, inverting the originally radical feminist notion that 'the personal is political' and further weakening women's power of independent agency. As Martha Minow has written, 'why, when it comes to our own arguments and initiatives, do feminists forget the very insights that animate feminist initiatives, insights about the power of unstated reference points and points of view, the privileged position of the status quo, and the pretense that a particular is the universal?'[51]

And why do feminists likewise forget their own history? There is nothing new about maternal feminism: it replicates the nineteenth-century American 'Cult of True Womanhood', the discourse which replaced the more progressive thought of the Revolutionary period. In this ethical system, selfishness of any kind was the prime sin for women, and independence, fiscal and otherwise, was a kind of selfishness.[52] During this period the economic rights of white American women reached the low depicted in Stanton's example, while the participatory and economic rights of free American men climbed from strength to strength. It is profoundly depressing to read a modern feminist like Robin West extolling women's dependence in much the same vein as did the Cult of True Womanhood, when she writes: 'To the considerable degree that our potentiality for motherhood defines ourselves, women's lives are relational, not autonomous. As mothers we nurture the weak and depend upon the strong.'[53]

So although I agree that the masculinist instrumental notion of property and the preference maximization concept of motivation are impoverished, I cannot accept this second strategy, rooted in maternal feminism – which I view as ahistorical and politically naive, lacking any sense of power relations. As Catharine MacKinnon so succinctly puts it, 'Women are said to value care. Perhaps women value care because men have valued women according to the care they give. Women are said to think in relational terms. Perhaps women think in relational terms because women's social existence is defined in relation to men.'[54]

In the next section of this chapter, I will also look at the inadequacy of maternal feminism in elucidating the connections between property, moral agency and virtue. But now let us move on to possibility 3:

(3) *Accepting the need for a general theory and basing it on a universal need for control and ownership, but demanding that women's need to control property be served equally along with men's* Following this third stratagem, we could note that women might well have much the same needs as men to enjoy the stability and security which property confers, accepting Munzer's psychological picture as genuinely universal. We would then castigate systems of property-holding which refuse this basic human need to women. This would be a mere glancing blow to Munzer's theory, in methodological terms, but it would require a radical shift in his policy formulations. We would be saying that his picture of human motivation and need is correct, although merely fortuitously, given that he has ignored the experience of women in propounding his psychological generalizations; but that he hugely underestimates the difficulties in making his theory work for women. They have been denied fulfilment of these basic needs far more systematically than he realizes. I am much more sympathetic to this view, which will be considered again in the next section.

There is, however, one supreme weakness in this strategy. It tends to turn women under oppressive property regimes into non-persons, into mere victims whose motivations we write off as too dissimilar to our own for real sympathy or comprehension. In this it is actually *not* conducive to women's liberation, returning to the second question at the start of this chapter. Despite its attractively egalitarian slant, it may even spell political suicide, if what most repels non-feminist women about feminism is what they perceive as its patronizing attitude towards women who are not independent minded.[55] We need to find some way of incorporating the insight that women's motivations may not be exactly the same as men's, in order not to castigate women for failing to succeed on the same terms as men in accumulating property.

So perhaps we need to rethink option 3 somewhat. We might accept that there is a 'universal need for control and ownership', and that women's needs are equally as important as men's. But we could look to women's experiences to colour in this broad outline, and we must remember that their experiences will not necessarily be the same as men's. That is, we need to make sure that we are not defining a property-justifying need in masculinist terms. In the final chapter, for example, I will return to the notion of stability and control, but turn it towards relationship, arguing that we need stability of expectations there – reconstructing a new sort of property.

I also wish to leave open the anti-realist or historical materialist possibility suggested by the last option:

(4) *Rejecting the objective notion of need altogether, and viewing property as a political arena of combat* Finally, and most radically, we might deny that needs are objective and empirical at all. As I suggested earlier in criticizing Munzer's moral realism, needs may instead be viewed as socially defined, the product of bargaining and negotiation, particularly within households. This is the approach taken by Henrietta Moore.[56] In Moore's opinion, 'needs' discourse is itself political and problematic; needs cannot be the objective basis of a theory, in naturalistic fashion. Rather, needs must be established as politically legitimate before they are noticed. A relevant example, although not one cited by Moore, would be James Mill's assertion in his 'Article on Government' (1820) that women *needed* no political representation because their interests could be subsumed in men's 'without inconvenience'.[57]

A feminist analysis, particularly a radical and/or a materialist feminist one, reveals that the choice of a discourse or vocabulary is itself political. 'Needs' discourse is intensely so. As Nancy Fraser puts it,

> From this perspective needs talk appears as a site of struggle where groups with unequal discursive (and nondiscursive) resources compete to establish as hegemonic their respective interpretations of legitimate social needs. Dominant groups articulate need interpretations intended to exclude, defuse, and/or co-opt counter-interpretations. Subordinate or oppositional groups, on the other hand, articulate need interpretations intended to challenge, displace and/or modify dominant ones. In neither case are the interpretations simply 'representations'. In both cases, rather, they are acts and interventions.[58]

In chapter 5 I shall examine materialist analyses of property in greater detail, counterposing Marx, MacKinnon, and Christine Delphy. I do not think I have to decide between positions 3 and 4 at this point, or indeed at all: both emphasize power, and neither is essentialist. For now, it has been enough simply to problematize the property-motivation nexus in a way that Munzer does not, but should.

Munzer is unaware of the need to counter any of these four alternative strategies to his own. This is because he misses the point about women, stability of expectations and need. He does answer the less comprehensive objection that property no longer offers the sort of security which allows human flourishing. The 'disintegration' of property, Thomas Grey has argued,[59] means that property no longer consists in material goods protected by the force of the law, as it did in the early stages of capitalism, but of a variety of specialized forms, heavily weighted towards intangibles. The speculator on derivatives or futures, to apply Grey's argument, owns no tangible thing, but merely an obligation to pay out or a claim to collect on the outcome of a bet in future commodity or share prices. The extreme volatility of electronic currency markets, the deregulation of financial services during the 1980s, the increasing proportion of individual wealth represented by pension plans and other holdings which cannot readily be translated into cash in hand, and which may even be plundered by directors – all these might cast doubt on how secure property really makes the propertied. Therefore, Grey contends, property as the ownership of material things is no longer an important concept in legal or political theory. Munzer considers this argument to be thought-provoking but overdrawn. I think he is probably correct: even eighteenth-century early capitalism was beset by speculation (witness the South Sea Bubble).

This lesser point does lead into an important distinction to which Munzer correctly draws our attention. Although the popular conception views property as objects, Munzer emphasizes that most legal commentators conceive of property *not as things*, but as *sets of relations and powers*: to exclude, transfer, and exercise other forms of *control*. Others see it as expectations and claim-rights: again, intangibles.[60] The influential analytical vocabulary proposed by Wesley Newcomb Hohfeld, for example, centres on four types of relation established by property: claim-rights, privileges, powers and immunities.[61] The no-property world, then, is not the world of futures and derivatives, but the world in which there are no expectations whatsoever that one's property claim-rights, privileges and so forth will be met. In the case of intangible property, they are merely met by another form.

But in the world inhabited by what is arguably the historical majority of women, there are no expectations of exclusive control and transfer rights of property. If such firm expectations are basic to stability and human flourishing, we must either conclude that women with limited or non-existent access to property have been unable to live fully human lives, or that Munzer is mistaken about the centrality of property to human flourishing and to moral agency.

Virtue, property and agency

Why does Munzer think that stable possession and reliable expectations about property are central to human action and aspiration? The answer he offers – a standard one in past theories of property as well – is that the power of action requires stability. Munzer identifies agency with the formulation of ends: 'Agency, in its philosophical rather than legal sense, involves actions done from needs, wants, motives, dispositions, inclinations, ends, purposes, plans, projects, and so on.'[62] Persons develop and formulate 'abiding ends', which require stable possession and use of those physical things that are instrumental to them. Although not all projects will necessitate material objects – developing friendships, for example, may not – those that do will be frustrated if the agent cannot depend on the availability of the means. 'It is no good trying to grow wheat if next week someone else can plow the field over for corn. Thus, stable possession and use are necessary to achieve some abiding ends.'[63]

Now this might appear a pretty humdrum way of looking at the universe, abysmally lacking in the tragic sense. As Martha Nussbaum argues, the Greeks believed that the good life for humanity depends on things that we *cannot* control. Not only our physical existence but even our moral excellence is fatally subject to uncertainty, risk and luck – for example, in what situations we are called upon to confront.[64] When Zeus forced Agamemnon to decide between sacrificing the life of his daughter Iphigenia or the lives of his sailors on the plague-stricken vessels, there was no morally right choice which Agamemnon could have made in the situation which he had the ill luck to encounter. On the other hand, although Greek *literature* was imbued with this sense of 'moral luck', *economic life* proceeded on assumptions very much like those Munzer makes, as I shall delineate in the next chapter.

Still, I want to begin this section with some doubts about the links which Munzer draws between agency, expectations and stability. His minimum condition is 'secure access to possess and use material things so long as the end in question requires them; [for] persons would never pursue many ends unless such access could be guaranteed.'[65] To repeat a key point, Munzer thinks that this is a bedrock requirement for agency, although he is willing to concede that stable expectations can be satisfied by something less than freely transmissible property rights on the developed Western model. Yet even this minimum was denied to the Athenian wife, or the South African wife under customary law, or, for that matter, Elizabeth Cady Stanton.

Nevertheless, I think Munzer is right to try to ground his theory of property in agency. Against my own objection that this entails a limited view of personhood, one which lacks the tragic sense, I have pointed out elsewhere[66] that the notion of moral agency as fatally undermined by luck is overdrawn, provided that we can limit the domain of responsibility to those areas we really can control. Notions of control and stability *are* central to agency, I think, although many feminists have rejected the model of the autonomous rational agent as inapplicable to women.[67]

But is this precisely *because* women have lacked the stable property expectations which typify the autonomous agent in Munzer's view? This speculation may seem too deterministic, but the question is worth asking. Lacking what Beauvoir would call the 'concrete means' for claiming the status of subject, perhaps women have had to make a virtue out of necessity. Perhaps they have been obliged to develop alternative means of creating stability and exerting control, substituting power within relationships for economic power? This highlights similar problems about the direction of causation to those which I mentioned at the end of the previous section. There I asked whether women are excluded from property-holding because they are not full civil subjects and moral agents, or the reverse. Does the direction flow from personhood to property, or from property to personhood?

Munzer does not mean that there is an indissoluble and necessary link between property and moral personhood, but he does maintain that property is 'conducive' to moral agency and personality – unless the privileged claim their rights so vigorously as to retard the moral and political personhood of the less fortunate.[68] Property in the sense of some limited personal movables over which one has exclusive transfer rights seems the best candidate for backing up this claim, he concludes.[69] And the private home is typically the locus of individual control, he thinks; in the workplace, for example, property rights may be limited by contract or by health and safety legislation.[70]

This seems a much weaker claim than Munzer's initial assertion that property is a central component of *moral* personality, personhood or agency. Indeed, as his discussion progresses Munzer's assertions become more and more limited. Property may not be necessary for moral personality, but merely helpful to it. 'With qualifications, private property is conducive to personality as moral and political personhood. It also has a bearing on personality in the sense of self-awareness, but only as one factor out of many. And its connections with different psychological conceptions of property appear difficult to ascertain.'[71] But property does assist in the development of self-integration through control, privacy and individuality, Munzer believes. Yet even this limited claim would imply that women in extreme patriarchal property regimes are moral non-persons.

Munzer seems entirely unaware of feminism's identification of the private realm as oppressive for women.[72] But following strategy 3 in our list on p. 26, we might want to accept that Munzer is right to highlight privacy as a universal need. It is just that the private home or the institution of private property have not satisfied this need for women, although we might want to insist that they should. To follow this course, however, we need to become aware of the background reasons in political theory which elucidate why the private has been a limiting rather than an enabling category for women. The discussion of Hegel in chapter 4, for example, will show how the private realm has in fact been construed as *excluding* women from public participation and civic virtue.

Even in relation to men, however, it is notoriously difficult to demonstrate that holding property *creates* personal or civic virtue,[73] although the attempt to do so has been a prominent plank in right-wing politics at the end of the twentieth century. Indeed, there is an equivalently strong view that holding property *debases* moral personality, exemplified by Plato's *Republic*, the writings of Thoreau, much of Marx, and the early work of Proudhon, as well as by Christian asceticism and Buddhism.[74] Even Adam Smith distinguishes between the *vices* produced in the indolent nobility by excessive property-holding, and the virtuous class of servants, labourers and journeymen, whose small portion forces them to be 'frugal, industrious, God-fearing and literate'.[75] Holding too little property, however, is just as brutalizing as holding too much, according to Smith; and certainly Charles Booth's accounts of extreme penury in late nineteenth-century London would bear this out.[76] The republican tradition relies on a similar view about moderate property and the virtues of self-reliance, self-governance, public-spiritedness, practical wisdom and desire for education. Nineteenth-century American feminism accepted this equation in pressing for property rights before suffrage.

We should at least consider the applicability to modern women of these ancient arguments. Women's exclusion from the public realm, including the realm of property-holding, may have produced the dependency which in turn dictates concern for relationships, as MacKinnon argues. If this is so – if the facts of power relations dictate motivations and needs, as well as ethical voices – then women have been denied the particular virtues which moderate property-holding has been said to instil in men. As Jeremy Waldron points out, the putative connection between property and moral virtue is actually a radical argument if we acknowledge equal rights to develop the virtues. It is less likely to become an apologia for existing property distribution if the concentration is on human agency and moral personality rather than on property itself.[77]

More strongly, the denial of property may actually produce vice. 'Maternal' ethics sometimes condones favouritism, for example, rejecting impartiality and other abstract rules of justice.[78] These are the character traits of subordination:[79] while they may be construed as virtues in maternal feminism, they can equally well be called moral deficiencies. The other side of the same maternal feminist coin is the vices condemned in Machiavelli[80] and Aristotle as typically female: putting family interests above those of the community, mean-mindedness and scheming. This is woman as the extinguished subject.[81] Nor is this adverse picture confined to theorists usually seen as misogynists. Mary Wollstonecraft makes a similar argument about the connection between women's economic dependency, their ensuing lack of education, and their tendency to small-mindedness.[82] In her essay comparing Wollstonecraft and Margaret Fuller, George Eliot likewise depicts uneducated, dependent women as 'your unreasoning animal ... the most unmanageable of creatures'.[83]

Munzer offers us a useful reminder of the possible connections between moral agency, an active relationship to property, and some kind of virtue. If there *is* any connection between property, agency and virtue – and I do not think that we can rule that connection out merely because it has only been made for men – then the current feminization of poverty[84] robs women not only of the material means of life, but of the conditions of privacy, stability and a certain calm which conduce towards the good moral life. Then deprivation of property becomes an *ethical* as well as a *financial* wrong done to women, a loss of opportunities to become a fully moral being as well as an affront against justice.

Again, if Munzer is right about property and women's moral personality, it is only by good luck, since he is consistently particularist, ignoring women's case. Nor, as he acknowledges, is he the first to suggest links between property and moral character. Whether in regard to vices or virtues, the affiliation between property and character traits is made most strongly in classical philosophy, especially in Aristotle. Some of these important connections have already been hinted at. In the next chapter I shall examine them in greater detail. Before that, let us recapitulate some of what chapter 1 has sought to establish:

1 A general theory of property need not be incompatible with a feminist emphasis on lived experience; indeed, the false universalism and abstraction which feminists have condemned in canonical theory can be ameliorated by incorporating women's experience of being something other than unequivocally autonomous subjects in relation to property.

2 The construction of property as sets of relations rather than things, which is the accepted model in most jurisprudence and political theory, may also be compatible with a feminist emphasis on relatedness. However, relationship as a criterion for property rights can be a two-edged sword for women; an individualistic model may actually turn out to serve them better (a point which will be further developed in the next chapter). We need to think in terms of two levels of relationship: the

preliminary entitlement to *enter into* the relationships which constitute property transactions, and those relationships themselves.

3 A motivational, developmental account of property as intertwined with personhood and agency could also be attractive to feminist theory. Such a model will also suggest some compelling questions about the direction of causation from property to personhood, or the reverse.

The various canonical traditions should be judged, then, by the extent to which they reflect women's experience, conceive of property in terms of relationships but allow women to enter into those relations on the same terms as men, and enhance self-development. Let us begin with the classical tradition as found in Aristotle.

2

Origins, Narratives and Households

Several puzzles were raised in chapter 1 about property, women, moral agency and political participation, and this chapter will explore them by taking these questions back to their earliest formulations, in classical political theory. Among the issues are:

1 The relation between property-holding, moral personality and civic virtue;
2 The connection between property and the public/private distinction; together with
3 The question of whether property is a genuine need in both sexes, and the related issue of how women make sense of their propertyless existence if property *is* such a need.

At the same time, as in the rest of the book, this chapter will also begin to suggest ways of construing property which are hospitable to women. At the end of chapter 1 I remarked that the various canonical traditions on property should be judged by the extent to which they reflect women's experience, conceive of property in terms of relationship, and enhance subjectivity. There is one more concern which a woman-friendly account ought to fulfil: an interest in property as narrative. That requirement can be suitably explored in relation to Aristotle, since, unlike Munzer and other hypothetical-wielding modern theorists, Aristotle is the theorist *par excellence* of the quotidian and concrete.

But why is narrative so important? I shall suggest that we have inherited from Athens a particularly limited 'storyline' about women and property, whereas other ancient societies operated far more favourable property regimes. Just as there are various constructions of property in the *theories* we inherit, many different property regimes in *practice* have moulded our views. Some regimes have been more hostile to women than others, needless to say. Unfortunately our heritage has been shaped by two of the most objectifying and least liberating for women – the regime of classical Athens and the English common-law doctrine of coverture. *These two cultures have been instrumental in creating the view that women are objects of property rather than subjects.*

Nevertheless that view of women *as* property is entirely understandable, I argue in this chapter and the next, in light of the particularly unfavourable property regimes for women in Aristotle's Athens and in Locke's England. (The discussion here also paves the way for chapter 3, on Locke and Carole Pateman's critique of him, by noting that women were as disadvantaged under the non-contractual property system of Aristotle as under Locke's contractual system.) We have inherited discourses conceived in singularly inauspicious property regimes for women. Understanding the historical roots of the prevalent notion of women as mere objects of property-holding – a portrait which feminists have ironically been all too ready to accept as a good likeness – is the first step to liberating ourselves as subjects.

A concern about property and narrative pervades this book, as it does much recent ethical theory.[1] In each of the next four chapters I tell a different story about women's actual property entitlements, in addition to delineating the theoretical position in a canonical writer of the time. In retelling the story, I attempt to demonstrate that the theatre of property which we have inherited is particularly limited in women's parts. Before I begin, however, I want to add some theoretical background to my concern with narrative by exploring the weight given to narrative as a founding myth in property regimes by the American academic lawyer Carol Rose.[2]

Property and narrative

Rose views community norms expressed in narrative myths about property in a rather Platonic fashion. They impart the same necessary but not strictly rational unity to a political community as does the Noble Lie. Effectively Rose reverses the usual truism that 'possession is nine-tenths of the law': the law of property is nine-tenths narrative, one-tenth the actual fact of possession. As Rose puts it, 'It is not enough, then, for the property claimant to say simply, "It's mine," through some act or gesture; in order for the statement to have any force, some relevant world must understand the claim it makes and take that claim seriously.'[3]

An example which might be cited (though it is not mentioned by Rose) comes from the imposition of colonial powers' narratives over indigenous ones. Before the British Raj, widows in Haryana (then in the Punjab) could legally inherit their husbands' property, but male elders sometimes informally circumvented this legal right by forcing them to remarry within the family, in a practice termed *karewa*. Rather than intervening to protect women's statutory entitlements, British colonial administrators actually strengthened *karewa* with legal sanctions against widows who resisted remarriage, all in the name of preserving customary law – even when the practice was challenged in the courts by the women of Haryana. The women's inability to enforce their property rights against British colonial administrators illustrates the triumph of a different narrative or ideology from that of their traditional law: one conditioned by coverture and the Victorian myth of domesticity. The women of Haryana could not get their story heard, even though it was actually the official one. We shall want to deconstruct our own founding myths of property in order to reconstruct a narrative in which we do have a voice, as the women of Haryana did not.

The use of narrative gets us round the ahistoric essentialism and the passive acceptance of victimization which comes out in Beauvoir's epigram that woman has 'no past, no history, no religion'[4] of her own. But it is a matter of choosing the stories that conduce towards women's liberation, and these are not likely to be the tales we have learned. In particular, as Rose points out, feminist theory uses a different model of the subject than the one that is common in most narratives about property. It aims to break the stranglehold of the self-interested, self-maximizing subject on political, economic and game theory. I shall return to the nature of the protagonist in the property story when I come to discuss a reconstructed model of the subject in chapter 7.

For the present, let us continue with Rose's argument. Individual property regimes rely on a particular ideology or story about women and property, such as the coverture-influenced model used by British colonial administrators in collusion with the Haryana male elders who stood to profit from the abolition of widows' inheritance rights. But in a metatheoretical sense, Rose argues, the very notion of property relies on 'an even bigger story', a founding myth to legitimize a property regime:[5] 'Classic property theory itself has a kind of explanatory glitch: for property regimes to function, some of us have to have other-regarding preference orders. These are preference orderings that the classical property theory would not predict and can only explain *post hoc*, through a story.'[6]

The requisite story in our dominant liberal heritage is, of course, the non-historical, avowedly fictional narrative of the social contract. Classical liberal property theory would not predict cooperation from an agglomeration of self-interested individuals, but any property regime requires an element of cooperation.

Cooperation, then, is a preference ordering that the classical property theorists weren't counting on in theory but that they can't do without. And so they have to tell a story to explain it, and rely on our imaginative reconstruction from narrative to paint a plausible picture about how we got those property regimes in the first place.[7]

Likewise, one might add, the Hobbesian story eventually requires a *deus ex machina*, the sovereign, to break the logjam of individual actors' unwillingness to trust each other sufficiently to lay down their right to self-defence. This is an alternative narrative, but still a story.

Any property regime requires a common core of agreement, what Rose presents as the ultimate form of community in property.[8] The agreement we are concerned with is not only the formal mechanism of social contract or sovereign, as in liberal theory, but the deeper, underlying unanimity in liberal theory on the motivation and background of the protagonists. The audience comes to the theatre with certain expectations about what makes the characters and the action plausible. The reason why the story about self-interest has predominated is explained by Rose, and perhaps feminism more generally, in a materialist manner, as ideological superstructure: 'the dominant storyteller can make his position seem to be the natural one.'[9] But we can choose to replace the Hobbesian story of 'men as if but even now sprung out of the earth . . . suddenly, like mushrooms' with a narrative featuring heroes and heroines who are not entirely self-interested, who set a greater store than classical liberal theory would predict on cooperation and relationship, development and self-development.

In other words, we can choose which narratives to accept, as agents; if we have them thrust upon us, they are only another objectifying tool of the despotic male subject. We have to claim our subjectivity. But many feminist theorists have assumed that the only choice is between the hegemonic story of property and none at all. On the other hand, some feminist theorists *have* returned to the reconstruction of history (or anthropology, or social policy) in order to reformulate our subjectivity: 'to rediscover ourselves in history as subjects with a historical subjectivity which can provide the basis for the creation of a future, grounded in an attitude to the past'.[10]

Furthermore, having stories as a weapon of argument is our inheritance from the feminist movement's emphasis on 'methodological subjectivism . . . a more adventurous idea of rigour which tears the fabric of acquired ideas and moves towards lands whose very existence is not guaranteed in advance',[11] as Le Dœuff argues. This 'tonic rigour, full of juice' is an addition to rational argumentation, not a substitute for it. Philosophy and narrative are entirely complementary, she asserts:

> *Capital* is made of bits and pieces, Descartes recounts his life story and his dreams, Bacon weaves his project with biblical memories, Greco-Roman

myths and quotations from Virgil, and Socrates often calls on strange bursts of imagination to help him in posing problems. Everything must be brought in to undo a world of commonplaces and at the forefront of the project is the demand for rigour: a tonic rigour, full of juice, and very different from the safe rigorism, the self-censored (and always ready to censor) puritanism that we have learned.[12]

So for all these reasons, Rose's concern with narrative is attractive, although not unique to her. In the introduction I was somewhat impatient with what I presented as navel-gazing by maternal or cultural feminists in America and by psychoanalytical or linguistic feminists in Europe. Too often these apparently distinct analyses, concerned so intensely with difference, melt into a common grey relativism.[13] Yet in one respect what they are attempting to do is entirely akin to my project. They offer a different *story* about what it means to be a subject, one that includes being a subject *and* a woman; I am trying to write a different narrative of what it means to hold property *and* to be a woman, one that emphasizes property-holding as an attribute of the active subject. Previously both pairings have often been seen in canonical political theory as mutually contradictory. It is now time to turn to Aristotle as the first illustration of that phenomenon.

Aristotle: 'Nature has distinguished between the female and the slave'

The realization that even within our Western inheritance there are multiple narratives about women and property helps to avoid ahistorical essentialism, along with the dead-end notion that women can only be objects of property-holding. In relation to Greek thought, that view usually comes across as the misconception that all women were effectively slaves. But even at Athens, where the property system afforded women almost no advantages, there were distinctions between married free women, slave women and (to a lesser extent) prostitutes, and I shall be concerned to delineate them in Athenian practice and in Aristotle's thought.

Aristotle poses an interesting problem if we try to apply Le Dœuff's proposition that a philosopher's 'stupid utterances' about women should not be objects of feminist derision but the key to understanding his entire work. The difficulty in Aristotle is a *lack* of sufficient utterances about women, stupid or otherwise. I shall begin by exploring the presence and larger absence of women in the accounts of property given by Aristotle and (to a lesser extent) Plato and Xenophon. In the last section of this chapter, using Aristotle's own will as a connecting device, I compare his theoretical account with the actual position of Athenian women. I conclude that their property entitlements were considerably fewer than those of other Greek women, particularly Cretans, and also fewer than those of Egyptian women. Just as we should be careful not to fetishize Third World women, we should beware of the historical ethnocentrism which sees all women before the twentieth century as equally oppressed. This is an Enlightenment approach, resting on a naive notion of linear progress. Athenian women were worse off than Egyptian women before them and Greek-Egyptians of the Ptolemaic period after them.

In Aristotle the point of property and indeed of economic activity as a whole is the maintenance of the family; yet women's activity in sustaining the household is not recognized. Although Aristotle is careful to distinguish women from slaves, and thus to deny that they are *objects* of property, he does not recognize them as full *subjects*. More specifically, he limits their economic activity to safeguarding, keeping and storing the household property, which is acquired by men. Women's labour adds no value, to put the argument in more modern terms. Wealth is generated by men in much the same way as babies are. There, too, women play the inferior role of mere receptacle; the active, energizing, soul-creating power is all male.[14] The male subsumes the female, in so far as menstrual fluid is merely impure semen, 'needing still to be acted upon'. As the god Apollo argues in Aeschylus' *Eumenides,* advocating Orestes' acquittal on the Furies' charges of murdering his mother Clytemnestra, a mother is not a parent, and therefore no crime of murdering a parent has been committed: 'The mother is no parent of that which is called her child, but only nurse of the new-planted seed that she grows. The parent is he who mounts. A stranger she preserves a stranger's seed, if no god interfere.'

So what need is there for Aristotle to mention the female at all? Only in order to introduce the problem which preoccupies Aristotle more deeply, because it applies to his sex: whether slavery is natural or merely conventional. From the beginning of the *Politics* Aristotle is at pains to establish that 'nature has distinguished between the female and the slave.'[15] Aristotle reinforces this distinction by noting that not even in poor farming households is the wife her husband's slave; the ox is.[16] Later he adds that the propertyless (*aporos*) man uses his wife and children as servants, in the absence of slaves; but this is not to say that they *are* slaves, although some commentators have blurred the distinction.[17]

The distinction between slaves and wives forms part of Aristotle's broader concern about the legitimacy of rule. The 'constitutional' rule of husbands over wives is different from the 'despotic' rule of masters over slaves and the 'royal' power of fathers over children,[18] although in all three cases it is the superior foresight and rationality of the male which legitimizes his authority. 'For the slave has no deliberative faculty at all; the woman has, but it is without authority, and the child has, but it is immature.'[19] When such distinctions as that between slaves and wives are absent, a state of barbarism prevails. 'Among barbarians no distinction is made between women and slaves, because there is no natural ruler among them: they are a community of slaves, male and female.'[20] In other words, barbarians are all objects; Greeks can be autonomous subjects, but only if the right distinctions are made between the various objects of their rule.

Yet Aristotle is much more troubled by the rule of master over slave than by the authority of husband over wife. The *Politics* spends considerable time on the question of whether slavery is genuinely natural or merely conventional.

> For some are of opinion that the rule of a master is a science, and that the management of a household, and the mastership of slaves, and the political and royal rule . . . are all the same. Others affirm that the rule of a master over slaves is contrary to nature, and that the distinction between slave and freeman exists by law only, and not by nature; and being an interference with nature is therefore unjust . . . But is there any one thus intended by nature to be a slave, and for whom such a condition is expedient and right, or rather is not all slavery a violation of nature?[21]

Aristotle's eventual solution is that slavery is both natural and conventional. 'For the words slavery and slave are used in two senses. There is a slave or slavery by law as well as by nature. The law of which I speak is a sort of convention – the law by which whatever is taken in war is supposed to belong to the victors.'[22] The wrong sort of person may turn out to be a slave through the ill chance of being on the losing side in a war, or, in a former period of Athenian history, having to surrender himself to a creditor in order to pay off debts.[23] The wrong sort of person cannot turn out to be a woman. In contrast to his lengthy disquiet about wrongfully enslaved men, Aristotle is barely concerned with the legitimacy of the husband's rule, although his account of women's position in marriage raises serious contradictions about citizenship, freedom and constitutionality. Yet although Aristotle propounds difficulties over why resident aliens, slaves and children have no entitlement to political participation, once more he shows no signs of being troubled about the anomalous position of citizen women.[24]

Wives may not be slaves, but non-alien adult freewomen are not citizens in terms of participation: only for genealogical purposes, in the production of sons who will be citizens. (Even here Aristotle is less willing to accord citizenship to sons of citizen mothers alone than to the offspring of two citizen parents.) The 'special characteristic' of a citizen is that 'he shares in the administration of justice, and in offices.'[25] In the reforms of Cleisthenes (508–7 BC) a citizen is defined as the head of an *oikos* (household) with means of independent living (usually a farm). He is exempt from regular direct taxation and is granted participation in the assembly and the law courts, but is required to fight for the state if necessary. Women do not share in the administration of justice, the defence of the city or the rotation of offices; yet Aristotle unconcernedly refers to them as citizens. Again, they are neither full subjects in rule, nor merely its objects.

Nor do they fully 'own' their bodies; their custodianship of the body that produces citizen sons is merely instrumental. (Although property in the body is a concept which I have already indicated that I shall use sparingly, it is vital to understand that Aristotle regards women's relation to their bodies and the fruits of their bodies as different from men's.) Women's role in reproducing the state's soldiery is not viewed as central to the defence of the *polis*. (Here the Athenian view implicitly foreshadowed Beauvoir's assertion that 'it is not in giving life but in risking life that man is raised above the animal; that is why superiority has been accorded in humanity not to the sex that gives birth but to that which kills.')[26] As Le Dœuff insists, this familiar truism should be problematized.[27] Women risk their lives in childbirth, and the state requires the potential soldiers to whom they give life. Why is women's contribution not rewarded with political rights? The question is central to subsequent accounts of citizenship, even though citizenship has now become 'feminized'.[28] Although it has become common to allege that the link between military participation and citizenship has been broken for men since the abolition of conscription in many European and North American democracies, this is to assume that citizenship usually flowed from and entailed military duties in the past.[29]

A clue may lie in Aristotle's examination of the anomalous position of the artisan class. He is uncomfortable with the notion that those who are too busy with servicing the more affluent should have the same political role as their economic betters. 'The best form of state will not admit them to citizenship; but if they are admitted, then our definition of the virtue of a citizen will not apply to every citizen, nor to every free man as such, but only to those who are freed from necessary services.'[30] If the necessary leisure and space for contemplation or education is denied to artisans, they cannot make sound political judgements, and they cannot be good citizens.

Aristotle does not bother to extrapolate to women, whose position so rarely troubles him, except in so far as he legislates the best age of marriage for the reproductive health of the offspring.[31] We are left to read in his reasons, but the inference is clear: what applies to the artisan class applies all the more strongly to the female sex. Women are never freed from the most 'necessary services': those of reproduction.[32] The average age of girls' marriage in ancient Greece was shortly after menarche; the average age of women's death, well before menopause.[33] Actually women's reproductive labour is valued in a perverse way, so much so that they cannot be spared from it.

It has been said that Aristotle asks of men, 'What can they *do?*'; of women, 'What are they *for?*' What Susan Moller Okin calls Aristotle's 'functionalist' view of women is part and parcel of his instrumental view of those who cannot be full subjects in themselves. Although tradesmen, husbandmen, slaves and women are necessary to the contemplative, leisured and yet active life which is the best existence for man, they cannot themselves participate in that life, or in the virtues which pertain to it. As Aristotle writes: 'Besides, the ruling class should be the owners of property, for they are citizens, and the citizens of a state should be in good circumstances; whereas mechanics or any other class which is not a producer of virtue have no share in the state.'[34] The life of husbandmen and tradesmen is 'ignoble, and inimical to virtue',[35] or at least to the full virtues, rather than the partial ones of obedience to the more wholly virtuous. So, then, is the life of women. That this is so is clear from Aristotle's denigration of the 'taint of meanness' which young children acquire from living with their mothers until his prescribed age of seven, when they can be committed to the more salubrious care of directors of education.[36]

In Aristotle women's absence from the public sphere is mirrored by their subordination in the private realm. It is not that women are simply identified with the private realm and men with the public, and the private realm then 'protected' from public scrutiny or civic duties, as in liberal theory. The private is not a compensatory realm in which women can excel, as Arlene Saxonhouse wishfully suggests: 'The female, as the symbol of what is private, of the home, and what is particular, as the source of children who are one's own and recognized as such by the city at large, is a vivid expression of the need all humans have to tie themselves to that which is particular and one's own.'[37] But this is simply projecting maternal feminism backwards. As Okin remarks of classical Greece, 'The family was simply not the locus for the expression of the deepest human emotions.'[38] It is anachronistic to identify women's private role as separate but equal to men's public one. Rather, I think, Aristotle's male is the 'symbol' or norm in *both* private and public arenas. In both realms women are less than full subjects. In each the justification for men's rule is the same: women cannot fully partake of the relevant virtues – either the informed participation of the citizen or the active acquisitiveness of the household head.

Aristotle identifies both the public and the private realms as political. But here again, anomalies abound. Although Aristotle calls the rule of husband over wife 'constitutional', he must then contend with his own definition of constitutional rule as taking it in turns to wield power, as rule of 'freemen and equals'.[39] In an uncomfortable moment, he admits that this is largely a fiction when applied to the rule of husband over wife:

A husband and father, we saw, rules over wife and children, both free, but the rule differs, the rule over his children being a royal, over his wife a constitutional rule. For although there may be exceptions to the order of nature, the male is by nature fitter for command than the female, just as the elder and full-grown is superior to the younger and more immature. But in most constitutional states the citizens rule and are ruled by turns, for the idea of a constitutional state implies that the natures of citizens are equal, and do not differ at all. Nevertheless when one rules and the other is ruled we endeavour to create a difference of outward forms and names and titles of respect . . . The relation of the male to the female is of this kind, but there the inequality is permanent.[40]

This is an unexpected avowal that men's rule over women is not natural but artificial, marked by the deliberate creation of 'outward forms and names and titles of respect'. It would be more appropriate to call the relationship with children 'constitutional' than the rule over women. Although male children will eventually take their turn to rule, women are always ruled: 'Again, the male is by nature superior, and the female inferior, and the one rules, and the other is ruled; this principle, of necessity, extends to all mankind.'[41] That this is so relates to women's ambivalent status as *neither* full subjects *nor* simple objects of property-holding.

Aristotle maintains that 'the members of the family originally had all things in common',[42] reflecting clan rather than individual ownership in the early Greek world.[43] Yet men rule the family by their very nature. What accounts for this tension between economic equality and political inequality? The answer, I think, lies in Aristotle's account of how the members of the family come to hold their joint wealth in the first place. Relations within the family, gendered relations, determine both the value of women's contribution and the nature of their membership in the household.

Early in the *Politics*, Aristotle asks 'whether the art of getting wealth is the same as the art of managing a household or a part of it, or instrumental to it'.[44] After little further ado, he concludes, 'Now it is easy to see that the art of household management is not identical with the art of getting wealth, for the one uses the material which the other provides.'[45] The next step is to elevate the 'art of acquisition' above that of maintenance; the final stage, to link the art of acquisition with the art of war, as in hunting – and thus by implication with men rather than women. Later Aristotle makes this identification quite explicit. Of husbands and wives, he writes: 'Indeed their part in the management of the household is different, for the duty of the one is to acquire, and of the other to preserve.'[46] In reality, of course, women's labours in spinning, weaving, food-processing and animal husbandry all create a product: wives acquire wealth for their husbands through their labour, adding value to what is by nature mere substance. Given Aristotle's consistent preference for what imparts form to mere substance, one might expect him to recognize that women's labour does add value. But here, as in physical reproduction, Aristotle recognizes only the male contribution as active.

In addition to this proposition about the *origins* of property, Aristotle also offers an argument based on the *consequences* of allowing women to hold property as full subjects in their own right: it leads to too much inequality. In Sparta there is an uncomfortable friction, Aristotle says, between the ideology of equality and the reality of large land concentrations:

> While some of the Spartan citizens have quite small properties, others have very large ones; hence the land has passed into the hands of a few ... And nearly two-fifths of the whole country are held by women; this is owing to the number of heiresses and to the large dowries which are customary. It would surely have been better to have given no dowries at all, or, if any, but small or moderate ones.[47]

By contrast, in a patrilocal and patrilineal society where women cannot inherit, the concentration of income is less, as was true at Athens.[48] In an equally patrilineal and patrilocal society where women *can* hold property in their own right, like Sparta, concentration often occurs in the hands of the rich. The daughter takes her dowry with her to her husband, and the father will marry her off to the richest man he can find for protection of the family capital. (A dowry in land is more valuable security for a woman than a dowry in capital; the transition from land to capital dowries during the Renaissance gave power over the money to the husband, which was merged with his own capital, and effectively limited a woman's control of her wealth.)[49]

It is often said that the comparative equality of land tenure at Athens, together with the system of payment for jury duty and other public service, helped to preserve democracy. Unlike the oligarchic city-states, fourth-century Athens did not even have a property census, and the city had long ago abolished Solon's division of the male citizenry into classes of political rights by wealth. The converse is that this broad spread of wealth and political representation was established on the backs of propertyless women. It was Athenian women's legal inability to control property in land, as full subjects, which equalized the distribution of wealth; and it was their labour which freed Athenian men for political participation. This is an unattractive aspect of Athenian democracy, like the better-known correlation between the more rigid distinction between slave and freeman in classical Athens as compared to the Homeric period, and the beginning of more extensive political participation for those who were fortunate enough to be born free males.[50] Yet as the Danish classicist Mogens Herman Hansen writes, 'It may well be thought that it was the work of the women even more than that of the slaves that provided the male citizens of

Athens with their opportunity to run the political institutions.'[51] Male civic
virtue was intimately related to female propertyless labour.

In both Athens and Sparta, none the less, women brought dowries to
their marriages. They, or rather their fathers, bestowed property on their
husbands. It is particularly odd, then, that the Aristotelian view is the other
way around. Although wives are not property in the sense that slaves are,
Aristotle considers them to be 'bought' in another sense, through vicarious
sharing in the male householder's virtues. The man's economic contribution
to the marriage is thus the greater: not only because he actively acquires the
wealth of the household, but because he allows the wife to participate at
a remove in the virtues which can only belong to men, and to share in the
children who are created predominantly by the male. Once more, I repeat,
only men can add value in Aristotle. The wife benefits from that added
value at a remove; she can create none herself. Although she is not bought
in any literal sense – and indeed was more likely in actual Greek society to
do the 'buying' in the sense of bringing a dowry – women's property status
in Aristotle is by no means that associated with an autonomous subject.

Elsewhere in classical thought, women's status is equally anomalous.
The French author Nicole Loraux has suggested that only in tragedy were
Greek women active subjects, and that even there their actions are limited
primarily to self-sacrifice, often suicide.[52] Certainly other classical philosophers agreed with Aristotle in denying women full subjectivity, even
though Aristotle is often seen as the arch-misogynist of classical thought.[53]
In Plato the abolition of private property leads famously to the demise of
the private family and to some degree of emancipation, at least for guardian
women.[54] However, rather surprisingly, Plato is far more prone than
Aristotle to assign women the role of objects which property-holding male
subjects may possess. In the *Laws*, for example, Plato typifies the second-
best situation as one in which 'women and children and houses remain
private, and all these things are established as the private property of
individuals.'[55] In the *Republic* Socrates discusses the 'right acquisition and
use of children and women' and 'the law concerning the possession and
rearing of the women and children'.[56]

This is puzzling, because in some senses women *are* full subjects in the
Laws. Plato allows women to take part in the common meals, if only
because their greater propensity to evil requires the legislators to keep an
eye on them. (As Aristotle sniffs, 'No one else has introduced such novelties
as the community of women and children, or public tables for women:
other legislators begin with what is necessary.')[57] The 'community of wives'
has been analysed extensively,[58] but little attention has been paid to the
question of the common meals (*syssitia*). Yet it is partaking of public meals
which enables women to be citizens, and full subjects, in the *Laws*. In so
far as they share in the common property and are fed from the public purse,

they share in communal, civic life and are removed from the domestic sphere. (This insight into the linkage between civic life and *communal* property, both extended to women, stands in sharp contrast to the liberal and republican views of citizenship as contingent on *private* property-holding.)

In Xenophon's *Oekonomikos*, the wife's share in the household's private property does not liberate her; rather it justifies her subjection. The speaker Ischomachos insists that although it is natural for women to be occupied with management within the house and men to concern themselves with the outside world, both sexes make an equal contribution to the household's economy. As Ischomachos remarks to his nameless bride:

> As to myself, everything of mine I declare to be in common, and as for you, everything you've brought you have deposited in common. It's not necessary to calculate which of us has contributed the greater number of things, but it is necessary to know this well, that whichever of us is the better partner contributes the things of greater worth.[59]

Xenophon makes his speaker refute the wife's modest disclaimer that she contributes no labour which adds value – the view which Aristotle resoundingly endorses. Furthermore, he regards her position in the household as in some sense political: she is to be 'a guardian of the laws regarding the things in the house', explicitly comparable to the rulers of the city.

> I taught her that in the cities subject to good laws the citizens do not think it enough merely to have fine laws, but in addition choose guardians of the laws to examine them, to praise the one who acts lawfully, and to punish the one who acts contrary to the laws. Then I suggested that my wife consider herself a guardian of the laws regarding the things in the house . . . and that, like a queen, she praise and honor the deserving to the limit of her capacity, and rebuke and punish the one who needs such things.[60]

This is an interesting evocation of property as a set of relationships, similar to those which prevail in the political realm, and it also challenges the public–private distinction. Yet again it is clear that the wife's domestic 'queendom' is at most a satrapy, in the gift of the husband-king. What immediately follows this moderately enlightened passage is the paradoxical assertion that it is actually the wife's equal share in the household property which makes her subject to her husband's rule.

> In addition I taught her that she could not be justly annoyed if I gave her many more orders in regard to our possessions than I gave the servants, displaying to her that the servants share in their master's wealth only to the extent that they carry it, attend to it, or guard it, and that no one of them is allowed to use it unless the lord gives it to him, whereas everything is the master's to use as he wishes. To the one deriving the greatest benefit from its preservation

and the greatest harm from its destruction belongs the greatest concern for a thing – this I declared to her.[61]

The master's and mistress's exclusive entitlements to enjoy the household's wealth do not make the wife independent; they justify a relation of subordination to her husband. At most she is allowed to be an extinguished subject; by identification with her lord, she becomes the ambiguous 'one deriving the greatest benefit' and must demonstrate 'the greatest concern' for their mutual property. What the household property gives her is not independence, but a motive for obedience and diligent self-sacrifice.

Wives, mistresses, slaves and prostitutes: women in Greek property law

The dependent status of Athenian wives is reflected in Aristotle's own will,[62] even though he had no wife. On his death Aristotle left a mistress, Herpyllis, by whom he apparently had a son named Nichomachos (of the *Nichomachean Ethics*), a son called Myrmex and a tellingly unnamed daughter. As befits the distinction between women, children and property in his political theory, Aristotle distinguishes them in his will. Together with five other men, his executor Antipater was to 'take charge as well of Herpyllis and the children and of the property' until the arrival of Nicanor, to whom the nameless daughter was to be given in marriage. 'And if anything should happen to Nicanor (which heaven forbid!) either before he marries the girl, or when he has married her, but before there are children, any arrangements that he may make shall be valid.' More specifically, if Nicanor does die before the wedding, the girl is to be married to Theophrastos if he will have her. If not, the executors are to decide on her husband.

'In memory of me and of the steady affection which Herpyllis has borne towards me', she receives considerable property in the will:

> Besides what she has already received, they [the executors] shall give her a talent of silver out of the estate and three handmaids, whomsoever she shall choose, besides the maid she has at present and the manservant Pyrrhaeus; and if she chooses to remain at Chaleis, the lodge by the garden, if in Stagira, my father's house. Whichever of these two houses she chooses, the executors shall furnish with such furniture as they think proper and as Herpyllis herself may approve.

This appears reasonably generous provision, as does the proviso that all Aristotle's slaves are to have their freedom – 'when they arrive at the proper age . . . if they deserve it'. But the last phrase gives the game away. Herpyllis is judged to have deserved this bequest, first, as a mark of respect to Aristotle, and second, in recognition of her fidelity to him. She receives nothing in her own right: everything is in relation to her dead master.

However, as a mistress Herpyllis retains an atypical degree of independence. What she does receive is hers, unless she chooses to marry, in which case it becomes the property of her husband. An Athenian wife could not possess property in her own right: her dowry passed from her father to her husband, the two partners in her marriage contract – to which she was not a party. And whereas Herpyllis has the freedom to choose whether to marry after Aristotle's death – although not whom she will marry, a matter for the executors – no freeborn Athenian woman could choose *not* to marry, or select her own husband. Classical Greek literature abounds in advice on choosing a bride or a son-in-law, but not on choosing a husband, since no woman could. As Okin points out, the shock of modern commentators at the *Republic's* insistence on eugenically dictated marriages, rather than 'love' ones, ignores the fact that no Athenian woman had anything but a dictated marriage.[63] Plato was only taking away *men's* freedom of choice. Similarly, Aristotle's anonymous daughter is to be married to Nicanor, or, if Nicanor dies first, to Theophrastus if *he* will have *her*. He is allowed to say no, in which case the executors choose again: but *she* will never choose.

Aristotle's will illustrates several features of the Athenian property regime in relation to women: above all, the power of a woman's *kyrios* or lord.[64] Herpyllis is entirely dependent on the whim of her dead *kyrios* Aristotle, however generous or mean he chooses to be. She is luckier than his unnamed daughter, or than she would have been as his legal widow, in that she has no *kyrios* on his death, unless she chooses to marry. Her position also illuminates the differential treatment of married freewomen and of the *hetaira* or mistress, who was usually not free – although she might have been manumitted by her lovers. To understand women's property position in Greece, we need to look at various social distinctions – freeborn or slave, artisan or aristocrat, respectable woman or prostitute; and at different cities or *poleis*.

But let us begin with the Athenian married woman. To understand the property regime which applied to her, it is necessary to take one step backwards and introduce the notion of the *oikos* or household. In archaic mainland Greece wealth was seen as belonging to the household, not to individuals. Classical Athens was beginning to make a transition towards the rival concept of independent ownership by a (male) individual, but Athenian law was still heavily influenced by the older notion. (The Spartan man, in contrast, was free to leave his property to whomsoever he wished – oddly enough, in view of the more communal ideology there.) Property in Athens belonged primarily though not exclusively to the household, the *oikos*; the head of the household, the *kyrios*, controlled it by virtue of his authority. A woman spent her entire life under the control of one *kyrios* or another.

> At a woman's birth, her father was her *kyrios*; at his death, her brothers. When she married, her husband assumed the economic responsibilities of the *kyrios*, though he did not have the right to give her in marriage to a third party (at least, not during his lifetime). After her husband's death or retirement, her sons became her *kyrioi*.[65]

The Athenian property regime for women thus depended on order generated through *relationship*, not on direct holdings in objects *by* women or *of* women as objects of property. However, the initial entitlement to enter into property as relationship in turn depended on prior relationships within the household, and those relations were far from egalitarian. This helps to elucidate point 2 at the end of the previous chapter (p. 36): the two-edged nature of relationship when it comes to women and property. In the more communal and traditional regime of Athens, compared to other Greek city-states which were beginning to operate more individualistic models of property, women lost out.

The *effect* of being a *kyrios* was to give a man the deciding power over the property of the *oikos*, although the *purpose* of the household was to accumulate wealth and provide security through the generations. If property is defined in the Hohfeldian fashion as claim-rights in relationship, then the Athenian *kyrios* owned the household as property, as well as the real property of the household – although that is not the same as owning his wife directly. Property as claim-rights also entails being bound by others' claims. The powers of the *kyrios* were limited by those of his legal heirs: he could not make a will or adopt a son if this would disinherit his own legitimate sons. They were also limited by the claims of his wife's family of origin: if his marriage proved childless or ended in divorce for any other reason, he was obliged to return his wife's dowry to her father or brothers, who resumed *kyrios* status over her. She relied on her dowry as *de facto* protection, but it was not hers *de jure*.

The husband's only legal obligation to his wife was to maintain her so long as he kept her dowry. The dowry could be confiscated to meet his debts, although in that case he had to stay in his wife's good books, to avoid the threat of having to return the non-existent dowry on divorce. But divorce was not in her interest either: a childless divorced woman had no legal claim to maintenance in any household, and she was dependent on the charity of her family of origin. In general, a wife's legal protection was greatest relative to her husband's in old age, bearing out my general hypothesis that a woman's relation to property is always different from a man's. Men had the *least* protection when they retired from their position as *kyrios* in favour of their sons, exchanging their economic power in return for maintenance, like King Lear; they then depended on others' good will, much as their wives had always done.

A married Athenian woman could not own land, the most secure and prestigious form of property. There are no records of women buying land; if land is mentioned, it is usually as security for a dowry, guaranteeing payment of the debt from the husband to the family of origin in case of divorce. To the extent that land is the source of wealth in a largely agrarian economy, we may have here one answer – inability to see beyond the gendered Athenian land tenure regime – to the question of why Aristotle could not conceive of women as acquiring wealth, even though he noted that in Sparta two-fifths of the land belonged to women.

Records of married couples jointly acquiring or holding land are non-existent in ancient Greece.[66] But there is epigraphic and statute evidence that women *did* own land on their own elsewhere in Greece besides Sparta: at Delphi, Gortyn, Thessaly, Tenos, Ceos, Megara, and Theta – although nowhere did women own as much land as men. Their holdings in land were most secure in cities where the archaic conception of land as belonging to the lineage rather than the individual was less marked. *In other words, an individualistic conception of land ownership worked to women's advantage.* This should make us cautious of automatically distrusting the notion of individual property rights, as the ethic of care does (indeed, it eschews the notions of both the individual and rights). More specifically, the comparison with other Greek states also tends to undermine Pateman's contention that the possessive liberal model of individual ownership oppresses women; it suggests the opposite, at least for ancient Greece.

Turning from land to other forms of property, we find another reversal of the expected: the nearer a woman came to being an *object* herself – to being or having been a slave – the easier it was for her to be a property-owning *subject* (although in Athens she still could not own property in land). Concubines had a legal entitlement to agree a payment from those who gave them as concubines. This sort of dowry was apparently paid directly to them, putting them in a superior position to that of respectable wives. In contrast, a married freewoman did not even have title to her clothes and jewellery. Personal accoutrements which she brought to her husband's household had to be returned to her family if she divorced; a *hetaira* could own her own accoutrements and furniture. Essentially a married Athenian woman owned no movables: they were either 'on loan' from her family of origin as part of her dowry, or her husband's property. She may have had *de facto* control, and normally her husband would bequeath them to her on his death. But they were his to bequeath. The *kyrios* could sell, mortgage or pledge any property belonging to the household, without the wife's consent. This was an even more repressive property regime than that of ancient China, where a wife's personal possessions in the form of jewellery and clothes were kept separate from the *jia* or family estate; they remained part of her personal fund.[67]

So when Aristotle says that acquiring property is something *men* do, he merely reflects the particularly extreme Athenian property law. Earlier I asked why women were not seen as contributing to the wealth of the household through their dowries. The answer is twofold: it was not their wealth but that of their previous *kyrios*, usually the father. And it was not given unconditionally, but merely on loan to the new *oikos*. What transformed the loan into property belonging unequivocally to the husband was normally the birth of legitimate sons, that is, the extension of the lineage to another generation. Note again the emphasis on property as created and conditioned by relationship.

Conversely, 'if the law could treat Athenian women as having no property, it was because they had, in fact, no real way of acquiring it.'[68] This applies primarily to married freewomen of the upper classes; there is ample evidence that Athenian women, usually poor widows or freed slaves, worked for pay as weavers, potters, milliners, cobblers, café keepers, drapers, grocers and perfumiers. By law these tradeswomen could not be paid more than a medimnus of barley (about six days' food supply), or buy any item worth more than that. Any larger transaction required the consent of the woman's *kyrios*, since a larger purchase could endanger the wealth of her *oikos*. Presumably a woman could not *receive* more than that without authorization because it would endanger the wealth of the household which paid it out.

The greatest commercial freedom was reserved for non-Athenian women, or widows living in distant relatives' houses, where the relationship with the *kyrios* was rather contingent. The *hetaira* also did quite well out of the law, even though (or perhaps because) she was formally outside it.[69] Like young freeborn male prostitutes, she had a formal contract with her 'protectors', with whom she usually had long-term connections, sometimes with more than one.[70] The financial independence of the *hetaira* might be restricted by her *proxenete* or go-between, however: because it was so difficult for women to acquire capital, and since it was so expensive to set up the gilded nest which a well-born client required, most depended on a go-between for their start in the trade.

Despite all these restrictions, the widespread economic activity under-taken by women even in Athens should make us wary of assuming that property is not a female need, is not a motive in the narrative. Where women did have opportunities to acquire (non-landed) property, they attempted to do so. Furthermore, Athens was atypical; throughout the rest of Greece women enjoyed a more active relationship to property. At Thespiae and Thera, for example, women could engage in large transac-tions without the consent of their *kyrioi*. Outside Athens it was more

common for Greek law to distinguish between property acquired by the
woman (which could generally only be alienated by her, though with the
consent of her *kyrios*) and that acquired by the man (which could only be
alienated by him). Clearly Athenian property law reflects an older conception on mainland Greece, as is evidenced by the archaic measure of the
medimnus. If all property, whether acquired by a man or a woman, is seen
as belonging to the *oikos*, then the consent of the head of the *oikos*, the
kyrios, is the only way to ensure that it remains within the household.
Again, the notion that property belonged to a communal body – the
household or the lineage – appears to serve women badly.

In Gortyn, south of Knossos on Crete, a more individualistic regime
prevailed. Daughters could inherit in their own right, although they
received only half of the sons' share. At Gortyn each member of the family,
male or female, was viewed as a potential individual property-holder,
although property was by no means equally distributed between men and
women. The archaic conception of wealth as belonging to the household
or lineage was less pronounced than at Athens, but still important: women
could not inherit the family house, or the cattle, which were an important
constituent of its joint wealth. Nevertheless, they could manage or dispose
of their inheritance without the consent of a *kyrios*. Gortynian law
specifically forbade a husband to alienate or pledge his wife's property,
including her dowry, or a son his mother's; essentially, it abolished the
economic autonomy of the *kyrios*.

Likewise, a Gortynian heiress (*epikleros*) had the right to refuse to marry
her *anchisteus*, the male member of her family of origin to whom Athenian
law would have given her as a bride in order to keep the inheritance within
the lineage. (Although the Athenian *epikleros* was formally the heiress, the
actual control of the property passed to the *anchisteus*; because it would
have been anomalous for him to be her *kyrios* but not her husband, he had
to marry her.) Gortynian law also allowed a girl to decide on her husband,
a privilege enjoyed by no Athenian woman. At Gortyn the dowry was
formally a gift to the bride from her family of origin; while she had no
further claim on the estate, this marriage portion remained hers throughout. Although a daughter's portion was limited to half of a son's share, the
Gortynian woman benefited from the fact that the amount was guaranteed,
that it was hers of right rather than as a boon from her father, and that it
was hers, rather than the property of her *kyrios*. She could own this and
other property independently, even as a married woman, and at divorce or
on widowhood she was entitled to a portion of the wealth which the
household had acquired during the marriage.[71]

In inheritance law, Gortyn recognized both paternal and maternal
property, indicating that a woman could bequeath her wealth as an
individual. Although an intestate woman's property could only be passed

on after her husband's death, he could not sell or mortgage it until their children were of an age to give or withhold their consent. The very concept of a will was new in Greece during the classical period, implying as it did the primacy of individual over lineage, and it was not extended to women anywhere but at Gortyn. Why was this? It seems plausible that Crete was a half-way house between mainland Greece and Egypt, where women's property-holding had long been assured. Gortyn was not involved in mainland Greece's wars, and may well have retained older influences, such as those of Egypt.[72]

From the earliest period, Egyptian wives could inherit from husbands, and daughters from fathers, without any of the restrictions put on the Athenian *epikleros*. As early as the Third Dynasty, an official called Metjen stated that he inherited fifty *arouras* of land from his mother.[73] Around the year 1900 BC, during the Twelfth Dynasty, the priest Wah left his estate entirely at his wife's disposal:

> Will made by the priest Wah: I am making a will for my wife . . . Sheftu called Teti – of everything that my [wifeless and childless] brother Ankhreni gave to me, with all the goods as they should be, of all that he gave me. She herself shall give [them] to any of her children that she shall bear me, that she wishes. I am giving her the three Asiatics which my brother . . . Ankhreni gave to me. She herself shall give them to any of her children that she wishes.[74]

Teti has not yet borne children, yet her marriage's validity is not dependent on her fecundity. There is no requirement that any sons she may bear shall inherit first, above daughters, or indeed inherit at all. Compare the Athenian laws as stated by Demosthenes:[75] the estate of a man who dies without sons cannot legally be inherited by the daughters in their own right, but merely 'goes with' them as *epikleroi* to their new male masters, their *kyrioi*. And this will is not an exception: throughout the New Kingdom, as in earlier periods, all children, both male and female, generally received equal shares from their parents, usually on condition that they gave the dead parent a proper burial.[76] A wife could frame her will differently from her husband's and disinherit whichever of her children she wished.

In one instance, a twice-married woman called Naunakht, who had inherited extensive property in her own right from her first husband, made a will disposing of this property and her share from the second marriage in favour of the children whom she regarded as having maintained her properly. The father, by contrast, included all his children equally in inheriting his share of the joint property.[77] The husband agreed to Naunakht's will before witnesses – an embarrassing circumstance that would never have arisen for an Athenian *kyrios*. In another case, a document of the late Middle Kingdom records a lawsuit brought by a woman, Tahenwet, against her father, alleging that he has given some of her own slaves to his second wife Senebytsy.[78] In Athens, of course, a wife could not own slaves or any other form of property, and an unmarried daughter could not bring suit against her *kyrios*, her father; if she was married, only her husband could launch the action.

In Ptolemaic Egypt, shortly after the period in which Aristotle wrote, the older Egyptian property regime continued to dominate over Greek influence. A papyrus of AD 133[79] records the will of Taarpaesis, also called Isadoura, who left both her male and her female children as executors and divided the property between them in much the same ratio as would have obtained at Gortyn: about twice as much to the son. Her daughters Bernice and Isidora receive two houses to share between them; these properties will remain in their own names, 'because of the agreement each of them has with her husband, under the terms of which she keeps her own possessions'. That such an agreement had to be made specially might argue that married Greek-Egyptian women's property-holding was not automatic; but that it could be legally valid at all is more than could have happened at Athens.

Although the son Ptolemaeus received the lion's share – his mother's house in Oxyrhynchus and her lands in the village of Phoboou – it is interesting to note that she had herself inherited this property from her own mother. No Athenian woman could bequeath or own land, although she could receive an inheritance as *epikleros* under strict conditions which ensured that the wealth remained in her lineage. It was not hers to dispose of, and she herself could be claimed in marriage – or taken away from her existing husband – by a male of her family of origin, so as to keep the inheritance in the family. If she had a son two years past puberty, the inheritance passed to him, under the minimal condition that he continue to feed his mother. Furthermore, Taarpaesis/Isadoura was able to alienate her property outside the family, as not even an Athenian man could without fear of a lawsuit from his male kin. Besides the bequests to her adult children, and a field to her grandson Eision, all other property and income went to a family friend, Psenesis.

All this implies, first, a conception of property as belonging to the individual rather than the lineage; and second, the notion that women can be property-holding individuals. Nor were Egyptian women's property transactions limited to matters of inheritance.[80] Women could administer family estates as heiresses, or, on a smaller scale, grow and sell produce. Women stewards were put in charge of grain storehouses; two queens in the Old Kingdom had women grain stewards, and another a female 'inspector of treasures', 'overseer of ornaments' and 'overseer of cloth'. Despite the nominal ownership of all land in the name of the Pharaoh, women as well as men could transact in land and houses, for income or investment. They could enter into business deals and bring lawsuits to enforce their property claims, a privilege allowed to no woman under Athenian law.

This economic autonomy seems to have been linked with civic member-ship and political agency. Whereas service on an Athenian jury was strictly a male privilege, women are recorded as serving on the court at Deir-el-Medina, the workmen's village near Thebes. Although this may not have been typical, there are more frequent mentions of women witnesses, plaintiffs and defendants in legal actions. At Athens women could not even appear in their own defence in court. The direction of causation is not certain – from economic to political personhood or the reverse? – but the correlation is clear.

Yet as in Gortyn, the Egyptian husband in all periods was still formally head of the household. Most houses belonged to men in the lists of property-holders, as did most tomb chapels. There was a firm boundary between male and female occupations, and the elite state bureaucracy was entirely male: sons could inherit their father's office, but daughters did not. Girls had no need of literacy, although there may have been a few female scribes, and women may have learnt enough to keep household or business accounts.[81] Most women would have been dependent on their husbands for basic support, and widows were vulnerable. Although women possessed almost completely equal rights before the law – in sharp relief against Athens – social and economic reality was less egalitarian.

Nevertheless the Egyptian and Cretan examples warn us against ahistorical essentialism of the sort which denies that women have a need for property on the supposed historical evidence that women have not had property in the past. Even with the limitations on women's property-holding in Egypt, Crete, and the rest of mainland Greece, Athens looks more and more the odd one out in the ancient world. It is all the more likely, then, that Aristotle's 'universalism' was intensely particularist, that his blind spots were influenced by his concentration on Athens; all the more plausible that we have been unfortunate to inherit canonical accounts from atypically patriarchal Athens.

It is also all the more unfortunate that many otherwise sophisticated feminist thinkers have been blinded by the dominance of Athenian models in our theoretical heritage. This is one bit of consciousness which feminism has not yet raised. Moira Gatens, for example, criticizes the view, found in J. S. Mill, that women have less independence in a natural state, where male strength dominates, than in a more highly evolved economy.

> Mill overlooks the fact that women are still disadvantaged, even though they are no longer excluded by the criterion of physical strength, in that power now becomes associated with wealth and property. Given that, in a patriar-chal society, women are restrained by the demands of the private sphere and often disadvantaged by the rules of patriarchal inheritance, they actually have less power than previously.[82]

'Patriarchal' is too blunt a concept here. Both Athens and Gortyn were undeniably patriarchal societies, as well as patrilineal. Yet the Gortynian woman had far more control in the private sphere, for example over the choice of a husband, and she could indeed inherit, although less than her brother. It is too general and simplistic to talk about 'the rules of patriarchal inheritance' as if they were uniform. I cannot emphasize too often that there are *various* traditions to draw upon in both theory and practice. But as I suggested in my introduction, feminist theorists too often lack sophistication about property; malestream property theorists typically lack awareness about women.

For the Athenian woman, the problems about agency, motivation and virtue first teased out in chapter 1 remain troubling. Stability and intergenerational transmission of the property belonging to the patrilineal household were central concerns of the Greeks, and Aristotle certainly believed that the good life for a freeborn male citizen depended on such control. Hannah Arendt has hypothesized that the ownership of a house was not merely of economic but of political importance to the Athenian man:

> What prevented the *polis* from violating the private lives of its citizens and made it hold sacred the boundaries surrounding each property was not respect for private property as we understand it, but the fact that without owning a house a man could not participate in the affairs of the world because he had no location in it which was properly his own.[83]

But Arendt's interpretation is only half correct: it is too anachronistic. What the Athenian *kyrios* controlled was not merely the physical dwelling, the house, but a *household*, including its women's reproductive value, their transferred dowries and the value which their work added to his household wealth. It was property in the private household which gave the master a place in the outside world. In men's case, the direction of causation seems clearer, and perhaps we can infer something important from that for women: the flow is from economic agency to political personhood. In classical Athens, citizenship was defined in terms not only of militia duty, but primarily as ownership of the means of independent living, such as a small farm. Women were excluded from political life not because they could not bear arms – indeed, we have records of Greek female naval captains – but because Athenian women did not own the means of independent living. Nor, even more importantly, did they own the property in their own persons: that belonged to their *kyrios* or lord, usually their husbands. Without autonomy over their own bodies and actions, they could not be given the right of political control over those who did own themselves, freeborn men.

True, the Athenian *kyrios* was in some senses the steward rather than the outright owner of the household's wealth; perhaps we might conceive of his 'ownership' more as a kind of entail, limited by lineage and *oikos*. But although the male householder was also constrained by relationship, his status *as* householder gave him a place in civil society. Conversely, the Athenian woman's propertylessness was part and parcel of her absence from the civil and political realm. Only the *kyrios* of the household – and neither women nor slaves, although the two were not synonymous – could participate in the Athenian democratic polity. Justice and the legitimacy of the *polis* depended on policing those exclusionary boundaries strictly. In the *Prosecution of Neaira*, for example, the prosecutor appeals to the jurors to enforce the founding rules of full civic membership against a slave-born, non-Athenian woman.[84]

Women had no place in the political realm, no location in it which was properly their own; and in the domestic realm they lived in a no-property world. Again, however, we would expect an Athenian wife's 'abiding ends', in Munzer's phrase, to concern the welfare of her children and the household into which she had married; yet she had no stable property expectations in regard to either. Possibly the Athenian woman was not fully an agent, in Munzer's terms? She certainly does not fit easily into the mould of the preference-satisfying, egoistic individual. Yet her projects and concerns for her children and household were doubtless central to her daily existence and to her moral virtue as a good wife. It seems patronizing and simplistic to say that she was something less than a fully human agent.

Munzer's 'no-property world' finds its extreme in the situation of the Athenian wife, who had no private possessions. If Munzer were to consider the situation of women, as he usually does not,[85] he would be forced to conclude that they lacked enough property to develop minimal control, privacy and individuality by his standards. Without some benchmark of the minimum, even conceding individual variation in what people can tolerate, Munzer's Floor Thesis would be meaningless; and it is difficult to see who could be regarded as failing the minimal test if *not* the Athenian wife. Essentially a married Athenian woman owned no movables, not even her clothes: they were either 'on loan' from her family of origin as part of her dowry, or her husband's property. Put another way, distaff Athens was a world of relationships and only relationships, but not one which even a 'maternal' feminist should find comfortable: rather, one of utter dependency. It is not implausible that a psychological sense of privacy, individuality and self-integration would be difficult to develop in such circumstances, especially when we add in the Athenian wife's inability to exclude her husband from her body.

Nevertheless, Athenian women were expected to conform to moral standards and to exercise an admittedly limited set of virtues, most prominently, *sophrosyne* or self-restraint.[86] It seems extreme and patronizing to conclude that they had no moral agency, individuality or personhood. Yet perhaps it is not mere coincidence that Athenian women were encouraged to develop only one virtue, and that they also had so few property rights. It is as if they could also own only an impoverished set of virtues – lacking the virtues of the householder and citizen.

Clearly virtues such as liberality and generosity, which are greatly extolled in Aristotle, can only be exercised by those who have something to give away. Was the apparently impoverished *moral* life of Athenian women actually rooted in their *literal* impoverishment? A correlation seems plausible: classical culture differentiated both virtue and property-holding by gender. But what about active causation? This question is of more than historical importance. If being barred from property-holding means that women are also deprived of full moral development and active agency, we are back to the questions raised in the introduction by Beauvoir's assertion: 'Woman does not claim the status of subject because she lacks the concrete means to do so.'[87] If women are 'extinguished subjects' because they lack property, they are less than full moral agents, and the range of virtues open to them may be circumscribed.

We saw in chapter 1 that Munzer accepts property as a moralizing force, good for a person's sense of identity and agency. This view is primarily rooted in later theories: in liberalism, and even more strongly in Hegelianism. But it is important also to acknowledge its debt to Aristotle, and, more crucially, to realize that property can only civilize *men* in Aristotle. Women remain outside its beneficial ambit. This is evident from Aristotle's explicit discussion of the two virtues which private property best promotes: 'first, temperance towards women (for it is an honourable action to abstain from another's wife for temperance sake); secondly, liberality in the matter of property. No one, when men have all things in common, will any longer set an example of liberality or do any liberal action; for liberality consists in the use which is made of property.'[88] Moderately enlightened modern male commentators tend to snigger slightly at this passage,[89] but this is to miss its point. As Le Dœuff says, a writer's most sexist utterances tell us most about his theory. This passage makes it plain that Aristotle exempts women *as subjects* from the moral development which private property promotes; at most they may benefit from the virtue of male temperance *as objects*.

The connection between virtue, subjectivity, civic membership and property is clearly elucidated by the example of Aristotle and Athens. I hope that this chapter has also demonstrated the need to distrust ahistorical essentialism, and the corresponding need for narrative. Unless we tell the story of women's property and propertylessness carefully, we as feminists may be as guilty of false universalism as 'malestream' theorists have often been. The story thus far has revealed some surprises: for example, that women are better served by an individualistic property regime, such as those obtaining at Gortyn and in Egypt, than by one which emphasizes the communal household, like the Athenian model. This will have a direct bearing on the argument in chapter 3, which concerns liberal individualism.

3

Contract, Marriage and Property in the Person

The classical antecedents of Munzer's views about property, stability and motivation have been examined, but the *locus classicus* of the position which attributes virtue to rational acquisitiveness, and agency to prudent control over property, is not classical at all. It is, of course, liberal – identified primarily with Adam Smith, John Locke, and, in the modern period, Robert Nozick and Friedrich von Hayek. What Munzer presents as empirical facts about human motivation are liberal assumptions, theoretically conditioned: a site of struggle, as Henrietta Moore suggests. In recent years that conflict has been fought between politically dominant neoliberalism and feminist challengers. My aim in this chapter is to strengthen the challenge by making it more sophisticated, not to give further ammunition to already well-munitioned neoliberals. But I shall also be arguing that feminists have been too quick to dismiss two concepts central to liberal thought on property: contract, and property in the person. Women *can* use both, I assert, to claim the status of subject.

In this chapter I shall be content to prove the *negative* claim that contract is *not* itself inimical to women's interests, setting this assertion in the context of liberal contractarianism. Contractual relations do not have to be unequal and oppressive, although many feminists have thought them so. Chapter 4 advances the argument further by positing *positive* benefits in contract for women, developing a style of thinking suggested by a feminist analysis of Hegel. The justification offered for contract by Hegel turns out to centre on self-development and agency, which are also crucial to Hegel's broader justification of property. Although Hegel does not extend the full benefits of either contract or property to *women's* self-development, I begin to formulate ways of doing so in chapter 4, and chapter 7 will take that analysis further when I come to reconstruct property.

I have argued all along that we inherit not one but many constructions of property and agency, and that some are more 'woman-friendly' than others. In this chapter I want to strengthen that claim: even the most allegedly inhospitable theories are not as relentlessly hostile as some feminists have claimed. Despite his supposed misogyny, Aristotle, for example, does not conceive of women solely as the objects of property-holding, although they are not full subjects either. If I can prove my argument in relation to contractarian liberalism here, and to Hegel in chapter 4, my argument will apply *a fortiori* to other, less frequently condemned strands in canonical political theory.

Liberalism and its recent political revival have given property a bad name as far as many feminists are concerned. Feminist lawyers and social policy scholars have castigated the liberal presumption that both partners have equal standing in the marriage 'contract'. Feminist historians have high-lighted the inconsistency between the crusading iconoclasm of nineteenth-century liberals in favour of men so that their lack of property should be no bar to their political participation, and the actual decline in women's economic and political rights which occurred during liberalism's hege-mony in the late eighteenth and early nineteenth centuries.

> Slavery, the divine right of monarchs, distinctions between aristocratic and bourgeois men, and literal views of religion all came under powerful and sustained attack during this period. But traditional ideas of women endured, and even were strengthened in the new developments of the age: in law codes and republican governments, in medical and scientific thought, in images of women, even in the clothing of the period. Women lost power, both relatively and absolutely ... Created in the spirit of reform, the new codes often discarded traditional inequalities among men. Aristocratic privileges were limited or abolished, religious qualifications and tests were often removed, distinctions were based on money rather than birth, and the principle of equality before the law was established. But these gains were for men only.[1]

It was not merely that women were slower to catch up, or simply overlooked in the rush, feminists have argued. The actual *worsening* of women's property position during the high tide of liberalism was no mere oversight, it is alleged, but a direct and intentional *result* of liberal thought. In this view, women's deteriorating status during the golden period of liberalism flows from the emphasis on *contract, rationality and property in the person* in Locke. These arguments, propounded most strongly and brilliantly by Carole Pateman's *The Sexual Contract*,[2] have left those concepts tainted in many feminists' eyes.[3] They consider the exclusion of women from the political realm to be deliberate and explicit in liberal theory. The body politic is construed as male: women's 'divided, birthing bodies', writes Kathleen Jones, disunite rather than speak for all. The state in contractarian liberalism represents a body 'not born of woman but fashioned artificially by human covenant'.[4] As with the despotic subject, men's liberation deliberately entails women's subordination as objects. 'If all men are created equal, is it only because women are their unilateral inferiors?'[5]

Liberal democratic theory is hypocritical, Carole Pateman charges: it does not *really* view the private realm as the sphere of individualism and freedom – or rather, it is only the realm of freedom for men. Through the marriage 'contract' – nominally freely arrived at, in fact imposed on women by the lack of other professions open to them in the nineteenth century, and by their continued inferior earning power in the twentieth – men attain male sex-right over women. They then justify their authority by telling women that they freely consented to the contract. Further, the sexual contract is prior to the social; women are barred from participating in the latter by their forcible inclusion in the former. Before men contract *in*, they contract women *out*.

Conventional writers on canonical political theory have sometimes agreed that Lockean liberalism implies women's exclusion from the political realm, but they rarely consider the matter central.[6] Other malestream commentators on Locke never consider women's position at all.[7] Those who do take women's exclusion into account tend to view it as an oversight, or, like Harriet Taylor and John Stuart Mill, as a vestige of a corrupt older system.[8] This is itself a liberal way of looking at the problem. But whereas Taylor and Mill thought that women's inferior position was the last vestige of force in politics, which would be ameliorated by the triumph of liberalism, recent feminist critics tend to see liberalism as obstacle rather than solution.

In relation to the two overarching questions first enunciated in the introduction and repeated at the beginning of chapter 1, recent feminism, particularly the work of Carole Pateman, has tended to give the following replies:

1 Liberal contractarianism[9] is indeed particularist, not universal; the individual by which it sets such store is implicitly a male person.
2 The property-holding individual *can* only be conceived as a male person. This defect cannot be remedied by consciously including women, because the underlying dynamic of contract oppresses women. Liberalism does not merely ignore women's situation: it actively requires their oppression, through the sexual contract.

In this chapter I want to argue that a reading of the canonical liberal theorists suggests that Pateman is largely correct about (1), but that this does not entail (2). If Munzer's 'facts' about human motivation are really only specific to liberal discourse, Pateman's pessimism about contract is also historically conditioned. Worse, it merely perpetuates the inequality of women which underpinned Locke's thought and which was embodied in the dominant legal doctrine of coverture. The sexual contract does oppress women, but although it is indeed possible for women's bodies to be property transferred through contract, and although modern forms of male sex-right still flourish despite some recent advances in family law, it is not the *mechanism* of contract itself which we should distrust: rather its *content* in the sexual contract, women's bodies. *What makes the sexual contract an instrument of domination is not that it is a contract, but that it is sexual.* What is false and fraudulent about the sexual contract is that it makes women into *objects*, and that it is made between men. Contract is explicitly egalitarian, I shall argue, allowing women to be *subjects*.

This thesis will involve analysing the distinction between property in the moral *person* and in the *body* made by Jeremy Waldron in his analysis of Locke.[10] We need not conclude, despairingly, that because contract theory presupposes a property in the *person*, but women's *bodies* have been and continue to be the object of the sexual contract, that women have no property in the person and cannot enter the social contract, with the advantages it confers. Still less need we assume that women can only be objects of property in any legal system which depends heavily on contract, as I think Pateman's theory rather unfortunately tends to imply. We have good reason to be sceptical of settling for any canonical male theorist's view of property, when it is almost certain to pertain to only half of humanity. But equally, it is our task as feminists to find a more empowering alternative to that which even some of the most extraordinary feminist minds have put forward.

Can the matter and the mechanism of the sexual contract be so conclusively separated? I think Pateman herself accepts implicitly that they can, despite her scepticism about feminists who see anything good in contract.[11] What is wrong with the sexual contract, if we read Pateman carefully, seems to be that it is not really a contract at all. The marriage contract, she notes, is unlike conventional legal and economic contracts for several reasons:

1 Other contracts can be undertaken by any two or more sane adults. Marriage is obviously restricted to two adults of different sexes, with the exception of the few countries which have begun to legalize gay marriage (such as Denmark).
2 In marriage, men and women do not own property in the person in the same way. 'The contractual conception of marriage presupposes the idea of the individual as owner. The marriage contract establishes legitimate access to sexual property in the person.'[12] This is demonstrated, for

example, by Anglo-American law's long unwillingness to regard rape in marriage as a crime.[13] Other contracts view all parties as possessing equal property rights. This may be a fiction in actuality, as Marxist critics would maintain of employment contracts, but it is a truth in law. Equal rights between men and women in property in the person do not exist in either life or law, Pateman asserts.

3 'To argue for the assimilation of marriage to the model of economic contract . . . is to assume that the public and private worlds can be assimilated and to ignore the construction of the opposition between the world of contract and its "natural foundation" within civil society.'[14] Liberal theories want to extend freedom of contract to all social relations. Therefore they need to present marriage as purely contractual, along with citizenship (obtained through the social contract) and economic activity (governed by liberal principles eschewing state intervention). Contractarian theory needs to incorporate women into civil society, but can only do so by the fiction of the freely-arrived-at marriage contract.

4 Women enter into the marriage contract as women, and therefore not as equal 'individuals' with men. Only men are full individuals in contract theory.

Arguments 2 and 4, in particular, actually support my contention that what is wrong with the marriage 'contract' is not that it is a contract, but that it is not a genuine contract because it is conditioned by gender. Implicit in all these distinctions is the presupposition that calling marriage a fraudulent form of contract must undermine the argument that *all* notions of contract are false. Distinguishing between real and fraudulent contracts assumes that there is such a thing as a genuine contract.

None the less, mine will not be a straightforward position to defend. It is certainly not a popular one among feminists: contractual relationships are often seen as debased, cold and individualistic. 'At best,' Virginia Held writes, 'society may contain contractual enclaves, but they should probably be embedded in noncontractual relationships of trust and concern.'[15] Then there is Patricia Williams's troubling psychological insight about the law of contract: 'a certain deadening power it exercises by reducing the parties to the passive'.[16] If this is true, however, we need to ask why men have not been reduced to the passive, why men's relationship to the law of contract has generally benefited them more than women's has. As I stated in my introduction, it is always useful to come back to that one clichéd but enormously productive hypothesis: that property is different for men and women.

Although Munzer is limited by his liberal outlook in his 'factual' finding that property is central to human flourishing, motivation and autonomy, none the less it is ill-advised to jump to the opposite conclusion, as some feminists have tended to do. To abjure property as a proper feminist concern is to be as much bound up in the liberal tradition as Munzer is. It is a form of adolescent rebellion against the liberal patriarch. We should at the very least be open to the negative proposition that *lack* of property might impair human flourishing, motivation and autonomy. But I want to go further.

If contract and property *are* essentially liberating – the stronger, more positive argument, which I undertake to prove in chapter 4 – that certainly does *not* mean that the liberal or neoliberal formulations of them are necessarily good for women. Because contractarianism gives rise to special rather than general property rights,[17] and because liberalism and neoliberalism have tended to stress historical entitlements – giving men the advantage of precedent – there are far more appropriate property theories for women's liberation than liberalism, I think. Better still, we can create our own theory of property, one which serves women's needs rather than honours any canonical male theorist purely for form's sake.

Property may look out of place in any feminist rethinking of political concepts, of the sort which has been performed for the problem of political obligation by Nancy Hirschmann, for power by Nancy Hartsock,[18] or for the state itself by Catharine MacKinnon.[19] It appears contaminated through and through by its intimate association with liberalism. As Hirschmann writes, 'If patriarchy is the basis for property, and property is the basis for the state, then is not patriarchy the basis for the state?'[20] Yet in Hirschmann this reading rests on a particular psychoanalytical connection between patriarchy, the state, and male neurosis about transmission of identity and inheritance;[21] we may or may not choose to accept the link between patriarchy and property which underpins her syllogism. If we do, we must acknowledge that we are conforming to a stereotype: that women can have nothing to do with property, except as its objects. It should be clear by now that I reject this stereotype.

In the next section, 'Contract, social and sexual: Locke and Pateman', I shall contrast mainstream exegesis of the *social* contract with Pateman's ground-breaking notion of the *sexual* contract, focusing particularly on property in the person and the marriage contract. I shall show how for male commentators the questions about property concern liberty,[22] but for Pateman, they concern subordination. The ensuing historical section, 'Women, property and marriage: the legal background to contractarian liberalism', considers women's economic position in the legal property regime which applied to marriage at the time of Locke. Although I conclude that Pateman's analysis confirms position 1, I draw on historical and theoretical arguments to discuss why I think that position 2 is none the less incorrect. To repeat those two statements:

1 Liberal contractarianism is indeed particularist, not universal; the individual by which it sets such store is implicitly a male person.
2 The property-holding individual *can* only be conceived as a male person. This defect cannot be remedied by consciously including women, because the underlying dynamic of contract oppresses women. Liberalism does not merely ignore women's situation; it actively requires their oppression, through the sexual contract.

The historical analysis of coverture in this chapter provides a further illustration of the argument sketched in chapter 2: that the *praxis* behind the canonical theoretical traditions happens to be particularly inhospitable to women. Just as Aristotle's Athens operated an unusually oppressive property regime for women, so did Locke's England. But just as there are passages in Aristotle which point towards transcendence of this conditioning context – for example, his inconsistency about the 'constitutional' nature of husbands' rule over their wives – so are there aspects of contractarian liberalism which outstrip their legal and political background.

If theory is typically a site of struggle, as Henrietta Moore alleges, there may well be such a contest going on within contractarian liberalism: between aspects that emancipate women and those that subordinate us. Pateman has productively enlarged our understanding of those that subordinate us, and of how deep they go. Although she recognizes that not all liberal theorists are equally hostile to women – Hobbes is not, she argues[23] – the unhappy converse is that she has encouraged undue pessimism about those aspects of contract that *are* genuinely emancipatory. Involuntarily, through an improper jump from the marriage 'contract' under coverture to *all* contract, Pateman has given aid and comfort to the enemy – if political theory is indeed a locus of struggle. It is bad enough that our traditions concerning women and property have been tainted by the *praxis* of Locke's time, coverture. Do we have to handicap ourselves further by ignoring the emancipatory aspects of Locke's theory?

I end this chapter with the suggestion that a Hegelian 'personalist' view of property which gives equal play to community and individuality might enable women *really* to 'claim the status of subject', against the limitations of the liberal claim that historical entitlement or contractarian views of property do that for everyone. Although there are liberating aspects of contractarian liberalism, Hegel's notion of contract and personhood is more sophisticated, and more congenial to a feminist emphasis on relationship. The Hegelian view embodies a communal consciousness which need not apply only to minority subjects, as it does in Beauvoir; it can apply to everybody, and thus certainly to the majority, women. In addition it may well be able to accommodate crucial feminist insights. This position will be critically examined and queried in chapter 4, which will also suggest the beginnings of an alternative model of rational behaviour to the liberal one – one which does recognize feminist concerns about women's embeddedness in relationships. My general concern in this chapter, then, is to deconstruct *both* the liberal model of property and the feminist rereading of contractarian liberalism.

Contract, sexual and social: Locke and Pateman

Like marriage and the family, property in liberal theory precedes the founding of the state and predates the social contract, just as the chapter on property in Locke's *Second Treatise on Civil Government* (1689) comes well before those on the creation of state authority. It is open to all comers in a state of nature to acquire property rights, which impose duties of respecting property on others. In more modern terms, this is an 'equal opportunity' thesis: there are no *a priori* restrictions on who may acquire property. Once acquired by the first comer, however, the right belongs solely to him, although it is tempered in its execution by every man's God-given right to the minimum necessary for existence. Thus historical entitlement enters the picture. While Locke is willing to allow a modicum of subsistence even to later comers – mitigating the strictness of his rule somewhat and departing slightly from his usual emphasis on special rather than general property rights – a modern neoliberal such as Robert Nozick is not.[24]

Special rights are contingent on the occurrence of some event or the satisfaction of some standard. General rights impose duties on others regardless of whether a particular contingency has occurred, on the basis (variously) of people's needs, interests or potential abilities. The right to property in the Lockean social contract is, famously, about the 'mixing of labour' with resources, and it is thus primarily a special right, though subject to some limitations imposed by the general rights of others. In addition, the right to possess the fruits of one's labour may or may not entail absolute freedom of disposal and transmission of that property. But with a few exceptions such as Locke's sympathy to later comers, liberalism is generally neutral as to the actual distribution between rich and poor – so long as their entitlements correctly reflect the extent to which they (or the ancestors from whom they have inherited, or the vendors from whom they have bought) have mixed their labour with the resources to which they lay claim.

This neutrality has of course been termed callous or inconsistent by most of liberalism's critics. Jeremy Waldron comments on 'the *strangeness* of the idea that private property – this regime dependent as it is, in the real world, on the arbitrary contingencies of fortune and endowment – could somehow be regarded by theorists in the Enlightenment tradition as one of the fundamental and imprescriptible rights of man'.[25] But to feminist commentators, that is still only half the story. Liberalism is not really all that neutral to the inequitable distribution between men and women. It does not merely turn a blind eye to property inequality between the sexes; it actively requires the existence of inequity, Pateman asserts. Pateman is very aware of what Waldron terms the 'strangeness' of liberalism, but she thinks that liberal theorists are as well. Where Waldron sees disingenuousness, she sees hypocrisy.

Pateman argues that rumours of Locke's commitment to liberty and equality have been greatly exaggerated. Although Locke speculates about the possibility of divorce and of married women holding property, he never questions the natural basis of conjugal power: only how far the husband's power should extend. David Held agrees that Locke's claims to be called a democrat are dubious because, among other things, 'he failed to specify adequately who were to count as "the people".'[26] But Pateman thinks Locke specified that all too clearly. Although husbands might choose to limit their authority over their wives, as for instance by allowing divorce once childrearing was completed, women are not to count as individuals who have a say in the social contract. One crucial reason why this authority is so obviously rightful to Locke, according to Pateman, is that married women cannot own their own persons. They are not the 'lords and owners of their faces', we might say – or of their bodies. To quote Pateman: 'The contractarian individual necessarily is the proprietor of his person and his attributes, or, in C. B. Macpherson's famous description, he is a possessive individual. The individual owns his body and his capacities as pieces of property, just as he owns material property.'[27]

If a person is not a possessive individual, then he – or much more likely she – cannot enter into the social contract, whose motivating force is the protection of property. In Hobbes this is property in the person, first and foremost. In the later theorists, economic property is added, but self-protection of property in the person retains its original force as the prime motivation. Even those who lack all other possessions will have that much, Locke asserts: 'Every Man has a Property in his own Person. This no body has any Right to but himself.'[28] But women lack a property in their own person, according to Pateman's interpretation of Locke. Therefore they cannot acquire property by 'mixing their labour' with unowned resources: they do not own the labour of their bodies in the first place, because they have no property in their bodies.

Pateman advances her claims mainly in relation to the classical liberal theorists, and to a much lesser extent in relation to neoliberals like Nozick, although she also implies that they also apply strongly to Rawls. Rawls's equivalent to the 'state of nature' is the 'original position': the just distribution of goods and rights is that to which individuals would have agreed if they had had to choose their position within that distribution in advance, from behind a 'veil of ignorance'. The veil of ignorance prevents them from knowing what class or status they will occupy, what fortune they will have in terms of strength, intelligence or other abilities, and even what psychological attributes and values they will possess. But Rawls never stipulates whether they will know their sex; that is a non-question to him. Further, Rawls assumes that the individuals who do the choosing in the 'original position' are 'heads of families', thus accepting hierarchy within the family – although the logic of the original position is that no other hierarchy is sacrosanct.[29] Justice within the family is another non-question to him.[30] So the original position is actually *not* original; it must be preceded by another sort of 'contract', some way in which the family is constituted in the first place. This is also necessary because the individuals in the original position are mature; somebody or something has been in charge of their moral and emotional development, most probably a mother.

The only possible rejoinder is that the patriarchal structure of the family is entirely natural, but we know that to be nonsense from the different forms which the family has taken even within our own memories – for example, the growth of single-parent families – and from comparative anthropology or social history. Pateman presents Hobbes as the exception to this general assumption among contract theorists that women have already been subordinated and the family already exists – an assumption even to Rawls, with his presupposition that men, as 'heads of families', will choose the best political order on behalf of women, just as James Mill presumed. Hobbes argues that the family is not a natural but a conventional institution, mothers' rights over their children being naturally greater than fathers'. But 'in civil society the husband has dominion because for the most part commonwealths have been erected by the fathers, not by the mothers of families.'[31].

To put Pateman's argument in terms of general and special rights, women are bound to be disadvantaged by special rights theories of property: although they create new life, when they 'mix their labour' within the household, they never do so on virgin resources[32] but on what belongs to the (patriarchal) family. (Athens would be a particularly clear illustration.) This is because the sexual contract, which establishes the distribution of male sex-right in women, is prior to the social contract, which establishes rights in other forms of property. The family, household or *oikos* always comes first in the story of origins. But 'the social contract is a story of freedom; the sexual contract is a story of subjection.'[33]

The genius of contract theorists has been to present both the original contract and actual contracts as exemplifying and securing individual freedom. On the contrary, in contract theory universal freedom is always an hypothesis, a story, a political fiction. Contract always generates political right in the form of relations of domination and subordination.[34]

The logic of this argument is akin to Gramsci's view that hegemonic ideology or culture maintains capitalism by preventing the perception of true class interests as opposed. Nineteenth-century liberal opponents of state interventions such as hours and wages legislation argued that workers had freely accepted their existing conditions when they took on their jobs: a contractarian argument. Something similar is done for the subordination of women by classical liberal theory. Both feminist and Marxist critiques assert that liberal theory's emphasis on free individuals masks the social reality of disadvantaged genders and classes – and even uses their existence as proof that they must have freely chosen their position. As Joan Cocks says of what we might call the 'contradictions of patriarchy':

> Its detachment from what it believed to be things to do with women allowed liberal theory to dismiss these contradictions as of no real importance and to turn a blind eye to all the curiosities of its position ... Their explanation required a move liberal theory had not the competence to make, one which its entire methodological apparatus was designed to forbid: a reference to relations between social collectivities irreducible to relations between individuals as the sole authors of their own thought and action. More specifically, it required an investigation of how a social order of sex and gender infused the self-understandings of all its members and ensured an asymmetrical set of experiences for women and men ... Whether or not they felt themselves to be self-determining, whether or not they were aware of only the most obvious restrictions upon them, all individuals were etched by the demands of a social system of sex and gender much larger and more powerful than themselves.
>
> It was not, then, that liberal analysis was simply the wrong way to come to grips with one of the most fundamental facts of social life. It actively seemed to obscure that facet under the veil of methodological individualism.[35]

Similarly, it is not simply that liberal democratic theory is written in a language which *excludes* women, Pateman asserts; it is couched in terms that actively *enslave* them. 'What it means to be an "individual", a maker of contracts and civilly free, is revealed by the subjection of women within the private sphere.'[36] This is strikingly akin to the importance for Athenian democratic identity of maintaining strict and legally enforced boundaries between slave and free, foreigner and Athenian, female and male. What it was to be an Athenian freeman was revealed by the subjection of women, although also of slaves and foreigners – as in the *Prosecution of Neaira*. However, contract had little or nothing to do with that exclusion: it simply was not a concept in Greek politics. That should sound warning bells about Pateman's insistence that contract is to blame for women's subjection.

Pateman reiterates that in contract theory 'men alone have the attributes of free and equal "individuals".'[37] The only source of political obligation is a social contract freely made by consenting individuals; but only men can freely consent, and only men can be individuals. Rather than concluding that women are not obligated to obey the state, however, contract theory posits that the question of whether to obey cannot arise for them in the first place: they are not free to question authority. 'Women are born into subjection' – or, more correctly, placed in subjection by the prior sexual contract, according to Pateman.

> Men create patriarchal civil society and the new social order is structured into two spheres. The private sphere is separated from civil public life; the private sphere both is and is not part of civil society – and women both are and are not part of the civil order. Women are not incorporated as 'individuals' but as women . . .[38]

But why must women be incorporated differently? Although the contract theorists conventionally argue that women lack a crucial ability (usually reason, impartiality, or strength) needed to become full members of civil society, women's problem is actually that they possess an ability which men lack: giving birth. This is particularly plain in Hobbes. If women were allowed to own their bodies the way men do, they would probably prefer not to hamper themselves in the state of nature with pregnancy, which puts them at a disadvantage in the war of all against all.[39] The generation in the state of nature could conceivably be the last generation, and there would be no point in instituting the social contract in order to bind future generations under political authority. Those few women who might choose to become pregnant would not be under the control of any one man, and no man could be certain that he was the father of the child.

It is this deficiency in men – their crucial inability to assure their own fatherhood – which motivates them to devise the sexual contract. The prior subordination of women to men and male sex-right over female bodies – the sexual contract – is required to ground the social contract, Pateman claims. The impetus of liberal models towards emancipation from all forms of existing authority stops here. Once the sexual and social contracts have been established, men then reverse the roles and claim the products of giving birth for themselves, by asserting their rights over the children. Not only do children of the marriage legally belong to the father; more broadly still:

> The story of the original contract tells a modern story of masculine political birth. The story is an example of the appropriation by men of the awesome gift that nature has denied them and its transmutation into masculine political creativity. Men give birth to an 'artificial' body, the body politic of civil society; they create Hobbes' 'Artificial Man, we call a Commonwealth',

or Rousseau's 'artificial and collective body', or the 'one Body' of Locke's 'Body Politick' . . . The birth of a human child can produce a new male or female, whereas the creation of civil society produces a social body fashioned after the image of only one of the two bodies of humankind, or, more exactly, after the image of the civil individual who is constituted through the original contract.[40]

Yet it seems more plausible to me that the subjection of women within the private sphere radically undermines rather than strongly underpins liberal contractarianism's view of 'what it means to be an individual, a maker of contracts and civilly free.' There is a serious inadequacy about the marriage 'contract', as seen from *within* liberalism. Alone among all relationships in civil society, marriage is *exempt* from the contractual way of looking at the world. A husband and wife may not contract with each other under the Anglo-American doctrine of coverture because they are *not* separate individuals. The marriage 'contract' cannot be renegotiated by an individual couple, because to do so would recognize women's separate existence – which the marriage contract denies. 'A man cannot grant any thing to his wife, or enter into covenant with her: for the grant would be to suppose her separate existence; and to covenant with her, would be only to covenant with himself.'[41]

The doctrine of coverture, in which Lockean liberalism generally colludes,[42] creates a crippling internal paradox for liberals. All things are open to contract in liberalism, including the very foundations of society. The fiction of a state of nature in which individuals are like mushrooms, shallowly grounded in the world, with no interconnecting roots – Hobbes's metaphor[43] – has primarily been criticized by feminists in terms of Gilligan's concept of the separate moral voice. Women do not see the world this way, it is said. This is a line of attack from *outside* liberalism, and it is the dominant one in feminist political theory. But there is also a Trojan horse *within* the liberal gates.

If followed through, Pateman's own analysis points in this direction. Women are not property to Pateman in quite the same sense as animals, slaves or things. 'Women are property, but also persons; women are held both to possess and to lack the capacities required for contract – and contract demands that their womanhood be both denied and affirmed.'[44] They have enough capacity to enter into the civil marriage contract but not to enter into the social contract, into which men enter allegedly on their behalf. It is the marriage contract which both proves their personhood and justifies their subordination. This is Pateman's interpretation. Mine is that women in contractarian liberalism continue to hold a property in their persons; that property in the person is the concept central to Locke, not property in the body; and that to the considerable extent that the marriage doctrine under the law of coverture in Locke's time denied women's property in their persons, it actually contradicted the central Lockean concept of property in the person. It is not contract *per se* which demands that their womanhood be both denied and affirmed; it is the 'marriage contract', *which is so internally contradictory as not to be a contract at all.*

This position emphasizes two distinctions crucial to the developing argument of this book:

- that between *property in the body* and *property in the person*;
- that between the *sexual* and the *contractual* aspects of the 'sexual contract'.

The two distinctions are linked: what is sexual about, and *wrong* with, the sexual contract hinges on its assertion of male property in female bodies, as epitomized by the so-called marriage 'contract' in *practice* under the laws of coverture. What is *right* with contractarian *theory* is that it insists on women's property in the person, thereby enhancing their moral and political agency.

This tension can be fruitfully explored in terms of Waldron's distinction between property in the body and property in the person, to which I shall now turn. Waldron asserts that what really concerns Locke is not property in the body *per se* but property in the *moral* person, in one's self, one's power of agency. I agree with Waldron, although he does not extend his analysis to women or the marriage 'contract'.

Waldron's distinction occurs in the context of a discussion about self-ownership.[45] To many feminists, of course, that term will be masculinist through and through, extending the instrumental notion of ownership quite inappropriately to one's self. In fact Waldron is aware of the inappropriateness of saying straightforwardly that we own ourselves: 'Now it is conceivable that an individual may have obligations to himself but unlikely that these would be expressed as obligations to respect property.'[46] But shorn of its terminology, the content of the concept can equally well be seen as the essence of feminism. Certainly it chimes with Beauvoir's assertion, with which my introduction began: 'Now what marks the specificity of woman's situation is that while she, like any other human being, is an autonomous freedom, she discovers and chooses herself in a world where men force her to assume herself as the Other.' So although Waldron makes no attempt to justify his concern as one which will be of interest to feminists, I shall do so for him.

Borrowing from Tully's demonstration that 'person' is a technical term in Locke[47] – 'a Forensick Term appropriating actions and their merit'[48] – and drawing on the account of personal identity in *An Essay concerning Human Understanding*, Waldron emphasizes that Locke's well-worn assertion, 'Every man has a Property in his own person,' does *not* mean or require that we have property rights in our bodies. Locke rejects Grotius's description of our life, body and limbs as our own, Waldron points out. Because we do not create our bodies – only God does that – we cannot be their owners. Waldron thinks this means we cannot own anyone else's body either, in Locke's system; here he obviously differs from Pateman's interpretation. 'Humans, then, do not have creators' rights over their bodies. But they can be regarded in this strong sense as the creators of their own actions (and *a fortiori* of their work and labour).'[49] So property in the body is simply an incoherent concept: it cannot rightfully be used to justify any assertion of property rights, including male rights over female sexuality. To the extent that coverture did sanction male sex-right, it actually offended against rather than illustrated the real implications of Lockean contractarian liberalism, to extend Waldron's interpretation into Pateman's territory.

Waldron's analysis is borne out, I think, by the contrast that Locke draws between property in the person and property in goods.[50] Property has a wide meaning in Locke, most commentators agree: not merely physical property, but 'lives, liberties and estates'.[51] We know that life and liberty constitute one form of property in Locke, property in goods a second form. If property in the person is not the same as property in goods, then it must be equated with life and liberty. Although life is bodily, of course, property in life and liberty is more akin to property in one's designs, projects and innermost feelings than it is to property in things. Locke ratifies this distinction in his discussion of children's minority, when he assigns to parents the management of children's property: 'By property I must be understood here, as in other places, to mean that property which men have in their persons as well as goods.'[52]

Waldron's distinction is also consistent with seventeenth-century usage. In 1665 the Bishop of Whitehall preached a sermon in which he discussed 'propriety of respect and honour' on the same footing as 'propriety in goods and possessions'.[53] *An Arrow against All Tyrants*, written by the Leveller Thomas Overton in 1646, derives a doctrine of natural rights, including conventional property rights, from property in the person, not in the body.

> To every Individuall in nature is given an individual property by nature, not to be invaded or usurped by any; for every one as he is himselfe, so he hathe a selfe propriety, else could he not be himself . . . Mine and thine cannot be, except this be . . . For by naturall birth, all men are equally and alike borne to like propriety, liberty, and freedome, and as we are delivered of God by the hand of nature into this world, every one with a naturall, innate freedome and propriety . . . [54]

Clearly Overton cannot mean that all men are 'equally and alike borne to like propriety' in bodies of similar constitution and strength, or that we have a 'selfe propriety', a self-identity, as bodies. Nature gives us 'propriety' twinned with freedom as individuals, as persons. This is a departure from the older usage of property or propriety as those entitlements in goods and land which were necessary and proper to maintaining one's allotted station in life.[55] But it also derives from that view in that neither sort of entitlement centred primarily on property in the body. Rather, property is what is proper either to a role in life (the view found in Jean Bodin, for example) or to individuals by virtue of their free nature.

It is not mixing our bodies with natural resources which gives us a claim to property, after all: that would be an incoherent metaphor. As Nozick has famously pointed out in his fantastical example of pouring his tin of tomato juice into the sea and then claiming he owns the ocean, mixing one substance which I own with another which I do not possess does not make the second one mine. Similarly, it is not the physical contact between my body and the hoe or the land which entitles me to claim the harvest. If there is anything special about my work, it is not that it is the labour of my body, but that it represents my agency, a part of my self, my person. It is intimately linked to my personhood, because a person is defined as a being conscious of free and responsible action. People own their actions; they do not own their bodies.

What good does this sort of hair-splitting do us? A great deal, I believe. In chapter 7 I shall apply this apparently abstract distinction to very concrete cases about property 'rights' in medical ethics, including third trimester termination and gamete donation. In this chapter, I want to emphasize that the distinction between property in the body and property in the person highlights the room left in liberalism's account of property and contract for agency and motivation, when we purge it of its repressive connection with ownership of female bodies by men. This is not to deny feminism's long-standing emphasis on the importance of the body, or still less to imply that I condone male property rights over female bodies. But to repeat, what is wrong with the sexual contract is not that it is a contract, but that it is sexual. In so far as it concerns male sex-right over female bodies, embodied in the historical doctrine of coverture, the liberal view of property and contract has nothing to say to us. But Waldron's distinction underlines how marginal that historical embeddedness is to the aspects of contract and property which emphasize selfhood, autonomy, choice and control.

Women, property and marriage: the legal background to contractarian liberalism

I hope that I have established the first distinction on p. 77, between property in the body and property in the person. Now let us move on to the second, the difference between the sexual and the contractual aspects of what Pateman terms the 'sexual contract', or of the marriage 'contract' under coverture. In political theory, as opposed to economic or social history, the feminist critique of liberalism, as *constricting* women's rights to property and political participation, is not literal. Like the social contract in most interpretations, the sexual contract is presented in Pateman as metaphorical or hypothetical, not historical. 'Malestream' political theorists have sometimes been quick to deride the sexual contract as fictional tosh, while accepting quite happily that the social contract was not an anthropological actuality.

None the less, without accepting this inconsistency, it is important to consider the actual legal and social situation of married women in Locke's time. I want to suggest that Pateman risks essentialism in mistaking a particularly unfavourable property regime for universal and inevitable subordination. As I argued at the start of chapter 2, our political theory – and here I include both feminist and canonical thinkers – has been moulded by particularly inauspicious circumstances. If we can see that the unusually oppressive property regimes which prevailed in Athens and seventeenth-century England were particular and historical rather than general and ubiquitous, we shall go some way towards restoring women's relation to property as a site of struggle. If we fail to observe that, we effectively accept a particularly patriarchal doctrine of property and agency.

Furthermore, it is most appropriate to locate Locke, of all the contractarians, within a historical context. Contending against Filmer's assertion that we have no historical record of any such thing as a state of nature, Locke makes references to the foundation of Rome and Venice,[56] and to the secession of Palantus from Sparta.[57] He relies on accounts by survivors of desert islands and of native American 'kings' – inspired perhaps by King Philip's War (1675–6), waged in New England by the Wampanoag Indian sachem Metacomet ('King Philip' to the English) against the colonial armies. Locke often situates his state-of-nature illustrations in specific geographical locations, such as Peru, Florida and Brazil.[58] By contrast, Hobbes's formulation of the state of nature is psychological, a 'thought experiment',[59] and Kant's version is a transcendental concept, the foundation of *Privatrecht*.[60] The modern liberal equivalent of the state of nature, Rawls's original position, is not intended to represent any actual historical period, but to provide a device for refining away our personal interests in the existing system of distributive justice. Rousseau does offer some history and geography, but it remains very vague, as in his assertion that increasing population drove humanity to the sexual division of labour, whereby 'women became more sedentary, and grew accustomed to tend the hut and the children, while the men went to seek their common subsistence.'[61] By contrast, Locke discusses very specific legal debates of his time, such as enclosure.[62]

It has been asserted that Locke was the pragmatic product of his times in his views on property: 'While Locke seems to recognise the importance of distinguishing between what one may call essential or natural and positive or institutional property rights, he appears, on the whole, to be so convinced of the pragmatic value of existing property arrangements that he is disposed to regard them as natural and necessary.'[63] If those arrangements were particularly bad for women, we ought to know about it. So it seems right to situate Locke in historical context, examining the economic and legal situation of women in his time. It was also particularly appropriate to locate Aristotle within the property regime of his period and adopted city, given that he is largely concerned to justify the existing order of things.[64] Indeed, all the canonical theorists whom I examine have a particularly close relation to actual historical circumstances, as I shall try to show in discussing Hegel and Marx in the next two chapters. This is a powerful reason for choosing those theorists in a book which tries to synthesize theory and practice.

In this section, then, I will try to delineate why and how the property regime prevalent in Locke's time became particularly hostile to women, married women especially. In so doing, the 'practical' section of chapter 3, like the equivalent part of chapter 2, will flesh out a rather skeletal claim made in the introduction: that women, now and in the past, tend to hold less property than men, or on some counts no property at all. The system of coverture, like the Athenian property regime for women, was one of those counts; both were 'no-property worlds' for women.

Coverture was the culmination and consequence of a long decline in women's civil rights, including their rights in property. During the Middle Ages women's economic activity and autonomy were substantial. In the late Middle Ages up to a quarter of all guild members were female, and some textile guilds exclusively so. The Parisian tax register of 1300 listed eighty to ninety crafts (out of two hundred) with both female and male members, and twelve professions limited to women alone. Fourteenth-century Cologne had forty chartered guilds, of which twenty-eight were open to women either in their own right or as widows, and three were for women only. In thirteenth-century Lubeck a woman could even pass membership in a guild on to her husband. Women masters took on apprentices and journeywomen just as men did, and these crafts provided sources of training and employment outside home or service for some girls. More commonly, a women carried on her husband's craft during his lifetime and afterwards, functioning as a full partner and, if a widow, as 'a masterly woman'. But the codification of guild membership, like that of the laws under more centralized government, limited access for women.

In the period up to and including the seventeenth century, with the centralization and consolidation of states into absolutist monarchies, inheritance through the female line was barred. The compilation of laws into codes – often influenced by Roman law, which gave near-absolute power to the father of the family – set forth the principles by which women were restricted from public participation and civil rights. Early 'democratic revolutions' in the thirteenth and fourteenth centuries, transferring authority in towns from feudal powers to craft and merchant guilds, excluded all women under the new definitions of citizenship. Capitalism initially increased women's opportunities, but in the long run the transfer of production from home to factory made the economic contribution of women appear less significant. Between 1550 and 1640 about 10 per cent of London's publishers were women, for example. The growth in the importance of towns and trade opened many routes of access for women. In fifteenth-century Florence single and widowed women could attain some measure of independence as holders of property in their own right. In these towns there were between 20 and 30 per cent more women than men, reversing the pattern of antiquity. The model of property-holding prosperity set by guildswomen attracted peasant women into the towns, in the hope of attaining similar good fortune.

Against these beneficial changes for women, however, were set the more pressing new imperatives of amassing capital. Great merchant families feared leaving too much property to their daughters, who would marry and take it to other clans. Land had frequently been divided along more equitable lines in older times, but early capitalist families increasingly gave the daughter her portion in the one-off gift of a dowry, with no further claims to an inheritance. The authority and status which a woman might have enjoyed from possession of land were transformed into additional capital for the bride's husband instead. In addition the portion for the girls was fixed at their weddings, whereas that inherited by sons on their father's death might have grown many times beyond the family's value at the time of the daughters' marriage. New Venetian statutes in the fourteenth and fifteenth centuries gave control of the bride's capital to the husband. Thirteenth-century German women had the right to possess property and trade in goods, but by the fifteenth century their husbands had taken over these rights from them.

These laws prefigured the English property codes which gave the husband all control over his wife's property and earnings, whether antecedent to the marriage or acquired during it, as *The Lawes Resolutions of Woman's Rights, or the Lawes Provision for Women* (1632) enunciated in the seventeenth-century doctrine: 'That which the husband hath is his own ... that which the wife hath is the husband's.'[65] The situation of married women was worse in England and America during Locke's time – in the countries most influenced by contractarian liberalism – than on the Continent. But, *pace* Pateman, it was not worse *because* of contractarian liberalism; it was worse because of the way the common law developed. Whereas the Continental doctrine of community of property allowed the wife some independent property interests – although the husband exercised considerable authority over the joint property – the common-law model of marital unity merged the wife's person and property into that of the husband. 'At common law a wife was a nonentity in most situations; her husband subsumed her legal personality. The law created an equation in which one plus one equalled one by erasing the female one.'[66] A married woman was effectively dead at law. In its most famous formulation, that given shortly after Locke's time by Blackstone, the common-law doctrine of coverture is stated in these terms:

> The very being or legal existence of the woman is suspended during the marriage, or at least is incorporated and consolidated into that of the husband; under whose wing, protection and cover, she performs everything; and is called in our law-french a *feme covert, faemina viro co-operta*; and is said to be *covert-baron*, or under the protection and influence of her husband, her baron, or lord; and her condition during her marriage is called her *coverture*.[67]

Blackstone presents this doctrine of coverture not as irrational, or anomalous under an entrepreneurial economic system, but as the revealed truth of reason, in conformity with natural law. In addition he gives a utilitarian justification for coverture: as the perfect instrument, in the upper classes, for the transmission of property to lawful heirs. For the lesser orders, coverture ensures that marriage will 'ascertain and fix upon some certain person'[68] the responsibility for the care and maintenance of children. The system of coverture distributes both assets and liabilities, but not equitably among classes or sexes; nor is it intended to do so. According to the strict doctrine of coverture, any personal property which the wife brought into the marriage became the property of the husband, as Elizabeth Cady Stanton's outraged account correctly relates. Any *choses* in action which she possessed – rights potentially recoverable through a lawsuit – were also reduced to the husband's possession. The wife's real property, such as land, was to be managed by the husband. She was allowed to make a will, subject to his permission, but since she had almost nothing of her own, there was little point.

A wife could only bring suit for injury to herself or her personal property with her husband's permission, in both their names. She could not be sued, since that would render her vulnerable to imprisonment for failure to pay a fine or settlement. That the law would not countenance, since it would deprive the husband of his conjugal right: 'a right guarded by the law with the utmost solicitude; if she could bind herself by her contracts, she would be liable to be arrested, taken in execution, and confined in a prison; and then the husband would be deprived of the company of his wife.'[69] The law was not similarly concerned that the wife might be deprived of her husband's company if he were imprisoned. There is no fiction of mutuality here, only a bare assertion of what Pateman would term male sex-right.

The wife under coverture could not sue her husband, since they were legally one person; he was likewise barred from suing her, but there would be no point in such a civil action from the man's viewpoint, since there was nothing to gain from someone who possessed no property. A husband could recover for the loss of a wife's services, or consortium; she could not sue for her own losses, or for any injury done to the husband. Departing from the fiction of marital unity, Blackstone presents the rationale for this last stipulation in plain terms of hierarchy: 'The inferior hath no kind of property in the company, care or assistance of the superior as the superior is held to have in those of the inferior and therefore the inferior can suffer no loss or injury.'[70] Although husbands could be prosecuted for failure to maintain, this quotation casts doubt on the reality of the husband's obligation to the wife under coverture, which might be construed as creating an interest on her part. The duty to support his family was the juridical basis of the father's rights, in Blackstone. If this obligation was less than genuine in practice, it leaves very few entitlements for the wife to counterbalance her many losses under coverture – despite the fiction of her husband's 'wing, protection and cover'.

The development of the separate law of equity, together with some allowable exemptions to coverture, did soften the position of women somewhat in Locke's time. As in Athens, under the rule allowing female traders to undertake transactions worth less than a medimnus of barley without seeking the approval of their *kyrios*, a wife was allowed to buy household necessaries, and her husband was obliged to settle such small debts incurred for the family. She could act as her husband's representative in contracting for things of greater worth, giving her some minimal agency. In the seventeenth century the law of equity recognized antenuptial contracts and trusts, usually drawn up by the woman's relatives to safeguard family wealth from predatory husbands. But these marginal exceptions only underline the harshness of the general principles of coverture.

We often assume, wrongly, that women's propertylessness under coverture is typical of all premodern societies: that women had no property anywhere until the twentieth century. But just as women held less property in Athens than in Gortyn or Egypt, so the Anglo-American model of coverture was more repressive for women than other contemporaneous regimes. In contrast to coverture, the Continental doctrine of community of property in civil law jurisdictions recognizes the wife's economic contribution to the marriage. There is some implication under community of property that marriage is an equal partnership. Each spouse retains all property acquired before marriage, and any property inherited during marriage; but the earnings of each spouse, plus all other non-inherited property acquired during marriage, become the couple's 'community' or joint property. However, under community of property, the husband has the right to control and manage such joint ownings (although in recent years this has been altered in those US jurisdictions which operate this system).[71]

Just as the Athenian *hetaira* without a *kyrios* – like Herpyllis after Aristotle's death – escaped some of the rigours of the property regime, so the woman without a lord sometimes fared better under coverture. Although they were just as often among the poorest in society, the legal situation under coverture was slightly more favourable for widows. The common-law right of dower, by which a widow automatically received one-third of her husband's estate, was still intact in Locke's day. (It would be revoked in England in 1833 by a Parliamentary statute stipulating that the husband could bar this right of inheritance during his lifetime – illustrating the continued decline in women's economic fortunes at the high tide of liberalism.) Furthermore, if there were no offspring of the marriage, the widow also received the one-third share reserved by testamentary law to the children. The husband might also bequeath her the final third, if he wished. If the estate was 'thrown into Chancery' for administration under the law of equity, the interests of *any* married woman – not only the widow – received indefeasible protection according to a judgment of 1638, whether or not her husband's interests were different from hers. But although a widow in the common-law system was entitled to a fixed percentage of the estate in dower, she of course had few entitlements *during* the marriage, and dower merely gave her charity in the form of maintenance after its end.[72]

The situation of a separated woman was far more tenuous, as shown by the case of Susannah Cooper, an American woman deserted (with her young son) in 1720. Her husband's creditors seized all the couple's property: her dower was not exempt, since she was not a widow. She managed to accumulate small holdings in real estate, paying cash earned from her labour for land; but she could not obtain credit, since she had no authorization from her husband. (In fact she was perhaps fortunate that her husband did not choose to exercise his right to her earnings.) But she could not sell her holdings without her husband's permission, or bequeath them to her son. She was of course barred from bringing a lawsuit, but in 1744 she appealed to the Virginia Assembly for a private empowering act, in these terms:

> No purchaser will treat with her on account of her coverture . . . In her present unhappy situation, she is exposed to many injuries, some persons committing trespasses on her tenements, and others refusing to perform their contracts and agreements with her; for which wrongs and injuries, she is advised she can maintain no action in her own name, unless her husband be actually dead.[73]

This case is a perfect illustration of the negative argument about contract which I have sought to establish. It was not contract which Susannah Cooper found oppressive, but its absence: 'others refusing to perform their contracts and agreements with her'. What she sought was the right to enter into contract as a fullly autonomous subject, and to benefit from the security which contract would have allowed her. Susannah Cooper's story – her particular narrative – suggests some interesting links between property and contract. She was a model of the virtues associated with property – foresight, initiative, resourcefulness – but without the protection of contract, these qualities of the active agent merely afforded her further exploitation. This is one sort of relation – a protective model – between property and contract. In the next chapter I shall also sketch in a more developmental model.

Anomalies like the case of Susannah Cooper could arise, one might argue, because the marriage contract was a site of struggle between common law and liberal contractarian theory. There is a conflict evident between the modern, capitalist notion of *freedom of contract*, and the doctrine of marriage as a fixed *status*, under the feudal Norman concept of coverture. In the doctrine of coverture the wife did indeed lose her agency and selfhood:

> Man and wife are one person, but understand in what manner. When a small brooke or little river incorporateth with Rhodanus, Humber or the Thames, the poor rivulet looseth its name, it is carried and recarried with the new associate, it beareth no sway, it possesseth nothing during coverture. A woman as soon as she is married, is called *covert*, in Latin *nupta*, that is, *veiled*, as it were, clouded and overshadowed, she hath lost her streame . . . To a married woman her new self is her superior, her companion, her master.[74]

The marriage *contract* could only be entered by two equal and independent agents, but paradoxically the woman lost all personhood upon assuming the overriding legal *status* of wife. Although both parties must have contracted for the marriage to be valid, neither could set the terms of the contract to differ from those recognized by coverture; nor could they terminate it by mutual consent. Further, despite their nominal freedom to accept or reject the marriage contract, women were assumed to be married. In law the *feme sole* did possess certain property rights, but there were considerable pressures on a *feme* not to remain *sole*: 'What of those who did not marry? Common law met that problem blandly by not recognizing it. In the words of *The Lawes Resolutions*: "All of them are understood either married or to be married." '[75]

This Weberian explanation in terms of contract versus status locates the contradiction *outside* rather than *within* liberalism, as Pateman does. The status conjecture is consistent with the view that women (and marriage) accidentally got left behind for a bit in the onward march of liberalism. To explain coverture as a mere holdover from a feudal legal system is attractive if I want to argue, as I do, that it is not *contract* which disadvantages women. Rather, it appears to be liberalism's *failure* to extend contract far enough. Reinforced by Christian notions of marriage as a sacrament, and by the adjudication in ecclesiastical courts of cases concerning adultery, bigamy, separation and annulment, the hierarchical relationship of man and wife, *baron et feme*, persisted in the doctrines of marital unity and coverture. These lasted long after other parallel hierarchies – master–servant, guardian–ward, noble–vassal – had lost most of their legal force.

But two difficulties are left unresolved by the Weberian explanation. First, why was it the *male–female* relation which remained cast in the hierarchical mode? The sacred nature of the marriage bond, and the doctrine of the unity of the flesh, did not entail male-dominant hierarchy in themselves. Canon law of the twelfth century simply required a private, mutual, verbal exchange of vows, between a male and female over the age of consent (sixteen and fourteen). It was common law, rather than canon law, which demanded a public ceremony as the price of conferring property rights on the man and the right of dower on the wife if she survived her husband.[76] Again, contrary to received thinking, we might view medieval ecclesiastical law as more egalitarian than common law by Locke's time.

Indeed, the relationship of man and wife became *more* hierarchical rather than less. The codification of the doctrine in Blackstone's *Commentaries* (1765–9) gave it additional strength at a time when early capitalism might have been expected to sweep away all hierarchies. The question is whether Blackstone was merely a prejudiced jurist – not an unfamiliar figure to feminists – or whether liberalism itself is implicated.

The notion that liberalism was actively to blame for women's increasing propertylessness and powerlessness does have the strength of historical correlation behind it. In political and legal theory, as in economic history, the early modern period in England saw a waning in women's rights at the same time that men's entitlements were waxing. The persistence, and indeed strengthening, of the doctrine of coverture in the common law 'signalled a decline in the status of English wives which reached a nadir in the early capitalism of the sixteenth and seventeenth centuries'.[77] By the high tide of liberal reform movements for male property and participatory rights in the early nineteenth century, even the few protections for women under coverture had been erased – for example, with the abolition of widows' right of dower in 1833. While liberalism excused men from property qualifications for the suffrage, it presided over women's increased propertylessness *and* powerlessness. The 1832 Reform Act, for example, lowered the property standard for voters but deliberately introduced the word 'male' into requirements for electors. The liberal movement ruptured the previous necessary link between property and political participation, but only for men. It may well appear that liberalism was the added variable which ensured that the male–female relation remained hierarchical, and indeed became more so. This would be consistent with Pateman's interpretation.

However, I think it is more instructive to see the rigidification of coverture as a form of *backlash* against liberalism's otherwise triumphal progress, rather than as a consequence of liberalism. As Lawrence Stone remarks, 'There must surely be some connection between the steady hardening of attitude by the courts to the contractual basis of marriage throughout the seventeenth century and the concurrent rise of ideas about divine right and passive obedience which were so much emphasized by those who wished to elevate the monarchy over its subjects.'[78] Legally, after the Hardwicke Marriage Act of 1753, there was no such thing as contractual marriage. The marriage 'contract' was not one in law: marriage was exempted from the increasingly influential liberal contractarian paradigm. This removes one arm of the paradox identified by Pateman – that women were considered rational enough to enter a contract which deprived them of all their rights. The legal reality in England and America was coverture, not contract,[79] even if the term 'marriage contract' persisted in popular usage.

The second difficulty with the view of coverture as an antiquated status category is that it assumes the wife's status was a vestige of feudalism. If so, we would expect societies with the weakest feudal heritage to be the furthest advanced on the path towards contract as the universal category. But in fact the doctrine of coverture flourished in the American colonies. It was not simply a vestige of feudalism which would pale before the dazzle of Enlightenment rationality. Those American colonies with Puritan or Quaker foundations, such as Connecticut and Pennsylvania, actually operated a more restrictive version of married women's property rights, especially in relation to land conveyancing and rights of dower, than those of Catholic or Anglican origin.[80] With their strong commitment to the family and their zeal for reform of a legal inheritance which they viewed as corrupt, the ultra-Protestant colonies abolished exemptions and equity provision for women, such as the freedom of the widow's dower from creditors' claims on the dead man's estate. Those colonies with the greater commitment to the light of individual reason thus afforded women fewer rights in property, although they took a voluntaristic line on divorce.

But this anomaly, too, can be seen as a form of backlash: not only against old corruption, but also against the threatening freedoms of Native American women. Native American marriage customs were frequently matrilocal and matrilineal, generally regarding the marriage as transient and the children as belonging to the woman.[81] The assured custody of her children was, to the colonists' puzzlement, a useful form of property to the divorced Native American women. Against the colonists' preconceptions,

> on the contrary, she is more highly respected for them, more honoured, more esteemed and richer. Accordingly she finds it an easier and quicker matter to get married again, for the man who marries her, in becoming her husband, becomes also the father and head of the whole family, and is therefore a person of more importance.[82]

A conscious propaganda action had to be mounted to convince potential female colonists that home ways were best. William Wood's pamphlet *New England's Prospect* (1634) turned the actual position under coverture upside down by claiming that 'since the *English* arrival comparison hath made them [Algonquin women in southern New England] miserable, for seeing the kind usage of the *English* to their wives, they do as much condemne their husbands for unkindnesse, and commend the *English* for their love.'[83]

To sum up the historical evidence: the doctrine of coverture, applied more harshly in England than in France and often, ironically, more harshly in the liberty-minded colonies, took precedence over the developing law of contract. What married women consistently sought was a genuine system of contract in marriage, and the right to enter into contracts outside marriage. These were denied them by the internal paradoxical 'logic' of coverture, by which husband and wife could not contract to change the terms of the marriage contract, because to do so would have implied the wife's separate existence – and the doctrine of marital unity was central to coverture. What was wrong with the sexual contract embodied in coverture was that it was emphatically *not* a contract: it was sexual.

The legal position does not indict contract itself, in the way Pateman wants to. After all, the doctrine of marital unity, the underpinning of coverture, is the very opposite of the notion of two independent individuals required by contract. So, too, is the notion that the marital contract, once made, could never be broken. Individuals retain their agency after the making of a conventional contract, and the contract can be broken. In keeping with Ockham's razor, it would seem simpler to conclude that women, and to a lesser extent egalitarian-minded men, are so constrained under the marriage 'contract' that it is not a contract at all, as did William Thompson in 1825:

> Each man yokes a woman to his establishment, and calls it a *contract*. Audacious falsehood! A contract! where are any of the attributes of contracts, of equal and just contracts, to be found in this transaction? A contract implies the voluntary assent of both the contracting parties. Can even both the parties, man and woman, by agreement alter the terms, as to *indissolubility* and *inequality*, of this pretended contract? No. Can any individual man divest himself, were he even so inclined, of his power of despotic control? He cannot. Have women been consulted as to the terms of this pretended contract? A contract, all of whose enjoyments – wherever nature has not imposed a physical bar on the depravity of selfishness – are on one side, while all of its pains and privations are on the other! A contract giving all power, arbitrary will and unbridled enjoyment to the one side; to the other, unqualified obedience, and enjoyments meted out or withheld at the caprice of the ruling and enjoying party. Such a contract, as the owners of *slaves* in the West Indies and every other slave-polluted soil, enter into with their slaves – the law of the stronger imposed on the weaker, *in contempt* of the interests and wishes of the weaker. As little as slaves have had to do with the partial codes of selfishness and ignorance, which every where dispose of their right over their own actions and all their other enjoyments, in favor of those who made the regulations; particularly that most unequal and debasing code, absurdly called the *contract* of marriage.[84]

Pateman's reading of Locke is innovative, perceptive and plausible, but it wrongly implies a necessary connection between all forms of property or contract and women's subordination under liberalism. This connection is ahistorical, even anti-historical in so far as it ignores the *illegality* of contract in marriage. It ignores the ways in which contract is practically and theoretically intertwined with the virtues and freedoms associated with being an individual who takes an active relationship to property – as the narrative of Susannah Cooper illustrates. It is also apolitical, or at least politically ill-advised. The notion of a freely arrived-at contract between individuals masks the reality of women's subordination in marriage, Pateman asserts. We must get rid of the mental baggage of contract and individual, and look the reality of subordination squarely in the face. But it is not quite clear how getting shot of the mental encumbrances will directly emancipate women. I want to suggest that it may actually do the reverse, encouraging women's quiescence and passivity in the economic realm. Ironically, the anti-contract, anti-liberal interpretation *magnifies* the adverse impact of liberal contractarianism and *increases* women's subordination – through discouraging a more active attitude towards property-holding and personal moral development.

Another way of putting my criticism of Pateman is to acknowledge that while she may be right about certain adverse effects associated with *special* rights theories of property, those justifications of property which rest on *general* rights remain untouched by her critique. The developmental justification of property found in Hegel is contingent on such general rights. This interpretation links rights in property back to the question of what it means to be an owner, rather than stopping at the mere fact of possession. In Hegel, control of property is connected to individual self-assertion, stability of the will, and recognition of each other's value[85] – all, incidentally and coincidentally, important second-wave feminist concerns. Contract likewise acquires positive value in the development of agency and subjectivity. In addition some commentators, such as Jeremy Waldron, believe that the Hegelian approach, despite its idealist roots, has practical, egalitarian distributive implications. Although Waldron does not ask about the implications for women, these corollaries could add theoretical weight to practical initiatives against the feminization of poverty. Because property is a general right in Hegel, rather than a special right accruing only to those who deserve it by Lockean standards, 'everyone must have property,' as Hegel puts it.[86] But where Hegel and his modern advocates stop short is at the door to the private home. There, Pateman's analysis of the private as a realm of subordination rightly directs our attention to property egalitarianism *within* marriage. And it helps us to understand the law's continuing absence from the private sphere, with the implication that women's concerns are devalued by the law.[87] These will be the concerns of chapter 4.

4

Property and Moral Self-Development

In this chapter I do three things:

1 I begin by introducing an alternative model of property rights to the Lockean liberal one. A Hegelian approach emphasizes the *developmental*, educative, identity-creating benefits of property to the property-holder. It does not view property as merely *instrumental* to the pursuit of already decided ends, in Lockean fashion.[1] Instead, it sees those ends as themselves shaped by an experiential process of identity formation and recognition of others' subjectivities, including the experience of property-holding. The self-developmental model proposes that there can be, and should be, satisfaction in work for its own sake, not simply because it brings the products of consumption. It also suggests a bond between myself and what I own, an extension of the notion of *relationship* rather than that of *appropriation*. In addition, this formulation incorporates a view of *contract* as a moral experience, a bond between myself and other owners – which, I argue, radically challenges Pateman's critique, suggesting that contract can be enabling and empowering. In chapter 3 I asserted that property and contract are not necessarily oppressive for women. Chapter 4 advances a stronger argument: that property and contract are actually *liberating* when construed as *developmental* rather than instrumental, and in terms of *general* rather than special rights.

2 The second section of this chapter asks why Hegel rejects the notion of the marriage contract, and whether this rejection is genuine – about which Pateman has doubts. I examine the countervailing proposition that Hegel *is* consistent in rejecting the equation of contract and marriage, as he rejects the notion that society is founded on contract. Hegel's attack on the notion of marriage as a contract, which he terms a 'shameful' idea, is

consistent with a non-liberal view that society is not contract all the way down. This notion is indeed particularist in Hegel, but it does contain a potentially liberating insight for women, setting the stage for the reconstruction of property in chapter 7. This distinction also helps to clarify the relationship between contract and property; contract in Hegel is not merely a means to protect property, as in liberal theory, but a more advanced condition of development. I have already argued that feminists have been unduly unimaginative in viewing women's only possible relation to property as that of object. From a Hegelian point of view, there is an even stronger case to be made for contract as instrumental to fully developed subjectivity.

3 Hegel insists that 'everyone must have property', and a Hegelian general rights account should be less likely to become an apology for existing inequalities of wealth than a special rights one such as those offered by Locke or Nozick. But in Hegel's own thought it is only men who are empowered by contract and by participation in civil society, with its economic base. Whereas in Hegel bourgeois men are incorporated into historical dialectic and modernity through their participation in civil society and the state, women's domestic sphere is ahistorical, unchanging and 'natural'. The nuclear family, based on affective bonds, is presented as a new, modern structure, but women's role within the family and their confinement to it remain unchanged. Indeed, one might argue that women take a step *backwards* in Hegelian modernity, from involvement in preindustrial home-based production to complete divorce from economic value creation. Although the notion of being 'at home' in the world is dear to Hegel, women are not at home in the economic world.[2]

Worse still, the only place in Hegel where they are at home – namely, in the private household – was radically threatened in Hegel's time by women's impoverishment under early capitalism. With the divorce of production for exchange from its classical and feudal location in the household, women could not be at home unless they had men who could afford to keep them there. With the concurrent absorption of women's property and legal identity into that of their husbands under coverture, though to a lesser extent under community of property systems, they could not be at home unless they had men who *chose* to keep them there, forgoing their right to their wives' earnings. In the third section of this chapter, I illustrate this argument with material on the poverty of women in Hegel's period. Hegel's account (and any separate-sphere model, including those in some modern feminisms) is radically undermined by failure to consider the feminization of poverty, I conclude in this section. Further, the feminization of poverty impedes political participation even when formal legal barriers such as liberal property requirements, or role stereotypes about women's confinement to the home, are abolished. Since political participation is meant to be good not only for the state but also for the participant – indeed, that is its principal justification in the Hegelian account – women's poverty strikes at the heart of a Hegelian analysis.

The use of narrative is slightly different in this chapter. Earlier I showed how the accepted 'story' about women and property has been conditioned by particularly punitive property regimes for women at the time when the theories which have most influenced us were being written. Here I use the nineteenth-century feminization of poverty, and women's increasing resort to prostitution, in order to underscore crucial omissions in Hegel's own thought. Where women are concerned, Hegel departs from history and retreats into essentialism. This points to the need to transcend Hegel in creating a model of property which incorporates Hegel's developmental notion of property and subjectivity, but which also remains true to the historical narrative about women and property.

Hegel: 'Everyone must have property'

Before I begin my exposition of Hegel's model of property and contract, I want to reiterate a point which first occurred in the introduction, which recurred in the discussion of Aristotle, and which I also argued in relation to Locke. The canonical property theories which omit women, or which are actively hostile to women, may not be as relentlessly inimical as some feminists have claimed. This is also relevant to Hegel, unlikely though it may seem in light of such comments as this: 'The theme of Hegelian feminism or feminist Hegelianism will strike many as being farfetched, to say the least . . . Among the major philosophers of the nineteenth century, probably only Nietzsche and Schopenhauer have a more antifeminist reputation.'[3]

There is little difficulty in spotting what Le Dœuff would call the 'stupid utterances' which Hegel makes about women.

> It must be noticed in connexion with sex-relations that a girl in surrendering her body loses her honour. With a man, however, the case is otherwise, because he has a field for ethical activity outside the family. A girl is destined in essence for the marriage tie and for that only . . .[4]

> Women are capable of education, but they are not made for activities which demand a universal faculty such as the more advanced sciences, philosophy, and certain forms of artistic production. (*PR*, 166A)

> Men correspond to animals, while women correspond to plants because their development is more placid and the principle that underlies it is the rather

vague unity of feeling. When women hold the helm of government, the state is at once in jeopardy, because women regulate their actions not by the demands of universality but by arbitrary inclinations and opinions. Women are educated – who knows how? – as it were by breathing in ideas, by living rather than by acquiring knowledge. The status of manhood, on the other hand, is attained only by the stress of thought and much technical exertion. (*PR*, 166A)

In Hegel's presentation of acquiring both property and understanding there is likewise an unsavoury element of the phallocentric:

A person puts his will into a thing – that is just the concept of property, and the next step is the *realization* of this concept. The inner act of will which consists in saying that something is mine must also become recognizable by others. (*PR*, 49A, original emphasis)

I do not penetrate an object until I understand it; it then ceases to stand over against me and I have taken from it the character of its own which it had in opposition to me. Just as Adam said to Eve: 'Thou art mind of my mind and bone of my bone,' so mind says, 'This is mind of my mind and its foreign character has disappeared.' (*PR*, 4A)

But against some feminist critiques,[5] Hegel's most redeeming characteristic is that he does not construe social difference as natural and unchanging; he is closer to Moore's construction of need as a site of struggle than to Munzer's naturalism.

Unlike the reductionist political theorists with whom he is often identified, Hegel distances his account of marriage and the family from approaches which focus on biological needs, which reduce the relationship between men and women to a natural biological basis. Instead of grounding his conception of the family in the biological dimensions of human existence, he describes the family as an institution which offers a means of transcending them.[6]

Hegelian feminists have generally concentrated on *The Phenomenology of Spirit*. Beauvoir is of course profoundly enmeshed in Hegelian concepts such as immanence, self-consciousness and transcendence. Her discussion of Subject and Other/object is informed by Hegel's master–servant dialectic, mediated through Sartre's version in which 'the final stage of Hegel's story – the externalization of self through labour – drops out altogether.'[7] Hegel's influence is obvious in Luce Irigaray's *Speculum of the Other Woman* and Judith Butler's *Subjects of Desire*. However, there has been little feminist interest in what Hegel has to say about property: once past the initial nod towards women *as* property, even the master–servant relationship has almost always been analysed solely in psychoanalytical terms – as, for example, an account of the developing self-consciousness in the servant and the link with the objectified 'other'.[8] The exploration of property in Hegel has been left to 'mainstream' theorists, whose accounts have only very recently become even moderately gender sensitive.[9]

So feminists' disregard of property in Hegel exemplifies their more general disinterest in the topic, mirrored by canonical commentators' neglect of women in Hegel's analysis of property. Yet I have become increasingly convinced that whatever the limitations of Hegel's own thought, a broadly Hegelian model of property and rationality offers a productive alternative set of concepts for feminism. Hegel's account of property is not a matter of egotistical triumph over the natural world: it has far more to do with recognizing others' subjectivities and enhancing one's own. Property in Hegel is not mere possession, but rather 'the social recognition that something belongs to me'.[10] Nor is his model so abstract as to ignore the realities of economic and social power; his rather anguished consideration of the tragic inevitability of poverty in modern society mitigates that criticism.[11] All in all, in relation to the two questions with which I began chapter 1: Hegel's own account of property is indeed particularist, but we can glean from it elements which are liberating for women. These are not particularly original interpretations in mainstream Hegelian scholarship; but their application to women and property is new, I think, despite the obvious potential for a feminist account of the emphasis on experience, relationship and others' subjectivities.

What inclines me to this view is not merely the redeeming legal prescriptions in Hegel which offset the quotations above: his willingness to allow marriage by free choice of the partners and divorce by mutual consent, for example,[12] or his condemnation of systems of inheritance which exclude daughters (*PR*, 180R). Nor is it his insistence that rationality and the ethical predisposition – the essence of subjectivity, of being a person – are inculcated in both sexes by maternal teaching, although that view is entirely compatible with some modern feminisms.[13] Rather, the elements which I find potentially liberating in Hegel, and which tie up with crucial feminist concerns, are as follows:

1 the justification of property in terms of self-development and *experience* of the external world;
2 the importance of *embodiment* in self-development, and
3 the connected thoughts that contract reflects *relationship*, but that not all relationships boil down to contract.

(1) *The justification of property in terms of self-development and experience of the external world* The *Philosophy of Right* concerns development and subjectivity, but begins with property and contract. The form of the

book has been said to be extremely significant,[14] not least by Hegel himself:[15] so why does property come first?

Development and subjectivity clearly belong to the world of subjects; property and contract initially to the realm of objects. In Hegel we can only become full subjects by engaging with the world of objects. 'The Hegelian subject always has to go outside itself to know what is inside; by seeing itself reflected in the world it discovers relations constitutive of itself.'[16] The sole route to *individual* autonomy and self-sufficiency is through the recognition of *others* who also possess self-consciousness. The essence of personality and subjectivity, the moral will, 'is essentially a striving to overcome the gap between the objective and the subjective, and to give itself a real expression in the objective world'.[17]

> If the will's determinate character lies in the abstract opposition of its subjectivity to the objectivity of external immediate existence, then this is the formal will of mere self-consciousness which finds an external world confronting it. As individuality returning in its determinacy into itself, it is the process of translating the subjective purpose into objectivity through the use of its own activity and some external means. (*PR*, 8)

Our individuality has to be created. It is conventional, not natural, as in Hobbes's metaphor of 'men as if but even now sprung out of the earth and suddenly, like mushrooms, come to full maturity, without all kind of engagement to each other'.[18] Neither is individuality developed through self-contemplation, or by meditation on cosmic principles, but rather by active relationship with our environment: the will's 'purpose actualized and achieved by means of its activity of translating its subjective purpose into objectivity' (*PR*, 9). Individuality 'translates' itself into reality, into objectivity, 'through the use of its own activity and some external means'. Property is the first such external means, or perhaps more accurately, the first such arena of interaction with the world outside the self; contract, the family, civil society and the state follow on, in the order of the *Philosophy of Right*.

Now this is not necessarily an argument for *private* property; it might be enough to participate in the creation and control of some collective enterprise.[19] Individuality does not itself require limitless individually owned property. If a private property system *is* preferred, self-actualization may actually require that we own *just enough* property. Hegel thinks the extremely rich are as likely as the very poor to manifest anti-social attitudes, laziness and mistrust; he refers to the 'ethical corruption' engendered by both extremes (*PR*, 185) and remarks that there can be 'rich rabble'.[20]

If there is an argument for private property in Hegel – and I think there is – it will not come from the Anglo-American emphasis on rights. Whereas in the liberal theorists private property rests on a foundation of natural rights, Hegel sees rights as *consequent* to society rather than *prior* to it. As the English Hegelian T. H. Green puts it, 'It is only through the guarantee which society gives him [its member] that he has any property at all, or, strictly speaking, any right to his possessions.'[21] Contractarian liberals would agree with the first premise – that society guarantees property rights – but certainly not with the second – that there is no such thing as property rights outside of society. In Hegel, however, it can be roughly stated that society creates rights. This follows from the metaphysical picture: we are not really individuals, not developed subjectivities, without social interaction. Since we are not really individuals at all, we cannot be rights-holding individuals.

Nor is Hegel's justification of private property utilitarian. The usual consequentialist arguments for private ownership centre either on the superior efficiency of private-property systems or on the security which it provides for the projects we hold dear. Hegel rejects the first approach;[22] his justification is closer to the second. On a developmental account of personality like Hegel's, our moral and mental well-being require security and certainty that our efforts to externalize our subjectivity will be respected. The externalization of the will does therefore require private property in Hegel. As Waldron puts it, 'Hegel's thesis is that by appropriating, owning and controlling objects, a person can establish his will as an objective feature of the world and transcend the stage in which it is simply an aspect of his inner and subjective life.'[23]

Yet much of the interest of the master–servant account lies in Hegel's explicit assertion that the servant gets more from the relationship than the property-owning master. Admittedly the servant is dependent, and his consciousness *unselbständig*, un-self-sufficient. He must put aside his own self-development and 'labor according to an alien will',[24] as Hegel says. But 'the truth of the self-sufficient consciousness is the servant's consciousness,'[25] Hegel adds: not the master's. Through the discipline of work in the external world, the servant undergoes a kind of *Bildung* – identity-formation or education – which the master does not acquire from merely owning the property on which the servant labours.

> By struggling with the world, by making nature conform to his purpose, he [the servant] experiences himself to be an active, competent being who can make a difference in the world. He makes things accord with his thoughts and designs. Through service to another the servile one establishes a sense of self.[26]

I have established that Hegel's model of property posits an active and attractive *relationship* to the world, implying an emphasis on lived *experience*. The role of property is not to provide the kind of security that allows us to ignore others, but to introduce us to other subjectivities. This is compatible with much feminist ethical theory, and it comes across most strongly in Hegel's account of the master–servant relationship. However, there are indications that the master–servant dyad is irrelevant to women in Hegel's original formulation. The prelude to the servant's developing awareness through servitude is the struggle for dominance in which he is defeated; by contrast, women's subordination in marriage – and Hegel himself would certainly not see it as subordination – is preceded by romantic courtship. The servant alienates his sense of identity through accepting defeat, and must struggle towards awareness from that humiliation; women are intended to fulfil their deepest identities in marriage, which is conceived as unity, not self and otherness. This disparity matters because it is the servant's consciousness of alienation and defeat which impels him to transcend his situation.

Carole Pateman insists that the relationship cannot apply to women, that master and servant must both be men. 'The mutual acknowledgement and confirmation of self . . . is possible only if the two selves have an equal status.'[27] Similarly, Genevieve Lloyd construes the master–servant dialectic as the rebellion of *male* self-consciousness against immersion in female-associated family life: both antagonists are struggling for recognition in the arena of civil society.[28] What master and servant share, says Lloyd, is successful transcendence of the female principle.

Yet there is certainly something about the master–servant parallel which is subversive to established ideas. Hegel's account may help us to see women who live in no-property worlds as something other than victims, although it would be a strategic blunder to read it as a justification of women's subordination on the grounds that propertylessness produces greater virtue. But as the master–servant relation demonstrates, Hegel does privilege those who actually *use* the objects of property, even if they do not formally own them. Both wives and male servants are frequently propertyless; or, more correctly, although wives may nominally share in the household wealth, as in classical Athens and seventeenth-century England, they have no control over its administration – not even under more equitable regimes like community of property. What is productive for women is Hegel's assertion that the propertyless gain greater agency and self-development from their labour in the external world than do men who rely on their property to protect them *from* the external world of work. So Hegel's account of property is attractive because it links self-ownership and property ownership in a rather subversive way, one which allows the dispossessed some dignity. It emphasizes private property and special rights less than the general right to enjoy some minimum of property; it is less concerned with the brute facts of mine and thine than with relationship, development, experience and agency.

(2) *The importance of embodiment in self-development* Another way of seeing this positive, developmental aspect of property in Hegel is in terms of *embodiment*. In Hegel my only real existence is as an embodied will; the political doctrine about property is thus connected to a metaphysical view of the self. There is no 'pure', transcendent self which exists apart from its embodied form. However, I do need to 'claim' my body; my embodiment is not natural, but is itself a developmental process involving training my body and mind in dexterity and control.

How does embodiment relate to property? This is a separate issue from property *in* the body, and irrelevant to the distinction between that and property in the person which I established in relation to Locke. We have seen that property belongs to the world of objects in Hegel, and that the subject needs to objectivize itself in that external world. But why does the will need property in order to do so? Why is property not merely ethically permissible, or instrumental to things which are morally valuable, but ethically important in itself? Waldron offers the following useful translation of Hegel's account:

> If I have worked on some material, it comes to embody the intentions that I had at the time, not in the Lockean sense of literally containing something of mine, but in the sense that the object is now in a condition caused by the fact that I worked on it with those intentions rather than any others. Once that has happened, I may not be able to change my mind – to decide, for example, to make something else using this material – because what I have already done to it places limits on what can be done to it in the future. Once a sculptor begins carving a *pietà* out of a block of marble he may not be able to change his mind and carve a man on horseback instead. The fact that the object registers one's intentions in this way therefore encourages a more careful selection of intention, for the agent knows that he cannot chop and change as he pleases once he embarks upon some project . . . [T]his is one interpretation (I think it is the best interpretation) that can be put on Hegel's account of the ethical importance of property.[29]

Our intentions and even our personalities become embodied in our projects and in the objects they involve. Identity and property are synergistic. The honing of the will required by purposeful activity on external objects makes us something other than random collections of erratic impulses and moods. (This is similar to Hegel's argument about the moral importance of marriage; the commitment which it represents keeps us from being mere playthings of flitting sexual desires and caprices.) Objects of property are not only instrumental to the achievement of steadiness, responsibility, and other qualities of will; they actually represent and embody those qualities.

The association of women with the body in most forms of Christian thought, and the relegation of the body to uncleanness, have been remarked upon by many feminists. Hegelian thought is attractive to feminisms which want to 'reclaim the body', although we also need to be aware that embodiment is a two-edged sword. In Hegel bodily differences between men and women signify intellectual and teleological ones. The bodily difference between the sexes is said to have a 'rational basis', and thus gender role differentiation cannot be said to be subordination.[30] This is, however, an entirely different criticism – and a more accurate one – than the position taken by both Julia Kristeva, that the Hegelian subject denies the materiality of the body altogether.[31]

(3) *The connected thoughts that contract reflects relationship, but that not all relationships boil down to contract* Ironically, if we want to avoid being ruled entirely by external forces, if we wish to become autonomous, we must direct our attention to external things and other people. What we are is the series of our actions, and our actions are constrained by those of others. This is a view of property which can accommodate relationship, which even glorifies it. The individual will alone is sterile: 'The laurels of mere willing are dry leaves that never were green' (*PR*, 124A). The environment in which we develop ourselves contains not only material objects, but other wills. The externalization of subjectivity requires that we recognize others.

This recognition occurs in Hegel through the simultaneously symbolic and practical mechanism of *contract*. Contract is not a realm of subordination and domination over women, or of fraternal bonding among men – the meanings assigned it by Pateman. Nor is it a means for letting each other alone, to paraphrase Thoreau's remark on contractarian government in his 'Essay on civil disobedience'.[32] In Hegel's terms:

> The first requirement of abstract right is 'the immediate embodiment which freedom gives itself in an immediate way, i.e. (a) possession, which is property-ownership. Freedom is here the freedom of the abstract will in general, or *eo ipso*, the freedom of a single person related only to himself. (b) A person by distinguishing himself from himself relates himself to another person, and it is only as owners that these two persons really exist for each other. Their implicit identity is realized through the transference of property from one to the other in conformity with a common will and without detriment to the rights of either. This is *contract*. (*PR*, 40, original emphasis)

Hegel thus takes a strong, positive line on contract, as on property. Contract is not merely the *means* by which property is protected, as in the liberal contractarians. It symbolizes the common will of the parties to the contract. In contract, two isolated individuals transcend their own individuality, and thus contract is more than the sum of its parts, the individual wills. In this respect contract represents an *advance* over private property, rather than a prior means to it. Contract is developmentally beneficial in the progress beyond self-immersion: it requires the recognition of other *wills*, not merely the acknowledgement of physical constraints and realities needed to acquire property. Although it is still 'only as owners that these two persons really exist for each other', even that shadowy existence is better than none at all.

'A person is a unit of freedom aware of its sheer independence,' Hegel writes (*PR*, 35A). This need not mean literal independence, as I construe it. Rather, it involves distancing myself from the notion that my actions and moral choices are entirely *dependent* on my surroundings, including other people. It involves seeing myself as in a sense 'owning' those actions. The next step in self-development is to see others as likewise 'owners' of themselves, their subjectivities and their choices. This is where contract comes in. Free will is to be developed not only in individuals *as* individuals, but in individuals as comprising a collective. From the viewpoint of individuals, their own subjectivities can only be fully developed in that collective. This in turn requires that we set up institutions to 'mediate' individual wills. As Waldron puts it:

> Free will is initially presented in the form of separate individual minds; but potentially it is a single rational entity. The realization of this potential must therefore consist in the embodiment of free will in forms which transcend the particularity of the organisms in which it is initially given. From the point of view of these organisms, the growth of free will must be 'mediated' by the establishment of institutions which transcend their particularity, such as the familiar institutions of property, contract, family, economy and state.[33]

Property instantiates *individual* wills in the external world. Contract is a higher form of self-development in so far as it transcends the substantiation of the self in objects and requires *mutual* recognition.

> The sphere of contract is made up of this mediation whereby I hold property not merely by means of a thing and my subjective will, but by means of another person's will as well and so hold it in virtue of my participation in a common will . . . Contract presupposes that the parties entering it recognize each other as persons and property owners. (*PR*, 71 and 71R)

Yet paradoxically and problematically, in contract, one party apparently agrees to *alienate* property: to sell it, for example. 'Contract is the process in which there is revealed and mediated the contradiction that I am and remain the independent owner of something from which I exclude the will of another only in so far as in identifying my will with the will of another I cease to be an owner' (*PR*, 72). We saw that an individual's aims permeate the object on which she has worked; it might appear that by agreeing to transfer ownership of that object, she agrees to lose her ownership in the self. But the importance of literally seeing oneself mirrored in objects is less, in terms of self-development, than the recognition of others which the contractual process requires. In Hegel's interpretation of property, I retain my property in what I have sold because the other party to the contract recognizes my interest and involvement in it. Property is not mere possession, but rather 'the social recognition that something belongs to me'.[34] This is why Hegel can make the rather surprising statement that 'in a contract my purpose is both to acquire property and to surrender it. Contract is real when the action of both parties is complete, i.e. when both surrender and both acquire property, and when both remain property owners even in the act of surrender' (*PR*, 76A).[35]

This will turn out to have important practical implications, to which I shall return in chapter 7. So will Hegel's insistence that social life is not contract all the way down: although contract represents a progress in the will's development, it is not the highest stage. Contract should not be the template for all social relations, and this, too, will have immediate application to practical ethics in chapter 7. The Hegelian model of contract is less voracious than the liberal interpretation: marriage, for example, is outside its grasp, and this can best be understood by returning to the notion of the sexual contract in Pateman.

The marriage 'contract': a shameful idea?

In Hegel certain things cannot be alienated by a free will, not even by contract: one cannot sell oneself into slavery, for example, or agree to cede all of one's time and work to another (*PR, 67)*. Where does that leave marriage? Certainly, at least under coverture, the marriage 'contract' cedes all of the wife's time and work to the husband.

Marriage, as the foundation of one of the institutions which 'transcend particularity' – the family – and the partial embodiment of another – contract – is an ethical command in Hegel. In marriage, one embodied free will recognizes another. This is a higher stage of self-development than either the appropriation of things which constitutes the basis of property, or the grudging and partial recognition of another's existence required by contract. Indeed, Hegel very explicitly denies that marriage is a contract; he denounces Kant's contractual interpretation of marriage as 'shameful' (*PR*, 75R). The most he will concede is that 'though marriage begins in contract, it is precisely a contract to transcend the standpoint of contract, the standpoint from which persons are regarded in their individuality as self-subsistent units' (*PR*, 163R).

Pateman makes a great deal of Hegel's admission that although marriage is a contract to transcend contract, it does begin in contract. 'Why', she asks, 'should a theorist who declares that it is shameful to see marriage as merely contractual still insist that marriage originates in a contract?'[36] The answer, I think, is that it is not so much insistence as acceptance for the sake of argument. What Hegel emphasizes most is the *transcendence* of contract in marriage. His strategy is to take the popularly accepted model, the contractual one, and to 'deconstruct' it, if the anachronism can be pardoned. Marriage represents a progression of the spirit from self-absorption, as contract does over property; but it represents a much greater advance towards a form of general or public will than contract does. Hegel puts very little emphasis on the formalities of the marriage agreement, and a great deal on its recognition by others as a *public* commitment through the wedding ceremony (*PR*, 164) – none of which is necessary to contract *per se*, as part of *private* law.

To put the matter in Pateman's terms, though not according to Pateman's interpretation: I think that Hegel denies both the sexual and the social contract, as improper generalizations of contract into 'a sphere of a quite different and high nature' in the case of the social contract (*PR*, 75R). It is well known that Hegel is no contractarian: the polity is not formed by such an incomplete acknowledgement of others' existence as contract represents. In the *Philosophy of Right*, the will's progress of development from self-absorption to being fully in the world proceeds from property to contract to family to economy to state. The realm of contract is distinguished from that of marriage and the family, just as it is from that of the state – although it is further away from the latter than the former.

Pateman, on the other hand, interprets Hegel as accepting the sexual contract, which, she alleges, undermines his rejection of the social contract.[37] The liberal contractarians, she argues, are at least consistent, though not terribly open: social life *is* contract all the way down, although the sexual contract has been hushed up. So Pateman thinks that Hegel, too, is guilty of the sin of the contractarians: the incorporation of women into civil society not as individuals but as subordinates, a status ensured by the marriage contract. 'Hegel's marriage contract that transcends contract', she concludes, 'replicates the sexual contract just as completely as the marriage contract in classic contract theory.'[38]

Communal life is *not* contract all the way down in Hegel, Pateman remarks, and this insight is correct in relation to the state, I think. But it also applies to marriage and the family. Hegel's account of marriage insists on the *distance* of marriage from the requirements of civil society. The marriage ceremony cannot be reduced to an 'external formality, a mere so-called "civil requirement"' (*PR*, 164R). To concentrate on 'the civil relation of the parties' at the expense of the wedding's spiritual significance is 'something not merely indifferent to the true nature of marriage, but actually alien to it' (*PR*, 164R).

Similarly, Hegel's account of divorce differs from the objective require-ments of the polity. If Pateman is right, there should be no divorce in Hegel's polity. Women must be incorporated through the 'free' marriage contract, in her account, but once they have agreed to that contract, they lose all rights, including the right to break the contract. If the secret agenda of the marriage contract is the control of women, they should never be allowed out of it, once in. Although Hegel thinks there is an ethical duty to marry, however, there is no legal requirement to marry or stay married: 'There can be no compulsion on people to marry; and on the other hand, there is no merely legal or positive bond which can hold the parties together once their dispositions and actions have become hostile and contrary' (*PR*, 176).

Yet although Hegel assigns marriage to a different, higher stage of self-development than contract, it is still not entirely clear *why* he does so. Why is it 'shameful' to see marriage as a contract? Hegel rather skates over that issue, pressing on to the fictiveness of the social contract (*PR, 75A*). So what might distinguish marriage from contract? Setting aside Hegel's sentimen-tal revulsion at the mere thought, there seem to be three logical possibilities.

The first explanation which occurs to anyone familiar with the law on coverture is that the wife might be seen as sacrificing too much for marriage to be viewed as a contract, according to a principle cited by Hegel in another context, *laesio enormis*. A contract in which one side surrenders too much (more than one-half the value of the goods) and gains virtually nothing in return is null and void (*PR*, 77R). But whether this is a correct interpretation of Hegel is dubious, I believe. The community of property system under which he lived would simply not see marriage this way; nor is it compatible with his own account of marriage.

The second possible reason why marriage is not a contract in Hegel might be that 'the object about which a contract is made is a single external thing' (*PR*, 75). Since we are embodied wills, the woman's property in the body cannot be that external *object*. I may withdraw my will from my body, even destroy my body (*PR*, 47 and 65); but since contract represents the presence rather than the absence of will, I cannot without contradiction both make my body an object of contract and withdraw my will from it. So the sexual contract cannot be the basis of marriage in Hegel.

Nor can the external matter which the contract concerns be property in things, since Hegel explicitly states that wealth, the family capital, is created *by* marriage. Marriage cannot be a contract about wealth which does not exist before marriage. This is a very different view of family property from the Greek one, and Hegel's preferred model of the family is correspondingly nuclear, not the extended *oikos*.

A marriage brings into being a new family which is self-subsistent and independent of the clans or 'houses' from which its members have been drawn . . . Thus an individual's property too has an essential connexion with his conjugal relationship and only a comparatively remote one with his relation to his clan or 'house'. (*PR*, 172)

This is also different from the liberal model of family wealth under the legal doctrine of coverture, because it is held in common: 'so that, while no member of the family has property of his own, each has his right in the common stock' (*PR*, 171). Hegel recognizes that this right 'may come into collision with the head of the family's right of administration' (*PR*, 171): the husband is the head, needless to say. But to recognize a potential conflict of rights represents an advance over coverture, under which the wife has no rights which may come into conflict with anybody else's. Here Hegel is clearly influenced by community of property; it is a historical inaccuracy to assume he and Locke both view marriage and property under the same aegis, as Pateman tends to do in her discussion of Hegel.

The absence of an external object does seem a good reason for excluding marriage from the realm of contract. But we also need to consider a third possibility. In Hegel marriage is primarily an ethical tie, or 'more precisely characterised as ethico-legal (*rechtlich sittliche*) love' (*PR*, 161A). Property is actually antithetical to love, in the view which Hegel expresses in his 1797–8 'Fragment on Love':[39] the virtue of property is to develop individuality, but love is about unity. To think of marriage as a civil contract cheapens the meaning of the couple's union, as surely as if it were no more than a series of chance sexual encounters. Whereas contract and property are intertwined though distinct, marriage and property are incompatible: so marriage is different from contract.

Pateman correctly identifies this argument in Hegel, together with its paradoxical opposition between the lovers' sense of themselves as autonomous beings and the deeper sense of self which the voyaging spirit discovers through unity with the other. None the less, she insists that despite Hegel's explicit assertion that marriage is the antithesis and abnegation of contract, 'the social contract (civil life) depends on the idea of the sexual contract (which is displaced onto the marriage contract).'[40] In my view, this argument was exaggerated enough in relation to the avowedly contractarian liberal theorists; it cannot fit Hegel, however thinly it is stretched. Particularly for a theorist working in the Germanic system of communal property rather than the English regime of coverture and marital unity, Pateman's approach is too Procrustean. Her extension of the sexual contract to Hegel forces the concept to bear too heavy a load. The concept gains theoretical sweep and unity only with the loss of accuracy and sophistication.

Pateman begins from the bedrock truth that 'one party to the marriage contract is a woman; conjugal relations cannot take the same form as civil relations between men.'[41] But Hegel never says that they do: marriage is considered under ethical life in the *Philosophy of Right*, property under abstract right – an earlier stage of the argument and of the progress of the spirit. I think it is more productive to take Hegel at his word: to explore why marriage is *not* a contract in Hegel, but why women's subordination is still inherent in his system. Even in the absence of contract, marriage may still be oppressive.

Men are identified in Hegel with modernity, civil society and human law; women with the archaic, the family and divine law. Their symbol is Antigone (*PR*, 166R) – at first glance a rather liberated choice on Hegel's part, or so some mainstream commentators have remarked.[42] But women remain immured in the cyclical, ahistorical preoccupations of the family, as Antigone did in the defence of her brother's body, of a dead thing.[43] Women are excluded from civil society and the modern state, from both sides of the public realm. Like Antigone, their immersion in the particular affections of the individual family and their unfamiliarity with impartial justice trouble the state. In George Lukács's view, Antigone, women's symbol, represents tribal society; Creon, the forces of modernity – what one might call the rule of law rather than the rule of relationship.[44] As the 'everlasting irony' in political life, Hegel accuses, womankind 'changes by intrigue the universal end of government into a private end, transforms its universal activity into a work of some particular individual, and perverts the universal property of the state into a possession and ornament for the Family'.[45] In this sense the communal and the feminine are incompatible; and yet the communal requires the feminine domain, that of the family, whose existence allows men to function as rational beings without losing their connection to nature and feeling.

Ethical life *can* occur within the family, and if women are to attain the universal, it *must* be within the family, through the transcendence of immediate feeling and partiality: 'In the ethical household, it is not a question of *this* particular husband, *this* particular child, but simply of husband and children generally; the relationships of the woman are based, not on feeling, but on the universal.'[46] But although the family represents a stage in the progress of ethical life, it is at a more primitive level than that of civil society: what Hegel calls a 'nether world'.[47] Both men and women transcend the merely natural in the family; Hegel is not a biological reductionist. But men transcend the natural more thoroughly. Their pursuit of property and wealth in the economic arena of civil society is significant not only for the individual family, but for the community.

This is why Hegel is really only concerned about *male* poverty: it is not merely a material deprivation for the individual, but a loss to the ethical life of the whole when a man is unable to pursue the active goals of property appropriation. For a woman there is no such concern; she shares in the more advanced stages of spirit 'in a curiously vicarious way, through her relations to man'.[48] This means that women's relationship to property is no less troubled in the Hegelian model even though marriage is not a contract. It is on the rock of women's poverty that Hegel's own developmental, general-rights model of property founders, although again that does not necessarily mean that a broadly Hegelian approach must also do so. What is wrong with Hegel's account is not its developmental account of property, but its separate-sphere ideology. The third section of this chapter will examine why.

Poverty and prostitution: Flora Tristan

Hegel's failure to treat women, property and self-development in a consistent fashion has serious practical consequences for his theory. In this section I shall argue that those practical inadequacies need to be explored for at least two reasons (besides the properly 'double vision' of feminist theory). First, although Hegel consigns women to the unchanging, ahistorical domestic realm and assigns an archaic heroine to represent their best virtues, he is actually perfectly well aware of historical and social differences in family structures.[49] Second, the 'owl of Minerva' passage implies that part of theory's task is to inform and be informed about social reality.[50] Although the owl only spreads her wings at dusk, following the day – that is, philosophy follows on from established *mores* and existing institutions – that does not necessarily mean that the task of philosophy is to do no more than to justify the rationality of dominant social structures.

Hegel recognizes that poverty is an insoluble conundrum in modern civil society, but what he does not realize is that it creates impossible contradictions for his account of the family. Like Aristotle, Hegel only worries about *men* who lack property or *are* property, paupers and slaves; like Aristotle, he is unconcerned about their female equivalents. Worse, perhaps: Aristotle, like Mill in a later period, does at least consider slavery a problem for an account of moral agency. Hegel denies that there can be any problem, because, as Ryan puts it, 'there is a conceptual as well as a moral impropriety involved in slavery: men, who are themselves the sources of the possessory intentions in terms of which he [Hegel] analyses property, already so thoroughly possess themselves that there is no room for anyone else's possession of them.'[51] Lacking the possessory attributes of full subjects, women 'wage slaves', however, *can* be objects of possession, undermining the universality of Hegelian theory.

Although Hegel asserts that 'everyone must have property', he recognizes that some social groups will be excluded from the accumulation of capital in modern civil society: the peasantry, for example. Women participate in property appropriation only vicariously, as we have seen, but this does not concern him because their requirements for self-actualization can be satisfied in family life. They do not have the spiritual need to realize themselves through appropriation and ownership. As far as financial need goes, both (male) peasants and (all) women are presumed to have alternative means of support, although Hegel only notices the problem at all for (male) peasants and paupers.

Hegel is genuinely but rather impotently concerned about the consequences of industrialization for the (male) urban proletariat. 'The important question of how poverty is to be abolished is one of the most disturbing problems which agitate modern society' (*PR*, 244A). Unlike the paradigmatic liberals, he is particularly disturbed because poverty is endemic and ineluctable in modern civil society (*PR*, 243), not an old evil which the progress of capitalism will dispel; and yet we cannot do without the self-realization which civil society offers. This is particularly terrible because civil society also has a responsibility for its members, a duty in which it has partially superseded the family.

> To be sure, the family has to provide bread for its members, but in civil society the family is something subordinate and only lays the foundations; its effective range is no longer so comprehensive. Civil society is rather the tremendous power which draws men into itself and claims from them that they work for it, owe everything to it, and do everything by its means. If man is to be a member of civil society in this sense, he has rights and claims against it just as he had rights and claims in the family. (*PR*, 238A)

Hegel is most troubled about the spiritual effects of poverty, even over and above its material deprivations. Lacking property, paupers also lack the recognition of their own worth in others' eyes which contracts over property embody. Furthermore, 'their poverty leaves them more or less deprived of all the advantages of society, of the opportunity of acquiring skill or education of any kind, as well as of the administration of justice, the public health services, and often even of the consolations of religion, and so forth' (*PR*, 241). They may then tend to become a 'pauperised rabble', 'when there is joined to poverty a disposition of mind, an inner indignation against the rich, against society, against the government, etc' (*PR*, 238A). Destructive though it is, this fury is not entirely unjustified: 'Against nature man can claim no right, but once society is established, poverty immediately takes the form of a wrong done to one class by another' (*PR*, 244A). This isolation of the poor from the rest of civil society by emotion (*Gemut*) or mind is profoundly destructive of the very impulse towards self-awareness which it represents: 'The poor man feels himself excluded and mocked by everyone, and this necessarily gives rise to an inner indignation. He is conscious of himself as an infinite, free being, and thus arises the demand that his external existence should correspond to this consciousness.'[52]

The male pauper's sense of himself as a subject is constantly violated by his awareness that he is, at best, a mere object of pity. Whether women of any class can be full subjects in Hegel is far more problematic. 'Hegel suggests that women are not individuals, at least, not in the same measure and to the same extent as men are. They are incapable of the spiritual struggle and diremption (*Entzweiung*) which characterize the lives of men.'[53] Nevertheless there are several reasons why Hegel should be *more* concerned about female paupers than male, and these obtain even if women are not full Hegelian subjects.

First, there is the troubling corollary of Hegel's view that women's spiritual development is vicarious. If their husbands share in the rabble mentality, they are exposed to it as well; most probably they will come to exhibit an even less desirable, bastardized form of it, since they have so few countervailing influences outside the family. Hegel views both sexes as freely surrendering their personalities in marriage (*PR*, 167); the difference is that men can gain another, more enlightened one in civil society. Similarly, it is only in the family that women can share the recognition of their identities through contract and the opportunity for self-development through property appropriation; they cannot fulfil these functions independently, since civil society is not their realm.

Secondly, Hegel is much concerned with being at home in quite a different, non-literal sense: that of *Versöhnung* or reconciliation, 'the process of overcoming alienation . . . overcoming the splits that divide the self from the social world and the attendant splits that divide the self from the self . . . being at home in the social world'.[54] Women have fewer ways of being 'at home' than men, but Hegel thinks they can be deeply and fulfillingly at home in the family. If they are forced out of the home by poverty, by the need to earn a minimal living, they cannot be at home in civil society: it is not their country. The weak version of Hegel's requirements merely insists that there should be 'a possibility *within the community* – a possibility for at least some of its members' to realize themselves within the social world. Michael Hardimon, who offers this interpretation in partial mitigation of Hegel's view on male poverty, thinks it also explains why Hegel believes that women can realize their subjectivities within the *domestic* world. Although 'women cannot realize themselves as individuals in the strong sense . . . Hegel could reply that women can enjoy the reconciliation of individuality and social membership the family provides.'[55]

So women are already deprived of the fullest possible personal identity; it would seem that Hegel's only possible defence must be that *all* women can find a satisfactory alternative fulfilment within the family. Women are not subjects to the same extent that men are, but their development does matter, and it is meant to occur within their separate sphere. Yet if some women are further deprived of the ethical life in the family, forced out of their particular realm of self-realization, this generalization becomes a nonsense. *The fact of widespread female poverty undermines the entire Hegelian ethical imperative in a way that male poverty does not.* Pauper men are only deprived of full individual subjectivity in one of the several possible ways men enjoy; but pauper women who must work outside the home lose their only hope of full self-realization as women.

Hegel does consider possible solutions to poverty, such as casual alms-giving or state work provision schemes, although in the end he concludes that the remedies would undermine the principles of civil society too radically. 'He would argue that although poverty is a structural feature of civil society, it nonetheless represents a *contingent* failure of this sphere to "protect its members and defend their rights".'[56] In the case of pauper women, however, the failure is not *contingent* but *necessary*, precisely because women are not full members of civil society and are not guaranteed its protections.

Finally, female poverty undercuts the deep logic of Hegelian modernity. Modern social life depends on dialectical opposition between dualisms: masculine–feminine, substantive–reflective, urban–rural[57], and indeed also archaic and modern. Each principle must be given separate institutional embodiment for a community to actualize itself, although it is not necessary for each individual to integrate these principles harmoniously within his own personality. The core dualism is that between masculine and feminine, since it reproduces and underpins the others: family–civil society, substantive–transcendent, archaic–modern. As Seyla Benhabib writes,

> Hegel, on the one hand, views the development of subjectivity and individuality within the context of a human community; on the other hand, in assigning men and women to their traditional sex roles, he codifies gender-specific differences as aspects of a rational ontology that is said to reflect the deep structure of *Geist*. Women are viewed as representing the principles of particularity (*Besonderheit*), immediacy (*Unmittelbarkeit*), naturalness (*Natürlichkeit*) and substantiality (*Substanzialität*), while men stand for universality (*Allgemeinheit*), mediacy (*Vermittlung*), freedom (*Freiheit*), and subjectivity (*Subjektivität*). Hegel develops his rational ontology of gender within a logic of oppositions.[58]

But if this crucial masculine–feminine division is breached, by female poverty, the others also fall. The result is utter distintegration – profoundly disturbing for Hegel, whose concern about poverty is its effect on social integration and individual fulfilment, rather than its economic injustice.[59]

The reason why female poverty breaches the masculine–feminine and family–civil society polarizations is that civil society is specifically the non-domestic sphere created by modern production: primarily that of the market, though also of voluntary associations. When civil society is invaded by women, the representatives of the domestic sphere, it loses its new and neat character. Conversely, when women can no longer live at home but must enter civil society, the family loses its archaic virtue, its 'piety', in Hegel's terms (*PR*, 166). It is in the domestic world that women 'overcome their merely natural being, and become ethically significant', as men do in the realm of civil society. There, in the private realm, 'the wife remains, director of the home and the preserver of the divine law.'[60] Particularly if women must enter prostitution – although Hegel is too polite to mention that possibility – they also lose their individual virtue, and that is the only honour a woman has (*PR*, 164A). No woman has what non-pauper working men have, the self-respect which comes from maintaining oneself by one's own effort (*PR*, 244).

Why might women be forced to enter civil society? One obvious reason is that Hegel specifically allows divorce; yet he seems not to see the possible consequence, that many divorced women will no longer be supported by men.[61] Furthermore, Hegel is aware of the economic dynamics of industrialization, its rhythms of overproduction, for example; yet he shows little awareness of the movement of production to outside the home, and of the growing dominance of production for exchange. Women fulfil no economic role at all in Hegel, in fact; even Aristotle at least affords them the role of maintaining the wealth that their *kyrios* has created. This is particularly ironic: the 'freeborn' Athenian woman was very effectively confined to the house, but in early industrial society enormous numbers of women were 'freed' by the enclosures of common agricultural land and the movement away from cottage industries towards production outside the home. This included sexual 'production'. Just as the separate sphere was becoming most firmly entrenched in ideology, through the 'True Woman' movement in early nineteenth-century America, for example,[62] its relation to the realities of female property and poverty became more and more tenuous.

Contemporary observers in Hegel's time considered female poverty to be worst, and the problem of prostitution greatest, in England, the most advanced early capitalist nation. That the two phenomena were linked was a commonplace; but that they were also associated with women's confinement to a separate sphere was a less common argument. That required a theoretical feminist analysis, such as that offered by the French socialist and union organizer Flora Tristan (1803–1844).[63] There had been feminist activist organizations attacking the rise in prostitution before Tristan: for example, the New York Female Moral Reform Society, founded in 1834, proposed to keep vigil at brothels and to publish a list of clients in the society's journal. But what makes Tristan's analysis particularly appropriate to my concerns in this chapter is its systematic nature; the manner in which it relates prostitution to women's propertylessness, including their deprivation of the means of wealth creation; and its particular implications for the Hegelian emphasis on the will, along with Hegel's separate-sphere views.

Writing before Engels and Marx – and indeed 'bequeathing' her concept of the wife as proletarian and the husband as capitalist to Engels, although he never acknowledged the legacy – Tristan consistently analysed women's propertylessness as the combined product of industrialization and patriarchy.

> By identifying the root cause of sexual inegalitarianism in the economic structure of capitalist society, she came to the conclusion that no real improvement in the position of women could be expected until the underlying restrictions on their financial independence (restrictions deeply embedded in the patriarchal family and the legal arrangements for property ownership) were removed. Tristan's feminism had thus moved beyond an appeal to the abstract natural rights principles of the 1789 Revolution to an appeal to concrete socialist principles. [64]

Tristan was stunned by the vast scale of prostitution in the English capital during her four visits to London in 1826, 1831, 1835 and 1839. In her account of these expeditions, *Promenades dans Londres*, she supplemented her own impressions with Dr Michael Ryan's *Prostitution in London*,[65] and reports of the Society for the Suppression of Vice (1837 and 1838), along with Metropolitan Police and Home Office reports for the same two years. Drawing on estimates by James Beard Talbot of the Society for the Prevention of Juvenile Prostitution, she put the numbers of prostitutes at 80,000 to 100,000, of whom she reckoned that two-thirds were in their teens or younger, and that one-quarter died every year. Talbot estimated that there were between 13,000 and 14,000 prostitutes in London who were under thirteen. The total female population at that time was only 596,000. Confusion over the actual figures was rife, in part because there was no system of police registration, as there was in Paris, and in part because working women used casual prostitution as a stopgap during periods of unemployment, or to supplement their paltry wages. Married and common-law couples, too, consciously used this stratagem: the degenerate prostitute and the respectable wife were often one and the same woman. Against the conscious and voluntary use of prostitution by mature women must be set the prevalence of child abduction (both male and female) and trafficking, which Tristan has no qualms in calling slavery.

It was women's enforced lack of property and education which directly caused prostitution, Tristan argued in her *Promenades dans Londres*. Indeed, with other professions barred to women, the oldest one was the most moral alternative open to a widowed or deserted woman with children: the other choices were theft or infanticide, Tristan starkly noted. To see prostitution as an indictment of the unequal distribution of wealth between the classes was not new: Owenite socialists, for example, viewed prostitution as the paradigm of class exploitation in early capitalism.[66] What was novel about Tristan's analysis was, first, that she extended the parallel to the inequality between the sexes of the rights to the factors of wealth creation. Lacking property in things, or even in the soul or will, women have nothing to lose by dissociating themselves from property in their own bodies.

> Prostitution is a blight on the human race, the most hideous of all the evils caused by the unequal distribution of wealth, an even more damning indictment of society than crime . . . If you [men] allowed women to receive the same education and follow the same professions as men, they would not be crushed by poverty while men prospered . . . The concepts of vice and virtue imply the freedom to do good or evil, but what moral sense can a woman have if she cannot call her soul her own, possesses nothing in her own name, and has been accustomed all her life to use her guile and seductive charms as a means to escape from tyranny and constraint? When she is tormented by poverty and sees the wealth of this world reserved for men's sole enjoyment, does not the art of attraction in which she has been schooled since childhood lead her inevitably into prostitution? Then let the society man has made be blamed for this aberration of nature, and let woman be exonerated. As long as she remains the slave of man and the victim of prejudice, as long as she is refused training in a profession, as long as she is deprived of her civil rights, there can be no moral law for her. [67]

Woman in this condition is outside the Hegelian sphere of moral agency. Further, as her biographers Maire Cross and Tim Gray point out, Tristan consciously put prostitution first of all the *social* problems she considers in *Promenades dans Londres*; but the order of the book shows that she also understood its relation to *political* life, and particularly to the public and private domains. This, too, has ramifications for Hegel.

> The positioning of this chapter in Tristan's book was significant: it was placed *before* a series of sketches on the social problems of crime, illness and poverty, in order to associate prostitution with social deprivation rather than with individual sin. It was also situated directly *after* Tristan's discussion of the House of Commons, in which she noted that women were excluded not only from the floor but even from the stranger's gallery. In the mother of parliaments, revered as the model of liberty, women were treated as pariahs. Ironically, therefore, the only way that women could enter the public domain was as prostitutes (*filles publiques*). Women were at one and the same time excluded from the kind of public life that was rightfully theirs, and forced into the kind of public life that was a shameful violation of their rights as human beings . . . [68]

Tristan specifically linked the high incidence of prostitution in England not only to the inequalities of early industrialization, but to the English law on coverture and inheritance: to property questions. Once again, women's deprivation of property robs them of moral agency. Aristocratic men, she charged, married for money and then dissipated their wives' fortunes in the gaming-houses and clubs of the West End. The passage quoted above continues in a vein which relates directly to the English legal doctrine of marital unity: 'As long as she can enjoy wealth only through the power she exerts over men's passions, as long as she has no independent legal status and her husband can rob her of any property she has earned or inherited, as long as she can ensure her right to her property and her freedom only by renouncing marriage, there can be no moral law for her.'[69]

By the light of women's actual circumstances in the most modern industrial nation of the time – and Hegel is modernity's great advocate – his discourse of the separate sphere emerges as naive at best; at worst, as mere ideology. It has been well documented that the ideal of female chastity and of women's natural devotion entirely to the home – what Bram Dijkstra calls 'the cult of the Household Nun'[70] – are not timeless truths; they were part of the new ideal of female 'passionlessness' which emerged in the late eighteenth century, arguably as a response to women's mobilization during the French and American revolutions.[71] In the mid-nineteenth century, feminists would resist this discourse as explicitly politicized and biased in men's favour: as an ideology which has to be 'inculcated', in Fuller's words.

> As to marriage, it has been inculcated on [sic] women for centuries that men have not only stronger passions than they, but of a sort that it would be shameful for them to share or even understand; that, therefore, they must 'confide in their husbands', that is, submit implicitly to their will; that the least appearance of coldness or withdrawal, from whatever cause, in the wife is wicked, because liable to turn her husband's thoughts to illicit indulgence; for a man is so constituted that he must indulge his passions or die![72]

Hegel's views slot into what Benhabib calls 'the "discursive space" of competing power relations'. The 'natural' purity of women in the 'passionlessness' discourse mirrors the 'piety' of home life in Hegel.

In the judgement of many mainstream commentators, Hegel's system founders on the inadequacy of his response to the problem of men's poverty. 'Though his account of the justification of property is deep, plausible and attractive, his central mistake was his failure to see that private property can be justified as a right of personality only if it can be made available to every person on whose behalf that argument can be made out.'[73] Hegel himself did *not* make the argument out on behalf of women, and so it might seem unfair to tax him with failure to consider women's lack of property. I have tried to show why this exclusion does not let him off the hook, why the problem of *female* poverty *should* matter for reasons of internal consistency within Hegel's system. (I also believe, of course, that female poverty simply *does* matter, within and without any philosophical system.)

Yet a Hegelian analysis can have something important to say about women's propertylessness. In this chapter I have sought to draw out the following elements:

1 The vision that 'everyone must have property' as a general right because property is instrumental to identity development, as a first stage;
2 The insistence that contract, the second stage of identity development, *is* only a stage, and not the template for all social relations (not for marriage, for example);
3 The recognition of experiential and relational ethical models which is implicit in Hegel's thought;
4 The importance of embodiment in self-development; and
5 The possibility of respecting the agency of the propertylessness which is afforded by the master–servant parallel. A Hegelian analysis helps us see how women make sense of their 'no-property' worlds.

Together with the perception that contract need not be all bad, which I argued in chapter 3, we now have in place several of the planks which we will need to rebuild property in the last chapter, but not all. In chapter 5 I want to provide some further building materials.

5

Labour, Alienation and Reproduction

This chapter builds on the concerns of the previous chapters in several ways, and it may be useful to provide an introductory context for each of the three main sections which follow.

(1) In examining the Hegelian developmental model of property-holding, chapter 4 raised the issue of whether only *private* property can satisfy the needs of an active moral agent, or indeed satisfy them best.[1] 'Everyone must have property,' but need that property be exclusively my own? Active engagement in a communal project may fulfil the self's need for interaction with the external world. But then why have property at all?

It begins to sound as if what the will's purpose requires, in order to translate its subjective purpose into objectivity, is not property *per se*, but that which produces property: labour. Property is merely the ossified remains of labour, in this formulation: generally the remains of my own efforts in the liberal view, but of someone else's labour in a Marxist model. And private property, in Engels's account, is inextricably entangled with patriarchy, which arises because of men's need to control inheritance. Once the original matriarchy is overthrown, along with its communal sexuality, men pre-empt women's exclusive sexual services, coming to 'own' both their wives and the fruits of their bodies, children. If this is so, if property *itself* (and particularly private property) is irrelevant or even opposed to women's self-actualization, then *no* theory of property will be appropriate to thinking about women's liberation – to put the matter in terms of the second overriding question in this book, 'Are some theories of property more appropriate than others to thinking about women's liberation?'[2] But a theory emphasizing the redeeming power of labour and economic activity might be. This was the thrust of much utopian socialism. In Owen and Saint-Simon, for example, women cannot be liberated so long as private property remains intact.[3] In Owen's case, at least, we might conjecture that this is merely a historically conditioned reaction to the extremes of coverture, not to private property *per se*.

But there is still a broader question to be answered. Is it labour or property which satisfies the agent's developmental needs, which makes the subject something other than object? *Very* roughly speaking,[4] the answer in Hegel is property, but not property so maldistributed as to create a 'rich rabble'. In Marx and Engels it is labour, *praxis*, productive work which transforms the material world to fit human needs and in the process also hones human consciousness to its ultimate potential – but also with certain conditions: not alienated or exploited labour. Yet both Hegel and Marx retain the Lockean assumption that 'every man hath a property in his person,' and thus in the labour of his person. This assumption is as gender-blind in Hegel and Marx as in Locke. Part of this book's purpose is to explore the possibility that *no woman* has been construed in any canonical theory as possessing an unbounded property in her labour power. But in both liberal and Marxist thought, it is essentially property in the person and in one's labour which generates entitlements.[5] Marx and Locke are equally committed to the apparent truism that even the person who has no physical property owns one inalienable asset, labour power.

Mainstream economists such as Partha Dasgupta[6] think that this proposition is false, but only because what the assetless person owns is *potential* labour power.[7] That requires decent nutrition and health care to become actual labour power, and Dasgupta rightly points out that most women around the world are denied those means to fulfil the potential. But this is a naturalistic argument which underestimates the strangeness of women's relation to property. So, in an apparently opposite manner, does the common feminist presumption that women simply *are* property, which I have questioned throughout this book, beginning with my treatment of wives and slaves in Aristotle. This ambivalence I share with Pateman: the richness of the sexual contract metaphor is that it presents women as both agents and objects, or more accurately, that the marriage contract allows women just so much agency as is required for them to will their own subordination.

Women are neither simple *objects* of property-holding, nor are they unqualified *subjects* whose property-holding may suffer under rectifiable practical handicaps. A materialist analysis might offer a less static and more activist possibility if it could categorize different sites of oppression rather than a simple dichotomy of victims and oppressors; and a materialist feminist position might also avoid the relativistic multiple essentialisms of cultural feminism.[8] In particular, it seems possible that the Marxist concept of alienation gets at some of this strangeness, allowing women to be agents rather than mere objects, but impaired subjects. The opening section below asks whether a possible answer to the query first raised in chapter 1 – how women have reconciled their lack of control over property with the necessity of their labours to create and preserve it – is that they are *alienated* from their labour.

As in previous chapters I begin by deconstructing a concept from a canonical theorist – seeing whether it will or will not help me reconstruct a theory of property which counts women in, as the canonical theorist fails to do. Other feminist theorists have also transferred the concept of alienation to wider domains, particularly those of culture and psychology.[9] But I want to do something different. I want to know whether we can transform the notion of alienation to fit women's typical *propertylessness in their labour*, even though the Marxist interpretation of the concept relies crucially on *ownership* of property in one's labour, and even though it is applied strictly to 'productive' rather than reproductive labour in Marx. Although I trespass onto non-capitalist forms of alienation, I shall be remaining mainly within the economic and political realm, drawing on Pateman's analysis of 'wives, slaves and wage slaves'[10] and Catharine MacKinnon's *Toward a Feminist Theory of the State*, which departs from a Marxist starting point but transcends Marxism. Throughout the discussion I attempt to evaluate whether alienation is the right concept to describe women's particular kind of impaired subjectivity as agents and property-holders, or whether we shall need to devise some hybrid or alternative concept, one that can include the other forms of objectification which women experience. So the concept of alienated labour is my concern in the first part of this chapter. I shall need that notion in chapter 7, as it turns out, when I come to reconstruct property.

(2) Marx's own definition of alienation specifically does *not* apply to women's domestic or 'reproductive' labour. In the view of Marx and Engels married women suffer an additional form of oppression besides that which imprisons all workers under capitalism. To them, this is *not* actually alienation, which is characteristic only of relations under capitalism: domestic work is a non-capitalist anomaly. (Prostitution, which like domestic labour predates capitalism, *is* characterized as a form of alienation, although 'only a *specific* expression of the *universal* prostitution of the worker.')[11] Yet the condition of the wife's exemption from alienated labour in the workplace is being an object of property to her husband, who disposes of her labour power and may even use her as a 'means of production', in the words of the *Communist Manifesto*.[12] This is a vestige of the original form of unequal distribution of labour and its products, including property: the sexual division of labour, under which the wife and

children are the husband's slaves.[13] The solution which Marx and Engels propound for women's specific form of oppression is to bring them out of the archaic isolation of domesticity, and into *productive* employment. As Engels wrote in *The Origin of the Family, Private Property and the State*, 'The first condition for the liberation of the wife is to bring the whole female sex back into public industry.'[14]

Many feminist critics have pointed out the inadequacy of this response in terms of women's 'double shift' and the undervaluing of *reproductive* labour, particularly in Marx.[15] Engels at least recognized the practical difficulty for the wife: 'if she carries out her duties in the private service of her family, she remains excluded from social production and unable to earn; and if she wants to take part in public production and earn independently, she cannot carry out her family duties.'[16] However, Engels failed to realize that the real reason that paid work is not necessarily liberating is not simply overwork and fatigue: it is that *paid employment does not give the wife ownership of her own labour*. The original property inequality in one's labour remains untouched by participation in 'productive' work, whether in a market or a socialist economy.

I argued in chapter 3, *contra* Pateman, that what is wrong with the supposed 'marriage' or 'sexual' contract is not that it is a contract, but that it is a form of sexual domination which in fact contradicts most of the principles of contract.[17] However, Pateman is certainly right in thinking that married women's relation to property in their own persons, and to the products of their labour, is different from and inferior to that of married men. Coverture in developing capitalist nations had much the same effect, although the beneficiary of the wife's labour was not the husband's lineage but the individual man himself.

While I do not intend to reproduce the debate over reproduction, I tend to accept that production and reproduction do not turn out to be groupings which we can use to rebuild an account of property that includes women's experience, although Christine Delphy's notion of the domestic mode of production is more helpful, as I conclude in the second section below. The site of oppression in relation to Marxism is not the mode of production, but the gender of the economic agent – just as the issue in the liberal context was not the mechanism of contract, but the 'sexual' aspect of the 'sexual contract'.

(3) There are many possible illustrations of women's alienation from and propertylessness in their own labour. Until very recently, for instance, UK tax law amalgamated the wife's income into her husband's tax return, implying that he owned it as a vestige of coverture. Another instance from the developed world concerns the 'proletarianization' of divorced women as delineated by Christine Delphy.[18] Delphy views divorce as the

continuation of marriage by other means: the exploitation of women's propertylessness continues even after the 'marriage contract' is defunct. However, the practical examples which I choose in this chapter come principally from the South. In the third section below I illustrate this problem in one of its most modern forms: the entry into paid employment by Third World women.

For example, the Indian landless poor, whether male or female, must hire out their labour; but the labour of women – the great majority of the casual workforce, at 60 to 90 per cent – is frequently a form of collateral offered by landless men seeking a loan from their landlord.[19] Bridewealth in sub-Saharan Africa is conceived as buying a woman's labour power, 'productive' and 'reproductive', for the husband's kin;[20] the Athenian *oikos* similarly pre-empted the wife's labour, although this was a dowry system. Women are propertyless under both dowry and bridewealth systems, and in both the productive and the reproductive modes; the question is not the mode of production, but the gender of the economic agent. This is one reason why the categories of production and reproduction have come to be the objects of considerable doubt among some feminist writers, who charge these conceptual dichotomies with reinforcing the equally misleading dualism of public and private economic spheres, and with having obscured women's economic importance, especially among the rural poor.[21]

The situation of women in sub-Saharan Africa stands Engels on his head, when he asserts in the *Origin* that from earliest societies men are always responsible for subsistence. For that matter, it also puts Locke through some uncomfortable gymnastics: although an agrarian society might be expected to develop straightforward laws of first possession by tillage,[22] *women's* labour input gives *men* 'first-possession rights' in the fruits of their labour. Sub-Saharan African women's productive labours create property in land and crops for men, as do the efforts of the children on whom their reproductive work concentrates. Men often have no responsibility to maintain those children, or indeed their wives.[23] Yet women have few or no property entitlements in land, crops or children.

Nor do they ultimately have property rights in themselves: *lobola* is paid by the husband to the wife's kin, but in order to divorce her husband the wife must pay him back the bride-price, of which she herself will not normally have seen a penny. The no-property world which Munzer treated as an unpleasant and unimaginable fiction is the everyday situation of many sub-Saharan African women. Labour alone, even labour in the expanding cash economy, does not liberate these women: rather the reverse. The harder they labour, the more they increase their husband's wealth and decrease his willingness to dispense with their labours through divorce. This is strikingly similar to the vicious dynamic identified by Marx and Engels in relation to the working class. As Jaggar puts it, 'Ironically, the more the working class produces, the more the capitalist class is enriched. The result of the working class's own productive activity is a constant increase in the power of its class enemy.'[24] However, the great difference is that the one thing which the male worker *does* own is his labour.

Three notes of caution. First, the treatment of Marx and Engels in this chapter is far less comprehensive than that of Hegel in chapter 4. This is because I want to make room for modern feminist materialisms, which are better developed and more influential than feminist Hegelianisms. Out of the vast Marxist opus I pull two principal questions: *alienation* and *reproduction*, both in relation to property in one's labour. These seem important at first blush: women are commodified through the value of their reproductive labour, and alienated from the products of that labour as well as from their own commodified economic value.

Second, the examples in this chapter are contemporaneous with our times, not with those of the canonical theorist studied. But as I have just remarked, this is as much a chapter about contemporary feminist historical materialism as about Marx and Engels. In addition, this departure seems justified because the merely partial adequacy of the Marxist formulations of alienation and reproductive labour has only come to be realized with the development of modern anthropology and economics.

Finally, there is need for great caution in discussing women's alienated labour in the South. Questions about Third World women do raise opportunities for feminist theory to develop notions of collective political agency, working through opposition rather than identification and challenging the notion that the personal is political as excessively in-dividualistic.[25] Although too much Western feminist writing about Third World women has left them firmly in the 'object' camp, implying only Western feminists are true subjects, I shall try to avoid that particular neocolonial trap. Donna Haraway has satirized 'the search for the fetishized perfect subject of oppositional history, sometimes appearing in feminist theory as the essentialized Third World Woman'.[26] Western feminists have also been accused of overplaying the importance of the conjugal role for Third World women, particularly African women. 'Theorizing the sexual division of labour as a simple opposition of male and female interests presupposes a degree of sexual individuation that may not necessarily apply in different societies.'[27] This may turn out to be a harder injunction to obey, since the sexual division of labour and property figures large in my argument. I shall also need to be sensitive to the tendency of Western feminists to see Third World women as their intellectual property, produc-ing or colonizing them as a field of knowledge and essentializing their difference from us.[28]

Labour and alienation: Marx and MacKinnon

To reiterate, alienation is likely to be a necessary addition to the building materials that we require in order to reconstruct property. If women are alienated from their labour, they are excluded from both developmental and instrumental models of property, both of which rely on ownership of labour as the precondition of property and contract. Conversely, in order to understand why both Lockean and Hegelian models exclude women, we may need to incorporate the Marxist notion of alienation as lack of control over one's labour.

Yet the concept of alienation may appear too general and patronizing to help us understand how women have endured and continue to endure their no-property worlds. Do I really intend to argue that all women whose property rights have been more limited than men's – and thus, effectively, almost all women – are alienated from their work and economic activity? Marx himself might well find it epistemologically inappropriate to use a concept derived under industrial conditions as a catch-all for other modes of production. Can a concept developed to describe the condition of the male proletariat under capitalism really have any bearing on the Athenian wife, for example? If alienation is arguably too broad a concept, it may also be too gender-specific. Many feminists might see alienation as yet another concept tailored to fit men only. To trot out one more male-centred concept when we ought to be creating radically new female attributes is antithetical to Luce Irigaray's project, for example.

There is also a risk of equating alienation with the root cause of women's oppression and of romanticizing pre-capitalist, 'alienation-free' systems as less exploitative of women. (This would be the converse of the equally impermissible error of assuming that women were equally alienated in all pre-capitalist societies; but I have already made it clear that Athens, for example, was exceptionally bad for women.) As the legal theorist Michael Trebilcock has pointed out, 'many internal (non-commodified) values may imply all kinds of oppression, hierarchy, and domination, as exemplified in many traditional family structures.'[29] The commodification and reification of practically everything under capitalism, to which the Marxist concept of alienation is closely linked, is not the sole cause of women's propertylessness; that much should be evident from the Athenian *oikos*. One might equally well argue that commodification, by putting a price on everything if a value on nothing, enables modern commentators to see what is wrong with women's propertylessness as Athenian observers could not. If everything must be bought, and is available openly to be bought, how can it be right to deny a sizeable proportion of purchasers – impoverished women – any means to buy? Conversely, the extremes of commodification in market systems create public debate which highlights issues around women's property in the person. For example, the controversy in medical ethics about legalizing paid surrogacy examines whether 'contract motherhood' valorizes surrogates as freely consenting and economically active subjects, or denigrates both surrogates and their babies as objects for sale.[30] I shall return to this example in chapter 7. For now, I merely note that these are all serious qualms about whether the concept of alienation can be transformed to suit a woman-centred theory of property.

On the other side, to see women as alienated is at least to *see* them – when they have been invisible in so much mainstream property theory. Although the concept of alienation may be accused of being patronizing in implying that women's consciousness is somehow not authentic, it does credit them with having consciousness and subjectivity; they are not just objects. There is an anomaly still to be explained, one which neither the Lockean nor the Hegelian model of property has answered: how women have found meaning in their no-property worlds, how they have continued to bear a disproportionate share of the work while reaping so few of its rewards. The concept of alienation answers that question by recognizing frankly that women's propertylessness *has* limited their participation in what Marx would term their 'species-life', the free productive activity which gives meaning to human existence. It chimes with a sort of psychological intuition which insists that even under very different sets of social beliefs, women may have had to blank out the bleakness of their condition in order to carry on with their work. And it may say something about how 'extinguished', impaired subjects lose their light.

The most obvious indication that alienation *has* already proved a useful explanatory tool to feminists is also the reason why it seems at first to have no bearing on women's situation. Marx notes that under the capitalist system which produces alienation, 'labour always appears as repulsive, always as *external forced labour*; and not labour, by contrast, as "freedom and happiness".'[31] At least in modern Western society, women are encouraged to think of their labours for their family as 'freedom and happiness'. From the early days of the Woman Question, however, feminist writers have insisted that wives' domestic labour is actually external and forced, even the creation of that most intimate 'product', children.[32] Thus feminists have extended the logic of alienation into marriage, where Marx and Engels feared to tread. In shrinking from applying the full power of the concept of alienation, Marx lays himself open to contradictions from which a feminist account is exempt. For example, in *Capital* Marx presents the sexual division of labour as natural,[33] which seems at odds with his earlier assertion (in *The German Ideology*) that it is also the origin of the first kind of slavery, that of the wife and children.

Pateman's notion of the sexual contract is the most sophisticated of many feminist rethinkings which *have* viewed women's labour as external and forced, and which rely implicitly or explicitly on the concept of alienation. Women's subordination as wives in the home is different from, and additional to, their subordination as workers under capitalism, Pateman argues.[34] No matter how low the (male) worker's wage, no matter how much is extracted from it in surplus value by the capitalist employer, the wage itself is a symbol of freedom. It stands for the worker's ability to divorce his labour power from his person, in a civil contract of employment. Although Marx views this as the source of the worker's alienation, it is a form of autonomy to Pateman. The commodity in the employment contract is labour, that in the sexual contract the woman's person. Extrapolating from Pateman's discussion, we might want to say that if anyone deserves to be called alienated, it is the wife, not the male worker. 'To be sure,' Pateman adds, 'men are also subordinates as workers – but to see the worker as no more than a wage slave fails to capture a vital dimension of his position in civil society; he is that curiosity, an *unfree master*.'[35] Surely this 'curiosity' is all the odder in women's case. What the conception of alienation might capture is the gendered nature of owning one's labour, or, more properly, of not owning it.

So it is at least worth trying the concept of alienation on for size, even if it will require alterations such as Pateman makes. The clearest explanation of alienation is in terms of subjectivity: of becoming a stranger to oneself, as the German *Entfremdung* more clearly conveys. In conditions of work over which labourers have little control, Marx writes, 'the work is *external* to the worker . . . it is not part of his nature . . . consequently he does not fulfil himself in his work but denies himself';[36] 'man's own deed becomes an alien power opposed to him, which enslaves him instead of being controlled by him. For as soon as the distribution of labour comes into being, each man has a particular, exclusive sphere of activity, which is forced upon him and from which he cannot escape.'[37]

The language of subjectivity is matched in Marx by a concern with false objectification. By becoming strangers to our own subjectivity, we falsely separate ourselves *from* ourselves, making ourselves objects when we should be subjects.[38] The commodification and reification of everything under capitalism extends to our subjectivity. In such circumstances it is impossible to enjoy the beneficial developmental aspects of labour, of transforming nature not simply to satisfy animal needs but to fulfil human potential. Marx and Engels originally held that the abolition of private property actually takes second place to the ending of such alienation: it follows from it rather than preceding it, reversing their usual order of economic determinism. 'Private property can be abolished only on condition of an all-round development of individuals,' as Marx writes in *The German Ideology*.[39]

Furthermore, the worker under capitalism is distanced not only from his or her own nature and potential, but from other people, and even from physical objects. So far as the latter are concerned, Marx writes in *The German Ideology* that 'private property alienates the individuality not only of people but also of things.'[40] This appears to make little sense: what kind of individual subjectivity can things possess? What Marx seems to mean here is that both owners and workers cease to see the full and true meanings of the means and objects of production, that the senses of things in common currency are cheapened. Land, for example, loses its emotional resonance and becomes purely instrumental. 'The central feature of alienated relationships is that things or people that in fact are interdependent or dialectically related to each other come to seem alien, separate from, or opposed to each other,' as Jaggar puts it.[41] The mutual dependence of employer and worker, master and servant in Hegelian terms, is erased.

To apply alienation to propertyless women, we must begin by recognizing that it is not the fact of working at home which makes women alienated from their labour. Marx and Engels, unlike liberal feminists, do not see immersion in the menial, repetitive tasks of housework as oppressive in itself. It is women's form of *praxis*, self-developmental productive activity – and in this Marx reveals his Hegelian roots. Domestic work meets the requirements of producing in a human manner, which affirms my own and other people's existence by giving a concrete expression to my individuality, allowing others to enjoy the product of my labour, mediating between others and the human species, and realizing my own communal and human essence.[42] I become more of a subject by producing objects which enhance the subjectivity of others. Arguably, domestic work even satisfies human need far more directly than does production for profit.

There is nothing intrinsically degrading about childbearing, childrearing and household labour, according to Marx and Engels: only about the conditions under which they are performed in capitalist society. *This* is the source of women's alienation from their labour. Exclusion from the public world typifies housework under capitalism. In previous societies, according to Engels's account in the *Origin*, women's household labour was not 'privatized', did not belong to a single man; and the tasks were performed cooperatively by all the community's women. Christopher Berry explains why this seclusion of housework under capitalism is in fact particularly oppressive to women:

Traditionally (after Aristotle's account) they [women] were creatures of the household, barred from the political world (the *res publicae*) of male citizens. But with capitalism, the economy displaced the household. As already noted, this meant that males went out into the world of work; but since in the liberal or neutral version the economy (civil society) was still 'private', it meant that in that realm too men were dominant. The upshot was that women had in effect disappeared ... Hence the claim that the 'individuals' who constitute the conceptual base of liberalism are *in practice* males, because it is their economic interests (their property/patrimony) that are to be protected by the State.[43]

This historical interpretation purports to solve the dilemma about the 'naturalness' of the sexual division of labour, but it does nothing to mitigate the oddness of the sexual division of property, including property in labour. *That* cannot be caused by women's work belonging to a more 'primitive' mode of production, or by seclusion of housework under capitalism, since women lack property under both archaic and modern forms of production. Indeed, I pointed out in chapters 2 and 3 that women's property rights were more extensive in some archaic societies, such as Gortyn or Egypt, than in the nineteenth-century capitalist economies of Great Britain and the United States.

Contra Marx and Engels, the commodification of women and the dominance of men are not limited to capitalist societies; nor are all pre-capitalist societies the same. Women's propertylessness in the body, in their labour and in their children precedes capitalism: the Athenian woman is a prime example. One may accept the basic feminist materialist tenet that women's oppression is historically specific without necessarily holding that it is specific only to capitalism.[44] It may also be distinctive to other property regimes: within pre-capitalist societies in which land is the main form of wealth, to the Athenian *oikos* more than the Gortynian, Spartan or Ptolemaic Egyptian regimes under which women *could* possess land. The real challenge is to see whether alienation can still be a useful concept even if it is not an 'unnatural' condition, as it is to Marx, who believes that the worker always rightfully owns the labour power of his person. For women, alienation from their labour power appears to be both *natural* and endemic, if not equally so in all periods. Why is this so?

One influential answer centres on sexuality, consistently with the argument which I developed in relation to Pateman: that what is wrong with the sexual contract is not that it is a contract, but that it is sexual. 'Sexuality is to feminism what work is to Marxism: that which is most one's own, yet most taken away,'[45] Catharine MacKinnon writes in one of her best-known aphorisms. Sexuality and labour, to embroider on MacKinnon's formulation, are both our own property, variants of property in the body,[46] of whose enjoyment and benefits we are deprived by patriarchy and capitalism respectively. Men's expropriation of women's sexuality parallels the capitalist class's appropriation of surplus value created by work. The woman worker is estranged or alienated from both, and propertyless twice over. But because Marx classes women 'within that "material substratum" that was not subject to social analysis',[47] he cannot offer an explanation of women's propertylessness as women: only as female workers.

What women do in giving life is, to Marx, like what the earth does: it is natural, not social, constitutive of an object rather than a subject. (This is radically to undervalue labour in childbirth, or labour in labour. I shall return to the practical implications of properly valuing labour in childbirth when I discuss property and abortion in chapter 7.) To Marx, what gives labour its transformative power is intentionality, control, imposing the subject's self on the environment. Women's labour in and for the household lacks these elements. Yet, as MacKinnon points out, 'Actually, factory work under capitalism possesses few of these characteristics, yet it is considered for that reason alienated rather than spontaneous and natural.'[48] To be consistent, Marx should also view women's domestic work as alienated; but he does not, and we will need to go beyond his interpretation in order to reconstruct property. We shall also need to transcend MacKinnon's account. MacKinnon herself does not define alienation in terms of ownership of labour power, tending more to the psychological feminist accounts of alienation in presenting male desire as that which commodifies women, most emblematically through pornography, and alienates them from subject into object:

> *Woman through male eyes is sex object, that by which man knows himself at once as man and as subject ... Combining, like any form of power, legitimation with force, male power extends beneath the representation of reality to its construction ... This works much like the way the social relations of production operate as epistemology, presenting the commodity form as objective thing rather than as congealed labor ... Except here the person is the product.*[49]

This is suggestive, however, for my purposes. Perhaps women do accept their alienated propertylessness in their labour because it is no different from their sexual objectification; perhaps both are forms of propertylessness in the person. '[F]rom the point of view of the object, objectification *is* alienation. For women, there is no distinction between objectification and alienation because women have not authored objectifications, they have been them.'[50] Conversely and consistently, having property is socially constructed as masculine:

> *To explain gender inequality in terms of 'sexual politics' is to advance not only a political theory of the sexual that defines gender but also a sexual theory of the political to which gender is fundamental. In this approach, male power takes the social form of what men as a gender want sexually, which centers on power itself, as socially defined. In capitalist countries, it includes wealth. Masculinity is having it; femininity is not having it.*[51]

This construction of property as something inherently masculine does accord with the subject's treatment by both malestream and feminist writers – and for that very reason, I tend to distrust it as strategically ill-advised. Yet perhaps it need not be so. Historical materialist analysis, derived from Marx and MacKinnon, bears out the original suggestion in my introduction that the way for women to 'claim the status of subject' is to end their economic alienation and propertylessness. *To the extent that one's economic condition determines one's subjectivity, changing women's propertylessness enables them to stop being objectifications. Helping women to attain property makes them subjects.*

This is a 'big' claim which needs to be pinned down with examples if it is to sound anything but rhetorical. I shall try to do so in the final section of this chapter. Before that, however, I want to deal with the criticism that alienation cannot be correctly said to apply to women's domestic labour under *reproduction*. I shall rebut that challenge by advancing Christine Delphy's substitution of the *domestic* mode of *production*, to which the notion of labour as alienated can then be said to apply.

Delphy and the domestic mode of production

Although Delphy has little to say about sexuality, her analysis, like MacKinnon's, focuses squarely on power within male–female relationships. Like Le Dœuff, she has consistently attacked the '*Psych et Po*' ('*Psychoanalyse et politique*') school for pursuing that will-o'-the-wisp, a new female essence. As the introduction to her collected essays in *Close to Home* puts it, 'To "revalue" femininity within our existing society is . . . to celebrate masochism.'[52]

What Delphy adds to my attempt to reconstruct property so as to count women in is an explanation of why women do not own their labour in the home, why their labour is properly regarded as alienated and the home correctly seen as a mode of production to which a Marxist analysis of labour as alienated can rightfully be applied. If it is lack of control which marks alienated labour, then feminists should be entitled to transform the concept of alienation so as to describe women's work in conditions of propertylessness and powerlessness. If we define alienation not by the conditions under which labour is done, but by whether that labour is one's own property – whether one is estranged from owning one's own person and its labour power – then men's factory labour is not actually alienated. Wives are more truly alienated from the ownership of their labour than are male 'wage slaves'.

As I stated in the introduction to this chapter, women's domestic labour is not regarded as alienated in Marx. Women's domestic labour is conventionally said to produce no use-values – so that an account of it cannot be 'bourgeois' – but neither is it seen by classical Marxists as production, the concern of 'proletarian' explanations. In fact women's domestic work, and the propertylessness in their own labour which typifies it, disappears down a black hole in conventional Marxist explanation.[53] But if alienation is really going to explain women's impaired subjectivity and propertylessness, it must be transformed to include non-waged labour, particularly child-bearing and childrearing. These are the most direct and intimate forms in which women's property in their person has been denied, as the discussions of the Athenian *oikos* and Anglo-American legal coverture have suggested.

Just as work in the home cannot be alienated because it lies outside capitalism, so is it also seen in classical Marxism as being outside production proper. Although Marx and Engels are far from consistent in their treatment of 'the production/reproduction of daily life',[54] the usual interpretation is that household work constitutes a twofold reproduction of the labour force: refreshing existing workers through providing food and creature comforts, and replenishing the future supply of labourers through childbearing and childrearing. However, much of women's work is not regarded as either 'production' or 'reproduction': work which does not produce surplus value (such as shopping or cooking) is defined principally as consumption, although occasionally (as in *The German Ideology*) women's entire domestic existence is regarded as slavery. MacKinnon dismisses the attempts of more recent Marxists[55] to accommodate house-work within a framework that does valorize women's work as mere 'fetishization' of the original categories, production and reproduction.[56]

Delphy's economic analysis of the family may be construed as showing how the reproduction of capitalism depends in reality on the reproduction of gender inequality within the family. But rather than attempting to fit women's domestic labour into the mould of reproduction, Delphy prefers to introduce a new category within Marxism, 'domestic relations of production'. This she views as shifting the methodological foundations of the Marxist structure, rather than the sort of mere redecorating which MacKinnon so dislikes. 'While these [Marxist] principles have supposedly been used to analyse the situation of women as women, the specific relations of women to production have in fact simply been ignored,'[57] Delphy writes. To put this insight in my own terms, women typically have had no property in the means of domestic production.

To call women's domestic labour reproduction rather than production, Delphy asserts, ignores the question of why women's labour is not seen as adding value, even when the products they produce and the services they provide would have to be purchased in the market if women did not make them for nothing. That is, Marxists presuppose that there is something natural and inherently non-exploitative about the division of labour within the family, by assuming that reproduction simply *is* women's domain.

Although women without paid jobs are not part of capitalist relations of production, the commodities they produce *do* have use-value, Delphy insists. Women are part of a different mode of production, one which the conventional Marxist categories miss, but a mode of production all the same, as well as of consumption and circulation of goods: the domestic mode.

The size and scale of domestic production's value can be illustrated by Gerda Lerner's classic claim that the concentration of resources made possible by appropriating women's labour was central to accumulation and take-off in early capitalist economies. Maria Mies likewise asserts that women's labour was not recognized as such by colonial regimes any more than by early capitalist ones. Yet it is not construed as the work of a *subject* which conveys rights of possession, but as a natural *object* ripe for appropriation.[58]

To develop Delphy's analysis further, in my own terms: just as women have no property in their own labour because they *are* women, they have no translatable property in the use-values created by the domestic mode of production because they are women. Housework is excluded from market relations because it is done by women, not because it is inherently not a source of market value, or because it could not be exchanged for money. For example, a study of 1,200 Bantu households in South Africa found that 55 per cent of the average family's income, counting income in kind, came from subsistence farming, clothes-making, house construction and maintenance, grain preparation, nursing and practising traditional medicine, performing ritual services such as funerals, and collecting fuel and water – all women's domestic activities which are not counted in conventional statistics of the national product. The value of these activities is demonstrated by the impoverishment of town dwellers who find that urban salaries do not confer prosperity because they must now pay for these services.[59] In the North, too, domestic services like childcare and cleaning can be and are marketed. Conversely, even when women leave the domestic sphere for the world of work, they can only obtain relief from their unpaid obligations by buying those services, payment which generally comes from their salaries rather than those of their husbands. It is also noteworthy that the UK tax system at the time of writing makes few allowances for such expenses.[60] Again, domestic production is assumed to be women's responsibility, for which they should not be compensated even indirectly through tax relief.

The apparent 'naturalness' of this situation is actually historically conditioned, and therefore potentially capable of change. As Leonore Davidoff illustrates in her historical account 'The rationalization of housework', the segregation of women from market forces was a political and ideological imperative under early capitalism.

The struggle to keep unlimited calculation ... from creeping into every sphere of life was a long-drawn-out and even bloody one. Nowhere was it more visibly demonstrated than in the segregation of women and of the home from market forces ... The resistance to the application of rational calculation to the family, and hence women, is of utmost importance; and because it reflects a primordial concern for order, for protection from pollution, it has a deeper basis in collective life than social theorists have so far acknowledged. In this sense, housework has remained not a residuum left over from a previous mode of production, but it is seen as a positive purposive activity in capitalist and non-capitalist societies alike.[61]

Because women's propertylessness in their domestic labour is historically produced, it could be changed: this is the merit of a historical materialist account. However, Engels's own solution – bringing women out of the home and into public work – leaves untouched women's exploitation *in* the home, since they retain their domestic responsibilities even as waged workers. So long as the domestic mode of production remains intact, entering capitalist production outside the home does not produce liberation for women, because their labour remains the husband's property within the home. We might even ask whether it is the husband's ownership of the wife's domestic labour which gives him title to her labour outside the home. Coverture did indeed grant him that right; in a moment I shall show that the same holds true of women's entry into paid work in developing nations. If this state of affairs is general, then gender relations under the domestic mode of production condition those in all other modes – rather than remaining an isolated vestige of a more primitive system.

But what gives the husband this title? We have already explored one answer, rooted in his expropriation of the woman's sexuality. In contrast to MacKinnon, Delphy writes that:

far from it being the nature of the work performed by women which explains their relationship to production, it is their relations of production which explain why their work is excluded from the realm of value. It is women as economic agents who are excluded from the (exchange) market, not what they produce.[62]

The difference between the capitalist and domestic modes rests with the actors, not the things produced: 'for one of the essential differences between the two modes of production lies in the fact that those exploited by the domestic mode of production are not *paid* but rather *maintained*. In this mode, therefore, consumption is not separate from production, and the unequal sharing of goods is not mediated by money.'[63] This mode is the economic base for the political institution of patriarchy.

Marxism recognizes that the bourgeois class makes the proletariat do the 'real work', but not that husbands also make wives do the genuinely productive labour. Delphy became sensitive to this pattern in her studies of the French peasantry, where the family remains the unit of production but the objects of production, such as choice foodstuffs, are regarded as the privilege and property of the head – just as the family lands, the forces of production, also belong to him under the usual forms of inheritance. When commodities arising from peasant production *are* sold on the market, 'the production of the wife is exchanged by the husband as his own . . . her work belongs to him.'[64] Yet despite the historical origins of her concept of the domestic mode, Delphy's account appears at first to be vulnerable to the same accusations of essentialism and ahistoricity as Marx's own. Although she maintains that workers in the domestic mode of production are not paid but rather maintained, in most of sub-Saharan Africa women's subsistence labour is frequently not paid, and neither are they maintained by their husbands. For example, Ester Boserup calculates that about one-fifth of Yoruba women receive no food, clothing or cash from their husbands, but still perform subsistence farming and domestic labour; about half of all Yoruba women work on their husbands' farms as well as their own, but the reverse does not occur. Many East African wives are said to prefer Muslim husbands because they have a religious duty to support their wives, unlike African men in their own customary codes. Can the 'domestic mode of production' be altered to accommodate radical difference of this sort? The following section of this chapter asks whether the building blocks of alienation and the domestic mode of production can really be used to reconstruct a genuinely universal theory of property, or whether they are effectively ethnocentric.

Dependency and the domestic mode of production: the case of sub-Saharan Africa

Contra Delphy, the source of the wife's propertylessness and the husband's title to the products of her labour is *not* the requirement to maintain on the husband's part, although that duty is found in European, Islamic and Jewish legal systems.[65] As Ester Boserup emphasizes, the communal ownership of land in many traditional sub-Saharan African systems, such as the Mende of Sierra Leone, is closely linked to the value set on female labour; where cultivation is shifting and soil frequently poor, it is not land but labour which acquires value. In these systems a man amasses property through the labour of many wives and their children. (An interesting corollary of this is that communal systems of ownership of property in land do not necessarily benefit women; we must beware of idealizing communitarianism because private property systems have also discriminated against women.)

The woman in many African codes lacks property in her own body, which is purchased through bridewealth paid to her kin and repayable by her to her husband on divorce, although she does not have access to it during the marriage. At the end of such a marriage, the wife will have cost the husband nothing; he retains the property in her person until she buys it back. Either returned bridewealth in the case of a divorced wife, or the proceeds from labour of her person if the marriage continues, can be used to buy the labour of another wife, to which a married woman is likely to acquiesce because more wives reduce her own workload. In an area where women are a productive asset because they do most of the farming, effectively a wife (to expand beyond Boserup's own thesis) becomes a capital investment; the return on one buys another.

Polygyny also lowers married men's subsistence agricultural productivity, while it enhances that of women collectively: studies in the Gambia and the Central African Republic showed that men with several wives to produce the 'female' crop of rice for them grew less of the 'male' crop of millet than did men with only one wife.[66] (Unmarried 'surplus' men in a polygynous system must hire their labour out along with that of unpaid wives; there are few unmarried women, excepting widows, because of their high exchange value, which induces fathers to marry their daughters off young.) This is partly because the subsistence labour of wives frees the married man for cash labour in other forms than farming. By contrast, it is difficult for women to find time for paid employment, although that is a requirement if they wish to pay back their bride-price. There is clearly an incentive for men to demand a high price for divorce, and to prevent wives from obtaining money incomes.

More recent feminist anthropologists and economists have accused Boserup of oversimplification, for example in overlooking the extent of autonomy which African women enjoy over the conditions of their labour – although these scholars continue to recognize her work as a dominant and generally beneficial influence in the women and development literature.[67] She has also been criticized for prompting too great a concentration on men's control of women's labour in the Third World, at the expense of studies of household income.[68] Nor does Boserup answer the chicken-and-egg question, 'Does the sexual division of labour form the basis of women's subordination, or is the sexual division of labour only a manifestation of women's subordination?'[69] Nevertheless, Boserup's work underlines the ethnocentricity of assuming that wives owe their subordination in the domestic mode to the husband's duty to maintain. In the domestic mode of production of sub-Saharan Africa wives are subservient and propertyless, although the husband has no such duty to maintain. They are neither dependent nor independent, and neither objects nor subjects.

Boserup has updated her original work to encompass urbanization and women's entry into paid labour, but she remains convinced that Engels's formula for liberation still proves a chimera: 'Whether the traditional family hierarchy is imposed by custom or is confirmed by formal legislation, men's customary right to dispose of women's labor usually becomes extended into a right to dispose of their income-earning activities.'[70] Thus married women remain alienated from their own labour. The husband may also retain the right to determine whether his wife can invest her profits in improving her enterprise. If he refuses to sanction her application for a development loan, as the law still requires in many countries, she remains at best a marginal trader in the informal sector, while men's businesses may grow into large-scale capitalist enterprises. Here Boserup's insights have been borne out by other studies of development's effect on women's property position.[71]

It begins to look as though what creates women's propertylessness is being married, not the domestic mode of production as such – the sexual 'contract', in fact. And the example of sub-Saharan Africa reinforces my point in chapter 3, that what is wrong with the sexual contract is not that it is a contract, but that it is sexual. Since marriage is well-nigh universal for women, we are back to what threatens to become simple essentialism: it is being a woman that is the cause of propertylessness in the marriage contract – not being a dependant, as Delphy would have it, but simply being a woman and therefore a wife.

Nor is it the mechanism of contract that oppresses such women. The sub-Saharan African marriage agreement is one 'contract' that *can* actually be revoked, as the marriage 'contract' could not under coverture. So it looks at first glance like a proper contract – but it is gendered so as not to be a proper contract at all. Payment for the wife is exchanged between the husband and the wife's kin; it appears that they are the parties to the making of the contract. The wife has power to break the contract, although she was not a party to it, but only on payment of the transfer monies which she never received. This is not a genuine contract, any more than the so-called marriage contract under coverture.

Strictly, it is not marriage itself which creates propertylessness here: unmarried men in sub-Saharan Africa are also propertyless, and so they must work for married men – although they receive payment, as wives do not. It is *marriage for women* which forecloses any property entitlements. This is true in both North and South. Even the state of having previously been married is enough to strip women of property in their continuing labour after divorce, as Delphy's compelling analysis of divorce in developed countries suggests. Here Delphy is more sensitive to the inadequacy of the explanation in terms of dependency. When women stay at home and are maintained by men, it looks superficially as if their labour power is merely being exchanged for maintenance. However, even when married women earn enough to support themselves, they remain responsible for domestic labour. 'It is therefore clear that they perform domestic work *for nothing*.'[72] This can only be because they have no property in the fruits of their own labour power under the domestic mode. As Pateman alleges, this is a more extreme kind of exploitation than any male worker suffers; here Delphy insists, 'women are exploited because they are women (wives).'[73] The wage-earner supplies fixed services according to a fixed scale, and can transfer his labour elsewhere; a married woman's services are not finite or paid on a fixed scale, and they belong exclusively to her husband as *his* property. She receives nothing for her work because she has no property in her labour or in the means of production. The allocation of property at divorce continues to reflect domestic relations of production.[74] Delphy's account goes some way to explaining divorced women's propertylessness as a continuation of the responsibilities and restrictions of those who are still married. In this sense marriage remains as much the universal norm in the North as in the South, despite the rising divorce rate.

What then explains women's exclusion from property in the labour of their own persons? In effect, it is the combination of alienation – which does hold true in both North and South, as the requirement to maintain does not – together with the domestic mode of production, minus Delphy's assumption that the wife owes her subjection to her dependent status. That is, married women are alienated from ownership and control over their own labour simply because they are married women, not because they are provided for by husbands. And the status of wife remains a matter of little choice for women, North and South, despite the ready availability of divorce. Another way of stating this insight is that full freedom of contract – to break as well as make – has not yet been fully extended to wives.

These appear grim if fascinating arguments. Yet their provenance, feminist historical materialism, suggests that they need not be counsels of despair. The synergistic, reflexive nature of subjectivity and economic condition in historical materialism means that it is at least potentially a theory which *can* work for women's liberation. As I stated earlier, '*to the extent that one's economic condition determines one's subjectivity, changing women's propertylessness enables them to stop being objectifications. Helping women to attain property makes them subjects.*'

There are numerous concrete examples of this sort of reflexive model in development practice. For instance, the Grameen Bank in Bangladesh operates a successful scheme – nearly half of whose beneficiaries are destitute women – offering no-collateral loans to households with less than half an acre of land who want to establish small-scale activities. The default rate is only 2 or 3 per cent, partly because the loans are made to between two and five women jointly. They are responsible for each other's debt and therefore have an incentive to choose and monitor partners carefully. This is an interesting practical instance of using women's embeddedness in relationships to enhance both their sense of agency – they are by no means mere objects of charity – and to improve their property status.

Not only do such projects – when successful – lessen women's poverty; in a functionalist manner, they also create habits of democratic participation, making women both economic and political agents. In Sri Lanka's 'change-agents programme', grassroots (mainly rural) independent women workers have organized in groups to bypass the middlemen who had taken their profits, to obtain direct access to resources, and to control resources they generate.[75] Particularly in Latin America, where the debt issue brought economic development issues to the fore in the 1980s and which has a history of two centuries of revolutionary movements, women's activists have been concerned with both the economic side of development and women's political participation.[76] Success of this sort is symbiotic. A review of 'better-performing' development organizations found that local organizations with charismatic middle-class female leaders were the most effective in enhancing and protecting the gains first made by poorer local women, alternately challenging and cooperating with powerful institutions like trade unions, banks and government offices.[77]

But even when women's property status does not improve, claiming the status of economic subject benefits their self-worth and political agency. Development scholars are often urged to differentiate between women's objective and subjective conditions, for although many indicators of income and goods suggest that women are worse off than before the UN Decade for Women (1975–85), 'women's organisations at all levels are giving women a sense of participation and power over their own lives they have never had before.'[78] Here is a way to maintain the value of *praxis* against the apolitical navel-gazing of much current feminist theory on subjectivity: *praxis* can itself transform subjectivity, as Marx (and Hegel) insisted. Yet there is a danger of patronizing poor women here, and conversely of infinite regress if we want to avoid patronizing them. That is, if we want to say that women's seizing property for themselves makes them subjects – better than being given it – we have to recognize that they *are* subjects and agents already when they take such action.

I do not think this is insuperable. Women's global campaigns against the feminization of poverty are evidence of a changed epistemological understanding, a liberation from the limited vision of women and property imposed by the dominant sex. Because, in a Marxist model, material life not only underpins social relations but also structures our understanding of them, the changed material conditions imposed by the worldwide feminization of property might be expected to result in a hard-won new realization of what it takes to make women subjects.[79]

In this chapter, I have argued for a transformed notion of alienation which de-emphasizes psychological aspects of estrangement, as much feminist thought has done, and goes instead for the jugular: women's peculiar and particular divorce from the labour of their persons. I have tried to show the need for inclusion of some such model of alienation, as forced labour external to one's subjectivity, in explaining women's propertylessness, which Lockean and Hegelian models largely ignore. Although alienation is presented in Marx as unnatural and peculiar to capitalism, a version which recognizes women's situation will have to see it as all too 'natural', although not inevitable or historically ubiquitous. A sensitive feminist historical materialism can do this, and much of the underlying rationale for the *praxis* sections in this book reflects such an outlook. Furthermore, a historical materialist analysis suggests that women can reclaim the status of subject by changing their economic situation. It avoids both essentialism and despair.

6

Another Sort of Subject?

Let us recapitulate some of the characteristics which will be required of a theory of property that counts women in. It will emphasize the Hegelian, educative, developmental role of property, which may be either public or private. It will be critical of the alienation from the products of their own persons, as forced labour hostile to one's inner subjectivity, which has typically characterized women's relationship to property under patriarchal systems. That interpretation of alienation will also extend to domestic relations of production, so that a woman-centred theory of property will also be sensitive to estrangement from the products of one's own reproductive labour. It will be consistent with a historical materialist analysis which suggests that women can reclaim the status of subject by changing their economic situation. However, it will not necessarily abandon the liberal notion of contract, as Marx and Pateman both do. It will borrow from Locke the notion of property in the person, which it will distinguish from property in the body. In keeping with much of jurisprudence, but in contradistinction to some feminist arguments, it will view property as a *set of relationships* rather than as *objects*. It will also allow women to figure as something *other than objects*, although we have not yet fully established what kinds of *subjects* they will be. That is the concern of this chapter.

Another way of framing this chapter's emphasis would be this. I stated in the introduction that I would establish property as central to women's subjectivity, not peripheral to it – or even opposed to it, as in Beauvoir's model of the despotic male subject who can only assert his own subjecthood at the expense of the female object. Both theory and case material has been advanced in support of that claim. But although the reader may by now be convinced that property is more important than feminist theory has thought, and women more important to property than mainstream theory has reckoned, she may still wonder what kind of subject I want to see. It would be a poor and not very feminist model of property which merely changed the sex but not the rational, acquisitive model of the subject, to *femina oeconomica*.

The depth and breadth of the feminist literature on subjectivity make this a particularly strong *caveat*. The very notion of a unified subject, and of labour under capitalism or patriarchy as alienated from that self, is cast into doubt by recent feminist deconstruction. A relational view of the subject, for example, does not posit one 'univocal' self with consistent self-interests or desires, as in the liberal model. Rather, identity emerges out of relations to others, in social practices.[1] However, this extent of revision is perfectly consistent with Hegel's developmental model of the agent as formed by the recognition of others implied in property and contract. It does not threaten my enterprise thus far, particularly because I, too, emphasize relationship in my model of property.

The picture of the Hegelian subject which I sketched in chapter 4 emphasizes relationship, recognition by others and experience. This implies an account of identity which has aspects that some feminisms could accept and incorporate quite readily. For example, both Carol Gilligan and Nancy Hartsock – from different standpoints – redefine the notion of the subject to stress persons-in-relations rather than autonomous selves. The *primary* other-directedness of the subject in Gilligan's work, who is guided by an ethic of care, *is* different from the Hegelian subject's underlying concern with his own emergence to full awareness and with self-definition. And an ethic of care would of course dispute Hegel's version of the path to personhood through property ownership.

Maternal feminists such as Sara Ruddick and Adrienne Rich[2] can be seen as accepting the Hegelian stress on self-development, but valorizing mothering and kinship as the primary means to liberated humanness. Feminisms which conceive of women as more virtuous than men can be seen as claiming an equal or even a higher subjectivity for women, precisely through their other-centredness; but they are actually indebted to the Hegelian model of subjectivity, in so far as such a claim remains within a model of subject-centredness and subjectivity that is entirely compatible with his. As Kathy Ferguson puts it, such feminism 'is outside modernity in claiming equal or even higher subjectivity for women, and inside in the subject-centredness that such a claim entails'.[3]

Other feminist theory, however, is sceptical to varying degrees about the model of development, identity and subjectivity which underlies the Hegelian dialectic. My discussion so far has made certain questionable and questioned assumptions about property, agency and rationality. In chapter 4, for example, the notion of *rational* as well as *relational* subjectivity underpinned my endorsement of a Hegelian model of property and contract. Whereas relationship poses few problems for my reconstruction of property, rationality seems altogether more troublesome. I cannot and do not want to do without it; yet much feminist theory has rejected it. True, the Hegelian model of rationality is neither instrumental nor acquisitive: it is intimately linked with identity, personhood, emotion, and, most important, with other agents. Does this alternative view meet the feminist critique of instrumental, Humean rationality? The second part of this chapter will examine that question, in the light of recent feminist deconstruction and reconstruction of rationality. First, however, I want to look at two feminist theorists who challenge the notion of the unified subject: Judith Butler and Luce Irigaray.

Butler and Irigaray: disjointed subjectivity

The Hegelian subject is problematized more profoundly by Judith Butler. The very need for others' affirmation, which I have presented as an embeddedness in relationship that many feminisms could find attractive, represents a hopeless paradox, Butler says. Inner self-discovery is premised on relation to externality; yet the outside world can never be wholly appropriated. The central motive in Hegel is desire, Butler thinks: labour is merely a form of inhibited desire, and recognition by others the means by which the progressively more self-aware and sophisticated subject seeks to satisfy desire. But the desire which typifies the Hegelian subject can never be sated, and no synthesis can be achieved. The Hegelian self is engaged in a quixotic quest to assimilate all external relations into 'relations of inner difference'.[4]

> The effort of desire to appropriate an object, and through that appropriation to assert its own identity, reveals self-consciousness as that which must relate itself to another being in order to become itself . . . The gradual yet insistent effort of Hegel's journeying subject in the *Phenomenology of Spirit* never relinquishes this project to relate itself to externality in order to rediscover itself as a more inclusive being. The insurpassability of externality implies the permanence of desire. In this sense, insofar as Hegel's subject never achieves a static union with externality, it is hopelessly beyond its own grasp, although it retains as its highest aim the thorough comprehension of itself . . . Hence, despite the alleged object of desire, i.e. 'this piece of fruit', or its more general aim, 'the consumption of this brute being which poses as other to me', desire has at base a metaphysical project which, while requiring determinate objects, transcends them as well, i.e. to effect a unity with the realm of externality which both preserves that realm and renders it into a reflection of self-consciousness.[5]

Butler's assertion that a final synthesis can never be achieved might actually make a Hegelian model of the subject *more* acceptable to feminisms which emphasize difference and deny the possibility of 'a mode of reason that can convey a fully transparent comprehension of life', as Kathy Ferguson puts it.[6] However, Hegel's account of subjectivity is more usually said to be challenged by 'genealogical' or linguistic feminisms such as that of Luce Irigaray, analyses which are concerned to *deconstruct* the very category of the subject. This also appears to mean trouble for the subject–object distinction which has been central to this book.

In a lecture on Merleau-Ponty, for example, Irigaray seems to approve his scepticism about subject and object: she agrees with him in demanding that philosophy 'must return to a pre-discursive moment of experience, take everything from scratch, all the categories of perception of things, of the world, of the division into subject and object'.[7] As Ferguson says in distinguishing them from 'interpretation' feminisms which *enhance* women's status as subjects by stressing their unique experience and voice, 'genealogical' feminisms doubt that there is such a category as the subject at all.[8]

> *Most analyses that call themselves phenomenological are premised on the priority of the speaking subject and on that subject's own accounts of her/his experiences, including Hegel's complex phenomenology in which the emergence of the individual to true self-consciousness is a manifestation and reflection of the same process in the life of the species. In contrast, the genealogist problematises the subject, claiming that our notion of the subject is itself an outcome of the disciplinary practices of modernity. Subjectivity and inter-subjectivity are themselves the effects of power, and thus provide no secure foothold for struggling against power.*[9]

It would indeed be ironic if Hegel, the arch-theorist of modernity, were undermined in his central project by this assertion that the subject itself is only a category created *by* modernity. Perhaps on a superficial level we might get round this claim by rephrasing 'our notion of the subject' as 'dominant notions of subjectivity and identity' in patriarchal culture.[10] After all, the central premise here seems to be that the subject is not a unified category. But this evasionary manoeuvre does not dispel the 'enemy' force altogether. We need to look at Irigaray's thought in more detail.

Irigaray's view resembles Butler's in so far as both present a self in interior conflict, a disunited subjectivity; both rely on the insights of psychoanalytic theory, particularly Freud and Lacan, in putting unresolved and unsymbolized desires and drives to the fore. This directly challenges the Hegelian model of the rational self moving consistently if sometimes erratically towards transcendence. But the more pluralist aspects of Irigaray's view also challenge essentialist feminisms, although Irigaray is often lumped together with other advocates of *écriture feminine* such as Kristeva and Cixous, of whom the criticism can more rightly be made.[11] Particularly in her more recent work, however, Irigaray appears to jettison the most essentialist aspects of her early work in favour of a more pluralist view of women's subjectivity as something to be *constructed*, in what is actually quite a Hegelian manner.

Although male subjectivity is generally seen as unproblematic and objective, both male and female identities are actually constructed, primarily by language. As Irigaray notes in 'The invisible of the flesh':

> The entire speaking body of the subject is in a sense archaeologically structured by an already spoken language . . . The fact that these sedimentary layers of language weave between past and future, and that my actual speech is rooted in what has already been said, completes the circularity between the subject and his or her word.[12]

But whereas the 'male' model of subjectivity, that found in Hegel, presupposes a single unified universal towards which the spirit progresses, Irigaray insists that there are not one but two 'particular universals'.[13] This, she emphasizes, does not entail wholesale rejection of Hegel, but rather an additional *caveat* about his notion of self-consciousness: that it is gendered.

> The most powerful consequence of this interpretation is the analysis of discourse as sexed and not neuter. This demonstration can be effected with linguistic and semiotic tools. To apply oneself to it is to realise an additional progress in self-consciousness which Hegel did not accomplish: the reflection on discourse itself as a tributary content of its forms, which are notably arbitrary. This task does not consist of a destruction of Hegel's thought: rather, it indicates a method.[14]

Hegel is unusually remiss in missing this dualism, Irigaray notes wryly, when he is generally so vigilant in questioning every postulate of unity. In particular, he is caught out in his analysis of the family as a unity, as it must be if there is no dialectic between the sexes. 'This imposed unity adds a false note to Hegel's entire construction.'[15] Instead, Irigaray proposes, the most we can have is a universal which mediates between the two sexed essences: a relationship, not a substance. Although this risks concretizing the male and female principles into undifferentiated universals – a paradox that should trouble Irigaray – arguably it preserves the Hegelian notion of subjectivity as dialectic better than Hegel's own analysis does.

Irigaray needs to be understood in light of her psychoanalytic training, and her association of women with the 'imaginary' taken not in the usual sense of that term in English, but in relation to Lacanian thought on the 'mirror' stage of the child's development in which subjectivity is formulated. (Here her thought must be distinguished from object relations theory in the work of Chodorow and the developmental psychology which

Gilligan's work represents, although some commentators tend to run all theories of differential psychosexual development together as psychoanalytic.) During the mirror stage in the formation of the Ego, the baby is enabled to understand its body as a whole, rather than as a fragmented welter of sensations, by means of a mirror or an image of itself reflected by its parent. But the male imaginary develops by a process of splitting or repressing the female unconscious. As Margaret Whitford explains,

> Subtending the rational subject (with his aspirations to universality, neutrality and objectivity) but unrecognized, there is a subject governed by unconscious desires, powerfully motivated and above all *sexuate* (so that the criteria of scientific epistemology should in fact be seen as shaped by the male imaginary). Irigaray's work, then, can be seen as a sort of 'psychoanalysis' of western culture and metaphysics, seeking what underpins its fragile rationality, looking for the 'repressed' or unconscious of culture ... [S]he attempts ... to theorize the conditions for a *female* subject which could not be simply incorporated back into the male imaginary as its 'other' (the 'feminine' of the male philosophers).[16]

To claim themselves as subjects – which, it needs to be noted, is an eminently Hegelian aim – women must distinguish the trajectory of their subjectivity from that which passes as the universal model, although it is grounded in the male imaginary. This also involves restructuring rationality, although Whitford is careful to note that it is 'not a prescription for female irrationality';[17] neither is it a claim that only men are rational. The Hegelian representation of rationality, Irigaray asserts, involves the repression or transcendence of the symbolic female. Instead Irigaray calls for a model of rationality which is not exclusionary but symbiotic. 'The model is that of a creative (sexual) relationship in which the two elements in intercourse bring forth offspring, rather than a domination/subordination model in which one part of the self is repressing another part (as reason may be said to dominate the passions).'[18]

In passing, although most analyses of Irigaray credit this notion as one of her more exciting and innovative insights, a similar sentiment is also to be found in Margaret Fuller's *Woman in the Nineteenth Century*:

> Male and female represent the two sides of the great radical dualism. But, in fact, they are perpetually passing into one another. Fluid hardens to solid, solid rushes to fluid ... Let us have one creative energy, one incessant revelation ... Jove sprang from Rhea, Pallas from Jove.[19]

Over one hundred years before Irigaray, Fuller also sought to allow the free development of a genuine female symbolic, one that would permit the expression of woman's 'electrical' being but would be otherwise unconstrained by nature or natures.

Irigaray does not assert that women possess natural virtues which are superior to men's; indeed, her recognition that women suffer from drives without adequate representations has led to her being labelled misogynist by some feminists. The result of women's inability to individuate themselves, and their debarring from the institutions which mediate social conflict – including property – is frequently callousness towards other women, Irigaray asserts. Women's subjectivity is formed by power – by men's power and women's lack of it. These insights are actually truer to the Hegelian project than Hegel's own view of women. Property and civil society are ethical influences in Hegel, but they are not extended to women except vicariously. More importantly, Irigaray's project is not so dissimilar to my own as may first appear. Although her work once looked largely apolitical, arguably she actually lays stress on social institutions such as property in shaping female subjectivity.

Irigaray has alternated between (1) rejecting an artificially unified category of the subject and (2) calling on women to define a new notion of subjectivity. To some extent this pattern represents growth in her work rather than inconsistency; her later work puts more emphasis on woman as subject and on the political and social construction of women's subjectivity, whereas her early writings seemed to disclaim such political aims as forms of masculine desire for control.[20] Although some feminists have found the second aspect of her work the most exciting, others think it antithetical to feminism's political origins. In addition, the second strain in Irigaray's thought risks undervaluing the forms of agency and subjectivity which women in past cultures have achieved, despite alien property regimes. By contrast, I argue, the multivariate notion of subjectivity is ultimately consistent both with my reading of the Hegelian subject and with my emphasis on women's relation to property as something other than mere objects, even in the most patriarchal of property regimes.

The most comprehensive reply to the doubts about the Hegelian subject which have been examined in this section is that their original source is Hegelian. This is true not merely in a different sense of the term 'genealogical' – the profound influence of Hegel on Beauvoir, and of Beauvoir on subsequent feminisms. Nor is it solely to do with the way in which both Hegel and Irigaray use Enlightenment values to criticize the heritage of the Enlightenment, although that same point has been made separately about both of them.[21] Rather, the argument is that the Hegelian account of subjectivity itself encourages women to become questioning, self-examining subjects. Deconstruction is parasitical on the claims it seeks to unfound, Ferguson argues;[22] and this is particularly true of its questioning of the self-aware, critical subject. Only such a subject can engage in the sorts of deep doubt we have indulged in here. Yet without a unified category of 'woman', there can be no political impetus towards the ending of women's oppression. A feminist deconstructionist therefore seems to be trying to make herself disappear.

But it is equally tenable that Hegelianism creates its own feminist resistance movement.[23] As social contract theory provided the weapons with which women have resisted contract theory's confinement of them to the private realm, so the eternally questing and questioning subject must ultimately exceed its confinement to the domestic realm, the more so because Hegel *does* concern himself with how women, too, can transcend nature and assume ethical selfhood. Antigone means rebellion as much as piety; she must question something, either male authority or family loyalty.

In her recent work Irigaray interprets Antigone's struggle as women's right to civil personhood,[24] but also as evidence of the profound enmity between female subjectivity and the state. Although Creon does not kill Antigone, he exiles her beyond the city, immuring her in a rocky prison that becomes her tomb. Though he is her kin, he cannot endure her everlasting rebellion in the name of maternal genealogy, the blood of the mother.[25] To Irigaray, Antigone initiates the patriarchal state's insistence that the daughter should break her bonds with her mother, becoming the property of her husband and lord. We are still fighting the particular propertylessness of the Athenian wife, to return to the concerns of chapter 2: for Irigaray, our loss of maternal genealogy, enforced by law.

While her immediate debt is to Heidegger, Irigaray is also close to Hegel in her emphasis on being at home, on owning a symbolic space we can call our own. Men have a home everywhere in patriarchal culture: they live in 'grottoes, huts, women, towns, language, concepts, theories, etc.'[26] As Whitford puts it, 'In the imaginary, woman *is* the material substratum for men's theories, their language, and their transactions. She is their "house" or "container".'[27] Woman is how man can be at home in the world. By contrast, women's fundamental state in our culture is propertylessness, homelessness, *déréliction*, which in French conveys lack of individuation as a subject. To some extent this indicates genuine difference between the sexes in Irigaray, rather than oppression. '*Habiter* [inhabiting] is the fundamental characteristic of masculine existence ... Might *percevoir* [perceiving] be the most habitual dimension of the feminine?'[28]

It would be stretching Irigaray too far to claim that real property is her prime focus: our principal residence is in language, and Irigaray distrusts money in particular as a capitalist and masculine concept.[29] But the broader function of property as recognition in Hegel is consonant with Irigaray's converse emphasis on women's *lack* of recognition by others through the instruments of culture and civil society, of which property is one and language another. (Following Hegel, we could add contract as a third form of mutual recognition.) Nor do Irigaray's recent writings oppose property claims or equal employment rights for women; she only insists that 'they must be demanded in the name of identity, and not equality.'[30] This shows how a non-liberal, developmental account can be made to work for women, with modifications that do not lessen the practical effect on women's property entitlements: only their rationale.

While Irigaray is often seen as one in a chain of postmodernist and post-structuralist attempts to deconstruct the subject, she is more concerned to create a subjectivity that women can *own*. Since they have been deprived of an appropriate symbolic, 'they have never had a subject to *lose*,' as Whitford puts it.[31] Instead Irigaray presents women as objects of exchange within the male imaginary. Female subjectivity as we now know it does not count: it is no more than the detritus which the male imaginary has jettisoned. When it is created, it will be multiple, fluid, full of becoming. Its language will be couched in the interrogative, like much of Irigaray's own writing.

Incorporating Irigaray's notion of propertylessness as lack of individuation, imperfect subjectivity, helps to hone the concept of property in the person which is so essential to my analysis. Having a property in the body is comparatively easy to understand; witness the play *Whose Life is it Anyway?* – a drama about a man kept indefinitely on life support against his will, and in contravention of the popularly accepted notion of property in the body. But property in the person seems altogether more vague. Perhaps it can best be understood by looking at its opposite, propertylessness in the person, as a lack of recognition by others. Without such a place in others' consciousness, women lack a place in the world, a home; and they also lack full subjectivity. This is what Irigaray adds to the analysis, together with a broader, more psychoanalytically conceived interpretation of property and propertylessness.

Feminists such as Nancy Hartsock present property as a redundant concept, or worse, an active impediment to both women's liberation and the betterment of the species. Women's experience of propertylessness, Hartsock argues, actually provides a truer vision of human potential, just as the proletarian's world-view is more genuine than that of the bourgeois. 'Women's experience of reproduction represents a unity with nature that goes beyond the proletarian experience of interchange with nature.'[32] As I hinted in chapter 5, I think this is both patronizing and ethnocentric towards the world's poor, who are overwhelmingly female. But a deeper criticism is suggested by Irigaray: that women cannot have a 'unity with nature' or a unity within themselves if they are the victims of *psychic* propertylessness.

As I first argued in chapter 3 in relation to Locke, what really concerns us is not property in the body *per se* but property in the *moral* person, in one's self, one's power of agency. I have sought to establish in this half of chapter 6 that even a reputedly deconstructionist feminism such as Irigaray's actually ratifies the notion of property in the person as unifying the disunited female subject. But does that necessarily entail accepting the Lockean notion of instrumental rationality? It is to recent feminist critiques of rationality that I shall now turn, as the final piece in the deconstructive puzzle, before moving on to apply my reconstruction of property in chapter 7.

Rationality and its discontents

Property in the moral person is generally connected with a notion of rational agency. Conversely, women's economic and political dependency on property-owning male subjects is usually justified in terms of their supposedly imperfect rationality and impaired subjectivity. To put it another way, control over blind nature is what distinguishes both the rational subject and the property-owner; womankind is disadvantaged in both categories because she is identified with blind nature.

If property has been an object of mistrust to feminist theorists, rationality numbers even more discontents.[33] As Genevieve Lloyd points out, the maleness of reason is more than a mere metaphor throughout political theory.[34] But it is also important not to view this link as fixed, ahistorical and factual, not to see maleness as part of reason itself, which then entails either women's irrationality or the affirmation of new 'feminine' thought processes. This is merely to subscribe subserviently to the assumptions made by canonical theorists, and to embrace essentialism.

The agency of the rational subject is linked in liberal theory to his ability to separate himself from nature, turning its fruits to property through his labour. Thus rationality is primarily instrumental in special rights theories, whereas it is developed (along with autonomy) *by* property in general rights theory.[35] Hegel restricts membership in civilization, in the body politic – which stands apart from the state of nature – to those who transcend nature and irrationality, demonstrated in their acquisition of secure assets and patrimonial property. So women, who do not have property, remain 'the everlasting irony in the life of the community' in Hegel's terms.[36] The effect of both liberal and Hegelian analysis, then, is to disadvantage women, to depict them as inferior in rationality and its correlate, property.

The feminist response has frequently been to reject rationality as tainted by association with this strand in canonical theory: as an instrument of male domination. Carole Pateman, for example, requires us to take a sceptical look at rationality. For her, as for many recent feminists, rationality is not the liberating force that Wollstonecraft imagined it to be, but a suspect component of subordination. 'The sexual contract is a repressed dimension of contract theory, an integral *part* of the *rational* choice of the familiar, original agreement.'[37] But it is hard to see how it can be rational for women to contract in to this regime. Again, the difficulty appears to be that women are *not* allowed to be rational under the sexual contract, or expected to agree voluntarily to it: it must be imposed precisely because it is *irrational* for them to agree to it.

I have already asserted that it is counterproductive to view women as the objects of male property-owning in female bodies by means of the sexual contract. Here I will be claiming that it is also a retrograde step to dissociate women from rationality.[38] Rationality – although not merely rational acquisitiveness – will also be one of the building blocks for a reconstructed, woman-centred theory of property. However, at this stage of the book it would be too time-consuming to justify at length my inclusion of a form of rationality in the final, reconstructed model of property whose foundations I attempt to lay. In any case, in both mainstream and feminist philosophy, other writers are already doing this task for me.

A profound critique of rational instrumentalism has proceeded apace in mainstream philosophy and economics, allowing for plural rational strategies and reviving altruism.[39] But my position may sound surprising in these deconstructionist days, when feminists have often allied themselves with post-structuralist distrust of rationalism.[40] Perhaps it may even seem a die-hard defence of the older rationalist strand in feminism, dating back at least to Wollstonecraft.[41] However, Wollstonecraft has been criticized for assuming a Cartesian *a priori* subjectivity which is not constructed by social participation.[42] I think this criticism can be bypassed if we employ instead a refined Hegelian notion of developmental agency and subjectivity, and I have put in some of the necessary labour in chapter 4 to prune away the unattractive aspects of Hegel's own interpretation, that reason transcends the 'nether world' of women. It is not the place of this book to fully develop an alternative model of rationality; the groundwork for a feminized concept of property-holding is quite sufficient to keep me fully engaged. However, the intimate connection between rationality and property in canonical theory requires me to state my position. It is roughly this: just as even the most apparently inhospitable theories of property are not so thoroughly hostile as has been supposed, so, too, rationality should not be rejected as an instrument of women's liberation – merely because it has been misused as an argument for their subjection.

This is admittedly a negative argument. However, my approaches to property and to rationality are not precisely parallel. Whereas I do want to lay the foundations for a new, woman-centred feminized theory of property, I am wary of what Genevieve Lloyd calls 'any positive reconstruction of either a new feminized reason or a new feminine alternative to reason'.[43] Both are suspect because 'femininity' itself has been defined in the canon by exclusion from ideals of Reason, and rationality seen as transcendence of the feminine.[44] But the ambiguous although consistent manner in which this has been done – with many philosophers making 'gallant acknowledgement of the impoverishment of male Reason'[45] – means that women cannot simply take as their ideal the opposite of everything that men have claimed for themselves.

> Making good the lacks in male consciousness, providing it with a necessary complementation by the 'feminine', is a large part of what the suppression, and the correlative constitution, of 'womankind' has been all about. An affirmation of the strengths of female 'difference' which is unaware of this may be doomed to repeat some of the sadder subplots in the history of Western thought.[46]

The notion of a particularly feminine alternative to rationalism risks essentialism in the name of difference. Lloyd counters by offering a third alternative: rereading Cartesian mind–body dualism through one of Spinoza's lenses. In Spinoza minds are not sexless by virtue of being separate from bodies, as they are in Descartes. Minds mirror the different experiences and possibilities given to the male or female bodies which house them. But this is not determinative of rationality, or restrictive on it; it affords a *rapprochement* between reason and emotion, mind and body. This seems a somewhat similar tactic to my consistent insistence on distinguishing property in the body from property in the person. A theory which focuses on property in the person does not *deny* difference of bodies and of bodily experience, together with the effect on the agent's thinking which those differential experiences produce. It simply does not allow that difference to be all-important.

Similarly, Karen Green argues for an embodied notion of reason, one more akin to Plato. Plato allowed for the motivating power of love of the good (in the *Symposium*) and for the inspiring force of the desire to do good, coupled with the capacity to judge that which is good (in the *Republic*). Green suggests that reason should be thought of as a kind of moral motive, like caring, to which it is complementary rather than opposed. This has the great advantage of not perpetuating the division between the public world of impartiality and universal values, and the private sphere of partiality and agent-relative value.[47]

If we are interested in a feminism of equality rather than a feminism of difference, to use Le Dœuff's distinction,[48] it might well be strategic to reject a feminized notion of reason, at least a simplified ethic of caring and altruistic response to others' demands and needs. An alternative, relational model of rationality, on the other hand, could conceivably concern itself with both self-development and mutual cooperation, not only with instrumental preference satisfaction. But it will not do so in a naive way. *Femina oeconomica* will not necessarily be indifferent to others, as is *homo oeconomicus*; but neither will she be their dupe.

Carol Rose demonstrates through game-theoretical scenarios that, in a situation involving bargaining, being thought to be more cooperative than men is a strategic disadvantage for women, even if that perception is erroneous.[49] The conventional *homo oeconomicus* assumes that rationality means maximization of one's own utility, and indifference to others rather than cooperation (or, for that matter, perverse non-cooperation). But a game-player who is not indifferent to others effectively has something to lose from failing to reach an agreement, in addition to what she loses from not attaining her own maximum utility.

Rose shows that this is a bargaining disadvantage for women in both marriage and divorce, as well as in pay negotiations with employers and in obtaining credit. Eventually women's 'choice' to pursue relationship and cooperation at the expense of conventional notions of advancement reduces their assets so radically that they have no choice but to cooperate with discriminatory pay policies or unfair divorce settlements. Asymmetrical cooperation does not induce men to follow suit: it increases the likelihood that they will pursue rational non-cooperative strategies, secure in the certainty that the cooperative partner will appease them every time. On the other hand, cooperation can be made *mutual*, and fully rational, through 'precommitment devices' – such as those illustrated in the example of the Grameen Bank. 'The taste for cooperation could be an asset itself, insofar as it helps . . . to make alliances with others and stick with them . . . [but the] issue that may be most difficult [for women] . . . is selective non-cooperation.'[50] In this analysis, contract also has an important role to play as a 'precommitment device'. In chapter 7 I shall take this discussion of contract and rationality further in three of my four case studies: those on contract motherhood, gamete donation, and the marriage contract. Before I begin to apply the woman-friendly model of property which I have begun to construct, however, let me recapitulate the model of the subject with which that theory will work.

I began this book by introducing three notions of the subject found in Beauvoir: as despotic, extinguished and minority. Beauvoir's concept of the subject – particularly the despotic subject – is essentially Hegelian, of course. The sovereign existence of the despotic subject requires an object, an Other. Although she believes women capable of being such subjects, and not merely the generalized Other, Beauvoir remains within this framework, pleading for women to have the rightful opportunity to view themselves as primary and others as inessential, as male subjects do.

In this chapter we have gone beyond this initial tripartite classification. Linguistic feminism refuses the dualism of subject and object; or rather, in common with deconstructionism, it views the modern subject as itself subjected. This may appear at first to undermine the entire enterprise of connecting women with full subjecthood, achieved by Hegel in part through property and contract. Neither sex can be claimed to embody such a notion of subjectivity, in a deconstructionist view. This is often said to put paid to the notion of rights, particularly positive rights in law. The law, Kathy Ferguson asserts, rests on a traditional notion of subjectivity according to which 'subjects are beings in possession of themselves and their property, and legal rights serve as property to be possessed.'[51] This notion of rights as possessions is typical of much feminist work; together with feminism's sensitivity to the maleness of property rights so conceived, it helps to explain why feminism takes little interest in property.

But I do not think this corollary necessarily follows. I have stressed throughout that most jurisprudence views property rights *not* as things, following the popular view of such entitlements as possessions in themselves – which would be an infinite regress – but as bundles of relations. These relations require other people to observe different behaviours, depending on the nature of the right: to exclude, to transfer, to bequeath, and so forth.[52] This polymorphous, pluralistic notion of property is actually rather similar to the notion of the subject as a profusion of past experiences and events. What is in fact the mainstream legal notion of property, as bundles of relations, is far more compatible with recent feminisms' deconstruction of the subject than most feminist theory realizes. Once again, we are ill-served by the chasm between malestream and feminist theories.

To the list of characteristics enumerated in the first paragraph of this chapter, then, I have now added interpretations of subjectivity and rationality which are consistent both with the interpretation of property as central, and with some though not all feminisms. The underpinnings are in place; it is time to start building.

7

Reconstructing Property

At the start of chapter 6 I enumerated the characteristics which a woman-centred model of property ought to possess. It is worth reiterating them here:

1 Emphasis on the Hegelian, educative, *developmental role of property*, which may be either public or private;
2 Sensitivity to women's *alienation* from the products of their own persons, as forced labour hostile to one's inner subjectivity, *including estrangement from the products of one's own reproductive labour*;
3 Compatibility with an interest in *narrative myths about property* and with a *historical materialist* analysis, which suggests that women can reclaim the status of subject by changing their economic situation;
4 Equally, but perhaps surprisingly, openness to the liberal notion of *contract*, but with an emphasis on *property in the person*, as distinguished from property in the body;
5 The view of property as a *set of relationships* rather than as *objects*, and hence a profound rejection of the notion that women's only relationship to property is as its objects.

In the previous chapter I added another characteristic:

6 In keeping with the polymorphous, pluralistic notion of property which is involved in construing it as a set of relations, a notion of the *subject as constructed* rather than as given – constructed not only by past experiences and events, in a passive manner, but by the active use of a *relational, non-instrumental model of rationality*.

These six characteristics do not constitute a full-fledged theory of property; I have never pretended that they would. At best they are the foundations of the edifice. But even in the absence of a fully gestated theory, they may lead to some compelling and unexpected applications. The purpose of this chapter is to explore four such possible applications, drawn from medical ethics and family policy: the sale and/or donation of gametes in IVF and other reproductive technologies; contract motherhood, frequently known as paid surrogacy; the sale and use of fetal tissue (which also entails a brief discussion of abortion); and the marriage 'contract'.

These four examples may all be conceived of as applications in a new form of the sexual contract; but although that is highly relevant, it is not how I shall primarily interpret them. In each of these interconnected examples I explore the extent to which women can claim themselves as subjects if a woman-centred model of property is applied. The reverse also holds: I am concerned with the Irigarayan notion that women's subjectivity is formed by power – by men's power and women's lack of it. The broader function of property as recognition in Hegel is consonant with Irigaray's converse emphasis on women's *lack* of recognition by others through the instruments of culture and civil society, of which property is one. In more Lockean terms, the four case studies all concern women's propertylessness in the person, as a lack of recognition by others.

Case study 1: Gamete donation and sale

A reconstructed theory of property requires the notion of property in the person, I have argued. It may or may not need that of property in the body; certainly it should not confuse the two. The example of gamete donation and sale will help to elucidate whether or not the notion of property in the body should be part of a woman-centred model of property.

There are many reasons for scepticism about that, despite the strategic uses to which the feminist movement has put the notion of 'our bodies [as owned by] ourselves.' Anglo-American law generally rejects the notion of the body as property: in most jurisdictions, for example, it is not strictly speaking part of one's estate after death, and legally it was formerly impossible to direct the disposal of one's own body.[1] Property in the body also seems to come with an unacceptably weighty freight of ideological baggage. To concentrate *solely* on property in the body, given the privileging of male bodies above female, 'would be to take for granted the intricate and pervasive ways in which patriarchal culture has made that difference its insignia'.[2]

Essentially property in the body is a tainted concept to Pateman, because the sexual contract is all about ensuring that only men have property in the female body. The political theorist Anne Phillips suggests that Pateman also distrusts freedom of contract not only because it legitimizes women's oppression, but because it is modelled on a male relationship with the body. Free contract, in this interpretation, justifies anything that free individuals decide to do, however they choose to dispose of themselves and their bodies.[3] That requires treating the body in what I would term an alienated manner, as estranged and separate from my 'real' self.

However, I want to argue that this is a faulty interpretation of contract in Locke, and of his notion of ownership of the body, which is at best equivocal. The neoliberal view cannot look to Locke to justify its assumption that we own our bodies unequivocally, wherever else it may locate its founding myths. We are not allowed to do anything we like with our bodies, because we did not create them; they are given to us by God, according to Locke. The implication might be that body transfer *by* gift is acceptable, as a parallel to the means by which we acquired our bodies in the first place, although transfer by *sale* would not be allowed. But can that hold even if we do not assume belief in God? Let us examine this in the question about payment for gametes, which will also raise other important facets of my reconstructed proto-model of property: contract, rationality and narrative.

At the time of writing men in the UK were usually paid for sperm donation, but women were not reimbursed in cash for giving eggs, although they were often offered treatment as payment in kind. This practice grew up in contravention of the spirit of the Human Fertilisation and Embryology Act of 1990. Section 12(e) of the Act states that money or benefits should not be given to suppliers of gametes unless authorized by the Human Fertilisation and Embryology Authority, and this seems to imply that payment will be the exception, at the discretion of the licensing body. The HFEA has indicated that payment would be withdrawn sometime after 1997, but in the meantime many IVF clinics still pay for sperm.

In a workshop sponsored by the HFEA as regulating agency, I was struck by the assumption that men could only be motivated by payment, whereas women would willingly undergo the far more painful and risky procedures of super-ovulation and egg extraction for nothing.[4] This assumes either that men own their labour and the products of their bodies in a way that women do not,[5] or that women's motivation is drastically different from men's, that it is not rational in the usual instrumental sense. Either way, the accepted narrative about women's property in their bodies differs from men's story, and the prevailing narrative directly affects clinical practice in the United Kingdom.[6]

Men can be dealt with by a recognizable contract, to sell a body *product*

– a renewable one which does not raise quite the same horrific issues as sale of kidneys or other body *parts*. Women donors are sometimes not even given reimbursement for expenses, and not at all for their 'sweat equity'. They are effectively *paying* to donate their eggs, sometimes to private clinics that will profit from them – a very odd sort of contract indeed, if a contract at all. Yet eggs are a non-renewable resource, unlike sperm: the full quota of oocytes for life is already present in a baby girl's ovaries. And there is an overall shortage of egg donors, with very few women willing to return a second time.

The greater objective value of eggs and the higher costs to the donor contrast so starkly with present practice that some UK commentators[7] have been led to suggest that both sexes should be paid, and that women should in fact be paid more. This approach does tackle the incongruity head-on, incorporating women into the 'normal' contract mode applied to men. But it assumes that women are being asked to act *irrationally* by the present system – rather than seeing both sexes as capable of being motivated by something other than instrumental rationality, of being moved by a relational, non-instrumental model of rationality such as that which I advocated in the previous chapter.

Are we in a position to sell our gametes? In Locke's interpretation, we cannot be said to have a property in our bodies because we did not create our bodies: God did. What we do have is a property in the person, in our moral agency and identity. The grounds for this distinction between property in the body and property in the person apply *a fortiori* to gametes. Let us distinguish between germ cells and somatic cells. All body parts might be said to entail relationship with our *progenitors*, since we are not their creators – whether or not God is. But even if we did want to claim ownership of other body parts, we ought to think differently about gametes, irrespective of whether we think that we owe our gametes and the rest of our bodies to God. Gametes are about relationship with *future* generations, and with our *present partners* – whether or not an individual gamete results in pregnancy. In a somewhat figurative but emotionally real sense, gametes *are not owned*. At most they might appear to be lent – although even that metaphor presupposes that someone did own them somewhere along the way.

The notion that gametes are actually not the sole property of the person in whose body they reside, but are instead held in relationship with past and future generations, is consonant with other cultures. The New Zealand Ministerial Advisory Committee Report on Assisted Human Reproduction refused to commercialize gamete provision for research and therapy because that would be inconsistent with the Treaty of Waitangi and with the Maori conception of gametes and embryos as possessing *mana*, a form of spirit.[8] The view of children as a product of the lineage rather than of the parents appears also to have operated to some degree in Athens, although men's reproductive potential was viewed as their own, limited only by the needs of the *oikos*, whereas women's belonged both to their husbands and to the *oikos*. In contrast to traditional interpretations stands the modern liberal instrumental approach to the body as a commodity. Already we can see an increasing use of market terminology in the new reproductive technologies, as in '*products* of conception' or 'egg *harvesting*'.

In fact, I want to suggest that the view which sees gametes as belonging solely to the individual is ethically wrong and politically ill-advised. In order to liberate women in this case, we need to wipe out the contradiction privileging men. We need to view both sexes as only possessing their reproductive potential *in relation* to past and future generations, not as owning it unequivocally. The practical consequence of my reconstructed model of property in the case of gametes, then, is that their sale should not be allowed for either sex.

Those who oppose payment for gamete or organ donation do often look for inspiration to a story about gifts: archetypally to blood donation.[9] That is a perfectly practical model, one which has informed the provision of blood in the UK. True, the Blood Transfusion Service of the National Health Service has been undercut by the closure of major collection centres, the sale of plasma and other products from donated blood to private hospitals, and difficulties over haemophilia and testing for HIV. But the fundamentals of the system in the UK remain donation rather than commercial payment, and public support is still quite high. It would be consistent to extend the same model to gamete donation, for both sexes.

It is often said that men will only donate if they are paid, and indeed the majority of donors in the UK are young single students who are mainly motivated by payment.[10] But to argue that it cannot be otherwise is a form of the naturalistic fallacy, and a variant of essentialism about male 'nature' which ignores evidence from other national systems. If feminism has learned anything at all about the social construction of gender, it is that motivations can be *produced* by gendering. The UK system does not just reflect gender differences passively; it actively perpetuates them. Experience from other countries, particularly Sweden, suggests that an initial drop in sperm donations under an altruistic system for both sexes is reversed over time.[11] France has run a system of free donations for over twenty years, actually achieving a higher rate of donor insemination cycles than the UK.[12] Some centres in the UK used to operate a system of altruistic sperm donation, but once the HFEA allowed other clinics to pay men for providing sperm, all centres had to pay in order to 'compete' on an equal footing.[13] This suggests a version of Gresham's Law: pecuniary motives ('bad' motives, in my argument) drive out good motives. The story of contract and sale is not the only narrative which can be written, but it tends to stifle other voices once it is allowed to be heard. The evidence from Sweden, Australia and France indicates that men *can* accept a new regime, a new narrative, about property in the body; why not write one?

Lewis Hyde has suggested that exchange is construed as a masculine realm in our society; gift – the stuff of nursing, teaching, social work – is female. The products of female labour are not genuine commodities, Hyde argues, and therefore are not deemed suitable for sale at the full price of their exchange value in a market system.[14] The example of gamete donation under the current UK system illustrates women's propertylessness in relation to their reproductive potential. In order to give women back a property in themselves, however, we should not extend a model of payment to women, but rather encourage the gift of gametes by men.

Another way of construing this example is in terms of the Hegelian property model which I have advocated throughout this book, particularly from chapter 4 onwards. Rather than a narrowly liberal and instrumental model of gametes as personal property, this case suggests the educative, developmental value *for men* of considering their sperm to be in some sense public property. The example of gamete donation absolves me of any charge that I merely wish to assimilate women to a male model of property ownership. Instead, the impetus of this case study is towards educating men in the relationship between gametes and other generations, as well as between themselves and potential recipients of their sperm, which already informs women's relationship towards their gametes. If men donate rather than sell their gametes, they will also avoid the risk of alienation and estrangement from their bodies. The model of sale by an anonymous donor is arguably the height of alienation from the consequences of gamete donation.[15]

What has become of the question of property in the body after the gamete example? I think this case shows the need to maintain some emphasis on the notion, but not to conceive of that ownership as anything like complete. In order to be able to give gametes, donors must be thought of as owning them in the first place. But the kind of ownership which we can be said to possess in relation to our gametes is conditional: we are not allowed to do anything we like with them, because they are not unequivocally ours. They are held in common with past and future generations; only a model of gift, rather than sale, can recognize this sort of dependency and indebtedness.

Although this is particularly true of gametes, there is some plausibility in viewing the body as a whole in this manner. Genetic endowment conditions our freedom to do what we like with our bodies, and lands us squarely in relationship to our parents and children. The increasing implication in many diseases and conditions of genetic contribution, usually multifactorial, illustrates that sort of relationship in a very concrete manner. To think of our bodies as entirely under our ownership and control is a flight from that reality.

My only doubt about generalizing women's story about gift and indebtedness to men is that it reinforces stereotypes about women's natural altruism – although it challenges the gendering of those stereotypes by asking men to emulate women. But surely what is wrong with the current gendering of altruism is not that it is about altruism but that it is about gender, just as what is wrong with the sexual contract is not that it is a contract but that it is sexual.

However, if gametes should be freely given rather than exchanged for cash under a conventional form of contract, that seems to suggest very little role for contract after all. Yet I spent much of chapter 3 trying to revive contract against the idea that it has nothing to offer women, that contractual relations are inevitably unequal and oppressive. Is this contradictory? In fact this case study is perfectly consistent with my earlier argument: it is the *absence* of contract in the assumptions made about women's motivation that alerts us to the unequal and oppressive nature of the current UK system.

The gamete example began from a recognition that there is something anomalous about a 'contract' in which women are effectively paying to donate their eggs. In fact, it is not a proper contract at all. The argument actually runs in much the same direction as Pateman's critique of the social contract: that looking at the so-called contract's application to women reveals that women are not given the status of subjects. In an admittedly negative sense, my way of proceeding in this example has established the value of looking at women and contract – because the contract model is simply not applied to women at all in the current way of doing things, because only men are seen to be the proper subjects of a recognizable contract. Once we do consider the oddity of the current UK system in terms of a conventional contract model, we can then move on to reject that model for women and men alike, as I have done in this case. This is more productive than simply regarding women as the exploited objects of contract, as Pateman tends to do; and there my method parts company from hers.

Essentially, I use the Hegelian model of contract as *recognition* to highlight the duplicity of *not* recognizing women as full subjects. However, I have rejected *for both sexes* the conventional neoliberal notion of absolute freedom of contract in body parts. This leads on to the next case study, contract motherhood. Points 1, 3, 5 and 6 of the six-point schema of a reconstructed property model have been illustrated in the case study on gamete provision. Contract motherhood will bring together several of this book's practical sections – those on coverture and prostitution, primarily – and others of the principal theoretical characteristics in a reconstructed model of property. It is particularly concerned with contract and with alienation, especially alienation from one's reproductive labour: points 4 and 2 of the six-point model of a reconstructed version of property.

Case study 2: Contract motherhood

At several points in this book I have emphasized that modern jurisprudence regards property as a set of relationships, rather than as an object or a thing. But these could be seen as mere weasel words if the relationship is simply one of exclusion – most famously in Blackstone's definition of a property right as a title which operates in favour of the holder 'to the total exclusion of the right of any other individual in the universe'.[16] Poignant examples of that exclusion can be found in contract motherhood,[17] where both sides have much to lose if they are excluded: the birth mother and the paying father, whose interests have conflicted in a number of American judgments.[18]

In the famously controversial case of *Baby M*, the lower court held that the father, William Stern, already had sole rights over the child, and that the contract with the genetic and gestational mother, Mary Beth Whitehead, merely covered her 'willingness to be impregnated and carry his child to term'. Note the term 'his' child: Judge Sorkow went on to say that Stern had not made a contract for the sale or surrender of the child because 'he cannot purchase what is already his.'[19] The debate over contract motherhood shows how many vestiges of coverture still operate in popular and legal narratives about women, children, custody and property. Although the state supreme court was more sensitive to those overtones of coverture than the trial court, ruling that surrogacy contracts *were* a form of baby-selling and therefore unenforceable, the Sterns none the less retained custody of the child on the appeal.

Surrogate motherhood may seem the ultimate extension of 'father-right', and indeed Carole Pateman argues that it represents the sexual contract in modern dress.[20] In chapter 5 I likewise remarked that the extremes of commodification in contemporary market systems create public debate which highlights issues around women's property in the body and in the person. There I promised that here, in chapter 7, I would examine contract motherhood as an instance of both commodification and debate. As an instance of women's alienation from their reproductive labour, contract motherhood can hardly be 'bettered'. 'A stranger she preserves a stranger's seed,' to put the matter in Apollo's language from Aeschylus' *Eumenides*. In more modern terms, the surrogate mother is alienated not only by expropriation of the surplus value of the 'product'; she is also emotionally alienated in so far as she has to repress her natural bonding emotions and her grief at the loss of her child. This, it has been argued, is the only way in which the surrogate 'industry' can control the worker's labour, since, like all putting-out systems, it faces the problem of extracting the final product from the worker.[21]

Yet perhaps that is to prejudge the issue: could contract motherhood actually be a vehicle for women's liberation, as some feminists have asserted? After all, I have consistently argued that feminists do not have to abandon the idea of contract. The logical corollary might well be that contract motherhood is perfectly consistent with a considered feminist approach to property. Particularly in the US, some liberal feminists have indeed argued that contract mothers must be held to strict contract observance – requiring them to deliver rather than keep their babies – if women's economic autonomy is to be taken seriously.[22] Other feminists have altered their initial anti-surrogacy positions to take a stance more in favour of contract motherhood.[23] Yet when we look at contract mother-hood in terms of the long narrative of women's deprivation of the products of their reproductive labour during the high tide of liberalism, we see something different from what a conventional liberal model of contract sees. Nevertheless, I argued in chapter 3 that although liberalism is tainted by its association with coverture, which deprived women of any control over the products of their reproductive labour, that is not really liberalism's fault; rather, the flaw was not taking liberalism far enough. So I do not want to rule the liberal view out altogether, at least not yet.

In reply to those liberal feminists who favour contract motherhood, Joan Mahoney has asserted that restrictions on absolute freedom of contract are inevitable and accepted under anything but barefaced capitalism. Preclud-ing gestational mothers from contracting away their babies, Mahoney claims, no more hampers their economic autonomy than does any other form of employment protection.[24] Elsewhere Mahoney has argued for a nurturance rather than an ownership model of parenting, defining the gestational mother as the mother who counts, whether or not she is the genetic mother.[25] The effect of this is not to outlaw contract motherhood as such, but effectively to eliminate any incentive on the father's part to enter the contract. This strategy bypasses contract, rather than views it as either conducive to women's liberation or oppressive. However, it is open to slippery slope problems: how do we define and monitor nurturance? If the contracting mother is poorer than the father, as she is almost bound to be if the arrangement appears financially attractive to her in the first place, is her home likely to be seen as less adequate than the father's? If she fails to provide consistently top-notch mothering throughout the child's life, is it open to the father to launch later custody actions alleging insufficient 'nurturance'? Perhaps the very fact of having signed a surrogacy contract will be interpreted as proving that the birth mother is insufficiently 'nurturing'. In the *Baby M* case Judge Sorkow accused Whitehead of proving her 'unfitness' as a mother by entering into the contract in the first place, although no such allegation was made against the father. But then contract is construed as a male domain.

Some advocates of contractual motherhood have argued that systems which pay women for oocyte donation but forbid payment for surrogacy are inconsistent. However, Mahoney points out – correctly, in my view – that the law should not treat oocyte providers as analogous to contract mothers because carrying a pregnancy to term and giving birth are even riskier and more laborious procedures than oocyte donation. (To treat them as the same is to fail to adequately recognize women's property in the labour of childbirth, a point to which I shall return in the next case example.) I have already argued that payment for gametes should not be allowed for either sex. By my previous reasoning, I could be expected to oppose contract motherhood. What applies to gamete donors ought to apply *a fortiori* to gestational mothers.

The 'good news' about contract motherhood is that it implies a recognition that the mother has *something* to transfer or sell. In Hegelian terms, it requires the genetic father, and society through the courts, to take women's reproductive labour seriously. What this implies, however, is that *breaking* a contract is what gets women noticed. Again, as in the case of gamete donation, a contractual model calls our attention to its own limitations.

The limitations are to do with *what* the mother has to sell. Clearly it cannot be the baby, unless we wish to revert to a model of property *in* children of the sort which so disadvantaged women under coverture. But that would be to view property as to do with objects, and to objectify children. In the *Anna J.* case,[26] the judge claimed instead that what the woman was selling was her pain and suffering in pregnancy and labour. Although that case went against the mother, it is actually closer to a notion which I find acceptable, for reasons which I spell out at greater length in the third case study. Essentially, the argument is that labour in childbirth is rarely seen as the sort of labour which confers a property right; but it should.

This emphasis on a property in labour also has practical advantages for the gestational mother, although at the risk of eliminating any incentive for the father to enter a surrogacy contract. That is, if the mother is not actually selling the baby, all that the father is purchasing is her pain and suffering. Provided he is not seen as having prior custody rights over the baby because he is the genetic parent, as was the case in the *Anna J.* judgment, the consequence is that the father cannot acquire custody of the baby if the gestational mother refuses to deliver the child to him. That is, if we eliminate an implicit model assigning genetic property rights in children to fathers – and I see no reason why we should allow any such rights, since I do not think that we own our gametes unconditionally – contract mother-hood arrangements may benefit women. Particularly if the fetus spontan-eously aborts, is stillborn or is born with a severe disability, a surrogacy contract needs to protect the mother.[27]

Rather than openly banning surrogacy, then, a contract approach could concentrate on overturning existing legal presumptions that favour men, such as the presumption of genetically conferred custody rights, and on ensuring that surrogacy contracts are worded so stringently as to eliminate exploitation of women. Non-liberal feminists have tended to see the source of exploitation in the economic imbalance between contracting father and gestational mother, and in the comparative low level of payment for surrogacy. This is important: but what is more important is to *ensure that labour in childbirth is viewed as women's property*. If women's labour is unequivocally theirs, with consequences for the abortion debate which I shall delineate shortly, then it must be theirs to transfer, by gift or sale.[28] But whether any potential buyer will wish to contract for labour rather than the product of labour, the baby, is open to doubt. The effect of the distinction between labour and baby, combined with the Lockean assertion that women own their labour, is to curtail women's propertylessness in their own labour, which surrogacy arrangements could otherwise exacerbate.

One important feature of viewing a surrogacy contract as purchasing the mother's pain and suffering in labour is that it is only very ambiguously a *sexual* contract. On the surface, at least, it is the very opposite of sexual pleasure for the woman, but that is not of course what Pateman means by the sexual contract. Both Pateman and Marxist feminists have tended to say that what is wrong with surrogacy is that it is a form of exploitation akin to prostitution. The economic imbalance between the genetic father and the contract mother may be similar to that between the prostitute and her client; but I have already argued that this is not the principal source of exploitation which we need to guard against in surrogacy, although it may be an important one. The real source of injustice is women's propertylessness in their reproductive labour. It is important to see that whereas the prostitute may be seen as renting out her body, it is quite wrong to see surrogacy as merely renting a womb. That is to radically downplay a woman's pain and suffering in labour. Pateman does distinguish between the prostitute as renting out her body and as selling her services, concluding that the surrogate is likewise selling her services as a childbearer. 'The womb has no special status as property. A woman could just as well contract out use of a different piece of property in her person.'[29]

I have argued against this approach as well; in addition to confusing property in the person with property in the body, it misunderstands what the woman is actually selling. She cannot sell her womb as such, in the sense of alienating it permanently; nor can her womb be used independently of the rest of her body. The surrogate mother is selling her labour in childbirth, with concomitant pain and suffering – not the usual definition of services, except perhaps to a sadist. Prostitution only entails pain and suffering in labour as an unintended byproduct. All in all, then, I think the prostitution parallel generates more heat than light.

Arguments against surrogacy which do not see it as a form of exploitation akin to prostitution often hinge on maternal feminist concerns about the commodification of emotion and relationship, including the impact on the children who will result.[30] A related argument turns on the narrow view of autonomy assumed by liberals who advocate that women should be 'free' to contract away their babies. As Elizabeth Anderson writes,

> Contract pregnancy commodifies both women's labor and the child in ways that undermine the autonomy and dignity of women and the love parents owe their children. Because the state has a legitimate interest in protecting the autonomy and dignity of women and the integrity of parental love for children, it is justified in prohibiting contract pregnancy ... Contract pregnancy transforms what is specifically women's labour – the work of bringing forth children into the world – into a commodity. It does so by replacing the parental norms that properly govern the practice of gestating children with the market norms that govern ordinary production processes.[31]

But 'parental norms' may equally well undermine women's value and autonomy: we have only to look to the Athenian *oikos* to see that. What is more troubling for my argument is the charge of commodifying women's pain and suffering in labour, even if I have avoided commodifying the child. However, I think there are some practical advantages for women in applying the law of contract in the way I suggest. If the contract is for the woman's pain and suffering in pregnancy and childbirth, the birth mother will be able to enforce a claim for payment against the genetic father even if the child is stillborn or disabled. If it is for pregnancy *or* childbirth, she can claim payment even if she miscarries. She has none of these protections if surrogacy contracts are void in law, as out-and-out opponents of surrogacy would prefer.[32]

Anderson argues that 'when market norms are applied to the ways we treat and understand women's reproductive labor, women are reduced from subjects of respect and consideration to objects of use.'[33] I think this is too starry-eyed about the respect accorded women as subjects and owners of their own reproductive labour *outside* contract motherhood. I have come – rather to my own surprise – to conclude that contract motherhood *can* enhance women's subjectivity under extremely tightly defined conditions. Contract and the market norms it implies can work for gestational mothers if the terms of the contract are set to compensate for genetic fathers' economic advantage, and to correct the assumption that genetic parenthood confers a sort of property right even in the absence of contract. Whether or not any genetic fathers would accept a contract framed in these terms is, as the saying goes, not my problem.

However, a difficulty which I *do* have to face is whether *women* would accept a surrogacy contract along those hard-nosed lines. There is some psychological survey evidence indicating that contract mothers, even paid ones, typically see what they are doing in terms of gift values rather than market ones.[34] They may identify with the couple receiving the baby, or feel that they are atoning for a previous abortion or adoption. Anderson argues that this non-economic motivation renders them ripe for exploitation: indeed, that exploitation is going on whatever the economic rewards if one party operates with norms based on commodity exchange while the other sees what she is doing as altruistic.[35] The surrogate 'industry', she claims, actually relies on women's altruism[36] (just as the IVF 'industry' does in the case of gametes, I would add). Without women's other-centredness, the pool of surrogate mothers would be minuscule. But of course changing the terms of the contract to favour women could increase the pool of contract mothers and decrease the supply of genetic fathers; life is too easy for the latter at the moment. I imagine that there will still be some 'takers' among contracting fathers for a contract in the gestational mother's labour, rather than in the baby; perhaps they will hope that the 'surrogate' will change her mind and hand over the baby of her own free will. This is actually closer to the adoption model of surrogacy which many commentators feel is the only morally admissible one.[37]

It may seem inconsistent for me to advocate mutual altruism in the case of gametes, but to allow paid contract motherhood, even if the rules of the surrogacy game are rejigged to protect women. But the parallel is not exact, simply because men do not give birth. Men and women alike provide gametes, and they should do so under the same system of rewards. To say that gamete donation and surrogate motherhood should be treated alike is to miss the special nature of women's property rights in labour and childbirth. It is to these that I will now turn, in the question of abortion and fetal tissue donation.

Case study 3: Abortion and the sale of fetal tissue

Women's property in the labour of childbirth is ignored by *both* sides in the abortion debate. The controversy is usually about whether the fetus is a person, and therefore deserving of rights which must either be balanced against the pregnant woman's,[38] or which must trump her rights altogether.

But even those few proponents of abortion who refuse to argue along such lines instead discuss the question as primarily an issue of *housing* the baby, of pregnancy rather than childbirth.[39] At most, opponents of abortion allow the procedure if the woman's life is in danger, but give no weight at all to her pain and suffering in labour and childbirth.[40] That is to assume that women are different from all other patients, who are presumed to have a right to refuse pain and suffering, to give an informed consent to (or refuse) treatment. No competent adult other than a pregnant woman can be forced to submit to a procedure on behalf of another party, even if the fetus is viewed as a full-fledged person.[41] (For example, a tissue-matched relative cannot be forced to donate bone marrow.)

This inadequacy in the ethical debate is peculiar, because Anglo-American law has traditionally made it quite clear that the fetus has no rights because it is not yet a person.[42] The anti-abortion argument relies entirely on the notion of the fetus as the patient, the holder of rights; but this view forms little or no part of Anglo-American law. Only through the woman's willingness to continue the pregnancy and to endure labour does the fetus acquire the rights in law of a person[43] – despite our unwelcome inheritance of coverture.

To put the matter another way, the moral significance of birth – in Mary Ann Warren's phrase[44] – is usually interpreted as its significance for the status of the fetus or baby. The rights of fetuses are, or are not, the same as the rights of infants, according to one's position in the abortion debate, depending on whether one views personhood as beginning at conception (alternatively, viability) or at birth. What I want to argue instead is that the 'moral significance of birth' concerns women's *property in the labour of childbirth*.

To properly value women's labour in childbirth is perhaps the most radical example of my Hegelian argument for property construed as mutual recognition. Without recognition of women's property in the labour of childbirth, not only are women estranged from their reproductive labour; the terms in which the abortion debate is commonly conducted, even by feminists, are themselves alienating. A notion of women's property in childbirth is urgently needed, particularly in the face of new developments in reproductive technologies such as fetal tissue transplantation, and of the lowering of the age of viability by improved obstetric techniques. Without a firm notion that women and women alone own their labour in childbirth, we risk tumbling down some increasingly slippery slopes.

The example of abortion primarily illustrates points 1 and 2 of my six-point model of property; but there are also elements of point 5, the notion of property as a set of relationships rather than as objects. In the mirror images which characterize ideological hostilities,[45] *proponents* of abortion are often accused of ignoring the 'future baby' as the other partner in the relationship. This is a particular problem if the argument for abortion rests on the pregnant woman's putative ownership of the fetus, making it an object of property. But it is still a difficulty if the argument is phrased in terms of the pregnant woman's rights in her *own* body. That version of the argument also seems to exclude the fetus, by merely collapsing it into the woman's body. However, the pro-choice position emphasizing women's property in the body *can* accommodate the pregnant woman's relationship with the fetus – if we conceive of property as bundles of relationships, not objects. But the anti-abortion stand cannot and usually does not want to count women in.

There are potentially two parties to the relationship between pregnant woman and fetus; but one of them *is* only potential. The fetus only becomes a full party after childbirth, when it is no longer a fetus, in fact, but an infant. It cannot enjoy rights until the pregnant woman elects to endow it with the status of an autonomous agent, cannot enjoy life until the pregnant woman *gives* it life. The life and rights of the potential infant are the pregnant woman's property until transferred to the fetus through childbirth; she retains the property right to exclude others from her body until such time as she transfers or abjures her property rights. British law reflects this position by affording no 'right to be born' to a fetus whose likelihood of surviving childbirth as a normal baby is minimal. But the current legal position is not fully consistent with its own internal logic.[46] If being born alive is the watershed, then the pregnant woman's giving birth should count more than it does. The law recognizes an asymmetry which, taken to its logical conclusion, should privilege the pregnant woman.

In abortion the property relations are severalfold. First, we must consider the woman's property right to *exclude* others from deciding on the abortion, stemming from her prior right under Anglo-American law to refuse treatment or invasive procedures. 'Anglo-American law starts with the premise of thorough-going self-determination. It follows that each man is considered to be master of his body, and he may, if he be of sound mind, expressly prohibit the performance of life-saving surgery, or other medical treatment.'[47] This sort of property right might be construed as a *privilege*, in Hohfeld's analytical vocabulary: a legal liberty or freedom. Unlike a claim-right, which generates a corresponding duty in others to *do* something, a privilege 'involves not a correlative duty but the absence of a right on someone else's part to interfere'.[48] There is also a case for calling the woman's property right an *immunity* from having her legal position challenged by anyone else. The right of ownership of real estate, for example, is an immunity against being forced to sell against one's will.

Second, there is the woman's right to *transfer* life to the fetus. In Hohfeld's vocabulary this is similar to a *power*, such as a power of transfer of land. A person has a power when by acting he or she can alter the legal position of someone else. The pregnant woman has a power to create a legal person with rights by choosing to give birth to the fetus. However, a person with a power retains the *right to choose* whether or not to act. True, in the case of the pregnant woman this is not a transfer in the sense that selling my property gives me no further interest in it. After childbirth the mother still has an interest in the baby's well-being; but she does not have a right to have it killed, because then it is a (potential) moral agent with countervailing rights of its own. However, the pregnant woman retains the power to terminate pregnancy up to and including childbirth, a power which does not depend on the degree of fetal abnormality. (I have argued this position in more detail elsewhere.)[49]

Third, the pregnant woman who chooses to undergo labour and childbirth *does so as a gift*: 'giving birth' means just what it says. The labouring mother embodies the most profound 'gift relationship',[50] that of life itself, and of the entitlements which a living human being possesses. She does not give birth as a *duty* entailed by the claim-right of the fetus, in Hohfeld's terms, because the fetus can have no claim-rights. The pregnant woman can, however, choose to *abjure* her own right not to give birth in favour of another *beneficiary*, for example, in favour of the father.[51] This, too, is a sort of gift.

Fourth, let us introduce another set of relationships, analysed in property terms. In the anti-abortion literature, the doctor is often regarded as having a sort of property right over the fetus, although it is rarely made explicit. The physician is seen as having either a right or a duty to *alienate 'custody'* of the fetus from the pregnant woman, justified by beneficence and duty of care to the 'fetus patient'.[52] In this view, both the mother and the doctor have duties of beneficence to the fetus: duties and only duties, so far as the mother is concerned. But the doctor can fulfil his duties to the fetus patient more effectively because he has the greater degree of knowledge. This might be seen as similar to the duties of social services departments to intervene in cases of child abuse or neglect.

But I have already made it plain that I think this is a sleight of hand. The fetus is not a child until the pregnant woman makes it one by giving birth, and it cannot be a patient without making the woman transparent.[53] However, we should not exclude the doctor from the relationship, even though the doctor should not be able to determine that no abortion will take place. It is entirely understandable that injecting potassium chloride into the fetus's heart – as is required in late termination of pregnancy in order to avoid the birth of a living child – should be felt to be a moral question, not just a technical procedure. Doctors whose consciences rebel at that step should probably be allowed to refuse participation; without this proviso, the doctor then becomes the invisible one. But doctors should not be allowed to deny the procedure altogether.

I have argued, then, that a woman has a property right, conceived alternatively as a privilege, power or immunity, in the labour of her person, in childbirth, and that this right should be recognized as paramount, in allowing abortion at any time during pregnancy. But I do not want to argue that the woman, or anyone else, owns the *result* of childbirth, the infant. That should be clear from the previous section on contract motherhood. Although I allow the contracting genetic father to buy the woman's pain and suffering in labour, which is unreservedly hers to transfer if she so desires, I do not allow him to buy the baby; babies are not objects of sale.

What then about fetal tissue which is extracted after abortion? Does the previously pregnant woman have a property right in that? There could be two grounds for thinking so: first, that the fetus is physically part of herself, and that she has an entitlement to her own body. But I have been sceptical of an unqualified right to property in the body, especially in matters involving reproduction: the case study on gametes made that clear. In addition there is the difficulty of knowing how much weight to allow to the genetic contribution of the father; the fetus's genetic endowment is not the potential mother's alone. There is also a strategic argument against emphasizing genetic relationship as a source of property rights: it plays into the hands of those who, like the judge in the *Baby M* case, think the father has equal or superior rights by virtue of his genetic 'ownership' of the potential child.

The second alternative is to argue that the formerly pregnant woman owns the fetal tissue because she has acquired a property right over it – through having already gone through some of the labour of pregnancy, and through having endured the insufficiently recognized labour of abortion, if not the labour of childbirth. There is no countervailing claim of personhood residing in the fetus, as there is with the newborn infant. A mother cannot own a baby, but can the formerly pregnant woman own the fetal tissue resulting from an abortion as the product of her labour? This second alternative is a better reason for thinking she can, but I am reluctant to accept the apparent logic of ownership unreservedly. Let me try to explain why not.

There is considerable interest in the commercialization of fetal tissue, including ovarian tissue, for research and transplantation purposes. Reproductive technologies are sufficiently sophisticated to allow fetus farming – the deliberate inception of pregnancy and 'harvesting' of fetal tissue for sale in the treatment of such pathologies as Parkinson's Disease. If we want to prevent that, we need to separate the decision to have an abortion from the decision to provide fetal tissue for transplantation.[54] But how can we be certain of a woman's motivation in this case? One way is to deny her the ownership of the fetal tissue; yet some feminists have argued that denying women the right to sell fetal tissue after abortion is inconsistent with their right to own and control their bodies.[55] However, I have already given several reasons for being sceptical about ownership of property in the body as a means to women's liberation.

The difficulty is that the alternative models are so unattractive: for example, if the fetus is regarded as a cadaveric organ donor, whose consent to transplant is being given by a proxy.[56] To construe aborted tissue as like any other bodily tissue removed during any surgical or diagnostic procedure seems simpler and less hypocritical. However, as Mary Mahowald notes, 'even the analogy with use of discarded tissue misses the uniqueness and complexity of the relationship between pregnant women and fetuses.'[57] That relationship is not contractual: society is not contract all the way down, as I argued in chapter 4. The example of contract motherhood was careful to distinguish between the woman's right to contract her pain and suffering in labour to another, and the absence of any right to sell or transfer the baby. Sensitivity to relationship, even with an aborted fetus, seems to require not doing certain things, including not selling the fetal tissue – or so Mahowald argues. But it is not entirely clear why this prohibition should exist, if the tissue belongs unequivocally to the woman concerned, and if the model is property in the body. However, if property in the *person* is distinguished from property in the *body*, or any other object,[58] we can make some headway towards reconstructing property in this case example, although my comments here will remain somewhat speculative.

Property in the person, or in Lockean terms, property in life and liberty, is more akin to property in one's designs, projects and innermost feelings than it is to property in things, as I summarized it in chapter 3. It is a strong way of stating that human beings are 'the creators of their own actions (and *a fortiori* of their work and labour)'.[59] In other words, someone who has a property in the person is unequivocally a moral agent, a subject. Allowing a woman to sell aborted fetal tissue seems to make her an *object* of possible exploitation; this is the concern which most feminists have about 'fetal farming'. In Lockean terms, this is inappropriate: having a property in one's person is connected to being 'Master'[60] of oneself.

In more existentialist terms, there seems to be something inauthentic, untrue to a subject's motivations, about beginning a pregnancy in order to be able to sell fetal tissue. Another way of putting this, in Kantian vocabulary, is that the fetus is being treated as a means to the pregnant woman's commercial end, as an object rather than a potential subject. This objection to trade in fetal tissue also captures something about the pregnant woman's relationship with the fetus during the pregnancy, or with respect for what the fetus might have represented after the abortion. In addition, we need to consider the relationship between the woman now, after her abortion, and her projects and values. These projects and values are what we mean by her property in the person. In the case of fetus farming, there seems to be something much less than ownership of one's own projects and values going on.

I have argued throughout this book that it is wrong to conceive of property rights as exercised over objects, rather than as sets of relationships, in the Hohfeldian manner. To think of fetal tissue simply as an object is false to the relationship between the pregnant woman and the fetus, I feel. It is perhaps also false to the pregnant woman's property in the person, rather than a concomitant of it. Finally, it is a particularly disturbing form of alienation or estrangement from the products of a woman's reproductive labour.

Case study 4: The marriage 'contract'

The previous case study suggests that there are some things which contracts should not be allowed to stipulate, and that the sale of fetal tissue is one of them. Yet elsewhere in this book I have argued against a general rejection of contract. In a negative sense, there is nothing wrong with the sexual *contract* as a contract; it is being sexual that invalidates it. In a positive sense, I have argued in favour of contract as an embodiment of mutual recognition, as an enhancement of moral mutual awareness. To a lesser extent, I have also accepted the liberal link between being a free agent and being a maker of contracts. When property is construed as property in the person, rather than the sexually tinged property in the body, property and contract can stand for ethical agency and moral self-development.

But is it possible to regard the marriage contract – a form of sexual contract – in this beneficial light? One might well think not, if what is wrong with the sexual contract is not that it is a contract, but that it is sexual. Yet in this most intimate relation, it would be good to think that there could be room for a vision of contract and property which sees the self as constructed *through* satisfactory relationships, the sort of model I posited at the beginning of this chapter.

What possibilities are open to us in regard to the marriage contract and women's liberation?

1 We could regard contract as hopelessly tainted by its association with subordination in the 'marriage contract', and the marriage 'contract' itself as a confidence trick;
2 We could admit the utility of calling marriage a 'contract' for pragmatic and strategic reasons, insisting that we could rectify women's subordination in marriage by making it a *genuine* contract. The aim of that, from a feminist viewpoint, would be to use contract as a way to recognize

women's property in the labour of childbirth and to ensure their reproductive freedoms. A real contract would have to afford both parties equal freedom to make and break the agreement along with equal freedoms during the contract's tenure;

3 We could deny that the marriage contract is a contract at all, and look instead to some other metaphor, myth or narrative: for example, the frequently made analogy between marriage and prostitution, or between marriage and domestic slavery. The marriage 'contract' is quite unlike other contracts: its provisions are unwritten, it is impossible to alter, and its full ramifications are not even known to the contracting parties.[61] Why use a pre-modern definition of marriage duties which really reflects status rather than contract as such? [62]

I construe Pateman as generally taking the first position,[63] which gets the worst of both worlds, in my opinion. It ignores the disparities between the sexual/marriage contract (collapsing the two for the time being) and all other forms of contract, which position 3 highlights. As I stated in chapter 3, Pateman implies that we must get rid of the mental baggage of contract and individual, and look the reality of subordination squarely in the face. But it is not at all clear how getting shot of the mental encumbrances will directly emancipate women, or why theorists who do not carry the full matched set of liberal luggage – like Rousseau – are every bit as guilty of subordinating women as the classic contract theorists. Position 1 conduces to a sort of despair about whether anything can be done to remedy women's sexual subordination, whereas position 2 is pragmatic and policy-oriented.

There is also a strategic advantage to position 2: it could be used to enforce equality between the contracting parties. But this is also the source of danger: assuming that the parties are equal *because* they have executed a contract. The example of contract motherhood illustrates both aspects: contract can protect gestational mothers who miscarry or give birth to babies with disabilities for which the contracting father declines to assume responsibility. But the greater financial power of the contracting father, and the social construction of women's propertylessness in the labour of childbirth, give rise to exploitation – unless, as I have argued, the contract is clearly about the woman's property *in* her labour, in childbirth, and not about the baby. Then contract becomes an instrument of recognition for what women do and endure in pregnancy and childbirth.

But if we are to use contract in marriage, we need a historical materialist awareness of how loaded the concept is. Whereas the law of contract generally disallows unequal exchanges,[64] the Anglo-American doctrine of coverture positively reinforced inequality in the marriage 'contract' until not so very long ago. So perhaps this is not recognizably a contract at all?

This is the essence of position 3, which prefers to describe marriage in other metaphors, such as slavery or prostitution. Think, for example, of the depiction of marriage by William Thompson and Anna Wheeler as 'such a contract as the owners of slaves in the West Indies and every other slave-polluted soil, enter into with their slaves'.[65] The same low view was taken by John Stuart Mill and Harriet Taylor ('Marriage is the primitive state of slavery lasting on');[66] by Margaret Fuller ('There exists in the minds of men a tone of feeling toward women as toward slaves');[67] and by Charles Brockden Brown, who denounced marriage as a 'compact of slavery'[68] as early as 1790.

But despite its sound historical pedigree, position 3 risks *ahistorical* essentialism and ethnocentrism, ignoring the very variety of marriage entitlements that I have documented elsewhere in this book. (I hope that diversity will mitigate the potential essentialism of saying that what is wrong with the sexual contract is not that it is a contract but that it is sexual.) If position 3 *underdetermines* actual marriage codes, it *overdetermines* the institution of marriage itself, 'fetishizing' the conjugal relationship as unique and separate from all other forms of women's economic subordination.

For example, despite the many forms of women's economic subordination in the more fundamentalist Islamic regimes, one of the most sexually egalitarian elements in Islamic law is the right it gives married women to make contracts – a right which Christianity has not always been so quick to defend. Marriage itself is a contract in *shariah* law, in contrast to the post-medieval Christian insistence that marriage is a sacrament and explicitly not a contract, despite Pateman's interpretation. The sacramental sanctity of Christian marriage is arguably more oppressive to women than the contractual basis of Islamic marriage. The contractual marriages of Mafia Island in Tanzania were mentioned in chapter 1, with their high degree of freedom for women. Under *shariah* law a wife may also demand all or part of her dowry at any time during the marriage, not merely on divorce.

But if marriage is a contract in the Islamic interpretation, a broken contract also carries no further obligations. There is no alimony requirement beyond the three-month *iddah* period, during which the husband waits to see whether his divorced wife is carrying his child. Nor is there any child support requirement on the husband after the first two years – although of course the children of the marriage are not party to the marriage contract which occurred before they were born. Finally, neither are the two parties genuinely equal in their ability to terminate the contract: the husband, not the wife, is allowed to pronounce 'I divorce you' three times, although it is the least desirable form of divorce in Islamic law. The Shah Bono case in India (1986) illustrated the depths of indigency to which a divorced Muslim woman with grown children can be reduced.[69] All this may spell trouble for position 2. Yet if both parties were *genuinely* equal in their ability to terminate the contract, and both equally responsible for the upkeep of children, there would be much that is attractive in the Islamic view of marriage as a contract. But other forms of economic subordination intersect with contract in many modern Islamic societies, drastically reducing the independence of married women.

Position 2 avoids ethnocentrism and essentialism, although perhaps at the cost of offering two contradictory notions of 'contract': the one that we recognize as the existing 'marriage contract', and a 'real' contract which would not tolerate the current reality of unequal economic power in marriage. Can the marriage contract itself be tailored to give women more equal power? Given that marriage has not withered away as was widely predicted in the 1960s and 1970s,[70] but has instead reconstituted itself as successive rather than lifelong – there is a greater likelihood of entering into marriage at some point today than ever before – we urgently need to bring marriage more fully into the realm of contract and to regulate its status anomalies.[71] With the ubiquity of marriage and, conversely, the handicaps against women's economic independence, it is certainly arguable that a reformed marriage contract is the most effective way to help women improve their economic lives. And as I stated at the end of chapter 5, a historical materialist analysis suggests that women can reclaim the status of subject by changing their economic situation. So let us explore the viability of position 2.

What explains the different entitlements of men and women in the traditional marriage contract? We have heard one answer, Delphy's concept of the domestic mode of production. An alternative, neoliberal explanation of women's propertylessness in marriage is offered by Michael Trebilcock. He focuses not on differences under the domestic mode of *production*, but on disparate treatment of male and female 'human *capital*'. Trebilcock castigates the inadequacy of the current law in remedying what he terms 'private ordering failures, resulting from unsatisfactory background entitlements . . . the lack of attention paid to a major class of family assets: human capital'.[72] Despite their differing ideological outlooks, the evidence that Trebilcock marshalls is quite similar to Delphy's observations on divorce, and he also employs a category of 'household production' based on the sexual division of labour. A divorce settlement, in Trebilcock's view, rarely reflects the foregone opportunities of market production by the wife, who must instead specialize in household production.

> In the course of this division of labour, she may have suffered a substantial depreciation of her human capital with respect to market opportunities and

thus, on marriage breakdown, confronts the prospect of limited employment opportunities and modest income-generating potential, while his earning potential is unaffected and indeed may well have been enhanced by the marriage.[73]

But Trebilcock actually goes further than Delphy. In order to fully compensate the divorced wife, we should include not only her opportunity *costs* in foregone career chances, but also her lost expectations of *gain* for those sacrifices, particularly in her husband's later high-earning years and in his pension rights.[74] The more time a wife has invested in household production, the more her compensation should be calculated according to lost gain, based on her expected 'profit-sharing' in her husband's increasing wealth over the term of the marriage as *his* human capital increases. That would probably give a higher value than the current standard of a 'reliance interest' in her foregone earnings (which will have stayed at the level of *her* human capital on marriage, or more likely declined).

Trebilcock proposes a detailed set of default rules that would apply in law unless the parties to a marriage validly contract otherwise by prenuptial or separation agreements. Freedom of contract is limited to reflect the inferior power base of the woman: the contracting parties do not have absolute freedom to devise alternatives which might put one party – presumably the wife – in a substantially inferior position to that under the default rule. Although Trebilcock recognizes that his proposed default rules legitimate and perpetuate women's economic dependency in traditional marriage, the compensating argument is more generous property allocation for women on divorce.

But would both parties agree in advance that the wife should share in her husband's property gains over his lifetime regardless of the marriage's success? Trebilcock is aware of the problem of moral hazard: his proposals give the wife no incentive – at least under a no-fault divorce system – to make the marriage succeed.

> The alternative and more powerful argument, however, is that by making economically dependent relationships much more expensive for men (and indeed, more reflective of actual relative investments) in the event of their termination, one may discourage many relationships driven by considerations of exploitation or subordination, rather than by genuine considerations of mutual advantage.[75]

This is rather similar to my strategy in relation to contract motherhood: retaining the possibility of contract, but altering the opportunity costs to discourage exploitation by the generally stronger party, men. To extend Trebilcock's argument in a more overtly feminist manner, the 'default rules' constitute a form of positive discrimination: they merely reverse the advantage which *men* have enjoyed. Although Trebilcock does not mention them, other systems have already devised procedures for discouraging men's economically rational disinterest in making a marriage succeed. The Jewish *ketuba* is a contract guaranteeing property rights to the bride, designed to make divorce financially punitive for the husband (since he can divorce at will, and only he can initiate divorce). The *ketuba* dates back to the second century BCE, when Rabbi Simeon ben Shetah provided a formula for the woman's credit (on the assurance of her *ketuba*) in lands, goods and chattels, down to her husband's garments – quite the opposite of the Athenian model, under which the wife's garments belonged to the husband.

> The principal function of the Ketuba is therefore to serve as a document that safeguards the position of the woman after she has entered the marital state, or in the words of the GEMARA: 'So that he should not deem it an easy thing to send her away.' The legal significance of the Ketuba in the life of the married couple can be seen by the fact that the husband was prohibited from spending even a single hour with his wife without a Ketuba document.[76]

Although the *ketuba* is generally now regarded as a symbolic contract only, it was upheld for enforcing child support in a 1970 US case.[77] Whether courts would ever take the more 'threatening' step of using it to allocate resources to the ex-wife is more doubtful; but it does provide a model to counter Trebilcock's fears about moral hazard.

Contractual enforcement of separation and divorce agreements, Trebilcock asserts, could benefit women if the law compensates for the power structures which result in 'unsatisfactory background entitlements' – the inequities which trouble MacKinnon and Pateman. *Again, what is wrong is not the mechanism of contract in itself, or even the application of contract to 'inapplicable' areas such as family law, but rather the use of contract to ratify rather than remedy the unequal entitlements of men and women.* There is an obvious strategic difficulty, however, with the neoliberal approach taken by Trebilcock – how far freedom of contract can be extended in the direction of remedying women's unequal entitlements before men protest.

Another way of putting this is in terms of Durkheim's insight that both contractual and non-contractual understandings bind individuals and continue to condition our notion of contract.[78] Men's non-contractual understandings of their superior entitlements in marriage will continue to condition marriage 'contracts' and divorce settlements. It is not good enough to wait until the divorce before the partners find out how closely their non-contractual understandings matched the way the settlement turns out in law. In order to minimize unstated background, non-contractual understandings at the time of marriage, Lenore Weitzman argues for explicit 'intimate contracts'. Such contracts would fulfil additional functions: to substitute what the couple actually want for automatic common-law provisions, to allow same-sex couples the property-related benefits and immunities afforded to heterosexual couples by the common law, and to extend support obligations to parents or children from previous marriages, if the couple so agrees. Intimate contracts, she asserts, do not threaten romance or undermine trust – except blind trust in common-law requirements whose existence is likely to be a nasty shock later on. Her emphasis, then, is on actively stipulating the property provisions which are to govern the marriage, and if necessary the divorce. Trebilcock, in contrast, relies on an automatic default – one which assures women more property entitlements than the common law – but allows couples to write their own contracts if they so desire, provided they do not write in too much inequality.

However, Trebilcock's default proposals will probably benefit more women than Weitzman's contracts. There will always be men, and indeed couples, who distrust contract as an invasion of intimate relationship (although I have argued that it need not be). Under Trebilcock's default rules, those who do not want to stipulate a contract will be protected by a more woman-friendly system of property distribution on divorce than the common law usually affords. Those who do want to opt out from Trebilcock's default rules will be unlikely to agree to anything more unequal than the default clauses, on Weitzman's own argument.

Models such as Weitzman's and Trebilcock's do something radically different from either liberalism or socialism: they extend the freedoms of the contractual public realm to the domestic mode of production. In so doing, I think they help to realize for women the Hegelian promises of the civilizing civic realm. They fulfil some conditions of a successful feminist materialism, avoiding the ahistorical essentialism of position 3 and the apolitical despair of position 1. And they hitch a ride on the prevalent neo-Lockean bandwagon, but to a very different destination from what the driver has in mind.

A reconstituted marriage contract, enforced through the mechanisms of divorce and family law, is the best example of the positive model of contract as enhancing rather than harming relationship. Contract itself is inherently a cooperative venture,[79] provided that individuals really are equally free to make or break it, and that they enter and leave it on terms which recognize them as subjects rather than objects. The law does not just rely on the freedom of contracting individuals as a given; 'normally,' in cases other than marriage or family law, it polices contracts to keep them more or less free of subordination, although the degree of clarity of the rules which it applies varies between 'crystals' and 'mud'.[80] Indeed, this is the more coherent story; the narrative about entirely self-interested individuals has a centre that cannot hold.

A brief conclusion

In the realm of property, we can choose to tell stories about Egypt, Gortyn or the Grameen Bank; we are not obliged to keep repeating the ones about Athens or coverture, although we had better be pretty familiar with their plotlines. Locke and his neoliberal successors are telling lies, I agree with Pateman, when they present property as improving the lot of humanity in general, or when they picture the advantages of marriage as so obvious to all that women enter freely into the marriage 'contract'. But too often feminist theorists have assumed that the only choice is between the hegemonic story about the connections between property, contract, virtue and subjectivity, and no story at all.

Other feminist theorists have returned to the social construction of history and subjectivity, and the reconstruction of key political concepts.[81] They have begun to question orthodoxies within earlier second-wave feminism which threatened to become almost as rigid as the exclusionary and excluding concepts of 'malestream' political theory. The notion that rights are opposed to relationships, for example, has been overturned in favour of the more productive insight that 'ascribing rights to someone implies a moral connection to her or him.'[82] With such theorists I feel much more at ease. They seem to allow what Beauvoir found problematic: the possibility of becoming a genuine subject, rather than the eternal Other. As Karen Green writes,

> By writing us out of history, as subjects, de Beauvoir leaves us with two options. We either return to essentialism and the attempt to forge our identity from some ahistorical given – maternity, for instance, or perhaps the female body – and/or we reject the project of becoming transcendent subjects as itself grounded in a patriarchal philosophy which has created a myth of the subject by denying women and bodily existence.[83]

I have stressed the importance of 'a property in her own person' to female subjectivity. If every woman 'hath a property in *her* own person', it is not over an object, the body: that merely perpetuates Cartesian dualism. This is another advantage of seeing things in terms of the person rather than the body, and of construing identity and subjectivity in rather Irigarayan terms as self-creating.

So a woman-centred theory of property will *not* require the misunderstanding which sees property as exercised over objects, not as sets of relationships. This has been something of a dead-end for feminists, I think, despite its polemical value. It is nearly always incorrect in anthropological terms to see women as simple *objects* of property-holding; although Lévi-Strauss, on whom Pateman relies a good deal, presented the 'exchange' of women as cementing male social bonds, the emphasis was on relationship, in which women do also participate, although vicariously.[84] There is no surer route to the patronizingly 'fetishized and essentialized Third World Woman' that Donna Haraway rightly condemns than seeing women, particularly women in traditional societies, as the mere objects of property-holding. That is also ill-advised in political strategic terms, I think: it perpetuates victimization.

We are not yet in a position to construct a grand theory[85] of property; Munzer only does so by counting women out. What I have tried to do is to provide some more solid foundations than the shifting sands on which, I have argued, so-called grand theories are built. To recapitulate for the last time, these foundational notions are:

1 Emphasis on the Hegelian, educative, *developmental role of property*, which may be either public or private;
2 Sensitivity to women's *alienation* from the products of their own persons, as forced labour hostile to one's inner subjectivity, *including estrangement from the products of one's own reproductive labour*;
3 Compatibility with an interest in *narrative myths about property* and with a *historical materialist* analysis, which suggests that women can reclaim the status of subject by changing their economic situation;
4 Equally, but perhaps surprisingly, openness to the liberal notion of *contract*, but with an emphasis on *property in the person*, as distinguished from property in the body;
5 The view of property as a *set of relationships* rather than as *objects*, and hence a profound rejection of the notion that women's only relationship to property is as its objects;
6 In keeping with the polymorphous, pluralistic notion of property which is involved in construing it as a set of relations, a notion of the *subject as constructed* rather than as given – constructed not only by past experiences and events, in a passive manner, but by the active use of a *relational, non-instrumental model of rationality*.

Even in their skeletal form, these undergirdings, beams, struts and joists are enough to be going on with. They enable us to analyse important current debates, such as those in reproductive ethics, in a woman-centred way, and to make some surprisingly concrete policy recommendations. They give us something to build with. But they are not the 'master's tools, which will never dismantle the master's house'.[86] They are women's own property.

Notes

Introduction

1 For example, Moira Gatens, *Feminism and Philosophy: Perspectives on Difference and Equality*; Joan Cocks, *The Oppositional Imagination: Feminism, Critique and Political Theory*; and Nancy C. M. Hartsock, *Money, Sex and Power: Toward a Feminist Historical Materialism*, esp. ch. 10 and app. 2. Distrust of dualisms is not unique to feminism, of course: Francis Bacon branded them as obstacles to thought, rather than its instruments. Nor has feminism always resisted dualism: Fiona Williams (personal correspondence) points out that Kate Millett, Shulamith Firestone and other 1970s feminists reinforced aspects of male–female dualism.

2 Simone de Beauvoir, *Le deuxième sexe* (Paris: Gallimard, 1986), cited in Michèle le Dœuff, *Hipparchia's Choice: An Essay Concerning Women, Philosophy, etc.*, pp. 55–6.

3 Carol M. Rose, *Property and Persuasion: Essays on the History, Theory and Rhetoric of Ownership*.

4 A. M. Honoré, 'Ownership', p. 108.

5 Samuel Pyeatt Menefee, *Wives for Sale: An Ethnographic Study of British Popular Divorce*. Although wife sale was most often used as a consensual means of divorce by the poor, who could not afford a parliamentary bill, there were also *Mayor of Casterbridge* style sales, in which the wife was taken to market in a halter and sold to the highest bidder

6 Catharine A. MacKinnon, *Toward a Feminist Theory of State*, p. 173.

7 *Thaetetus* 160b, cited in Le Dœuff, *Hipparchia's Choice*, p. 102.

8 Cited in Donna Dickenson, *George Sand: A Brave Man, the Most Womanly Woman*, p. 47.

9 Beauvoir, *Le deuxième sexe*, vol. 1, p. 21, cited in Le Dœuff, *Hipparchia's Choice*, p. 100.

10 MacKinnon, *Feminist Theory of State*, p. 120.

11 Georgina Ashworth, 'International linkages in the women's movement', p. 139.

12 The law has nominally moved away from treating children as property in

divorce settlements, and indeed from the concept of custody as a form of parental rights (which are replaced in the Children Act 1989 by parental responsibility). However, the notion of children as property figures large in the more traditional doctrines around coverture, examined in chapter 3.

13 Here I draw on the contrast in Erich Fromm's *To Have and To Be*. The desirability of autonomy has of course been questioned by much feminist moral philosophy, as has the related but distinct notion of self-respect. See, for example, Robin S. Dillon, 'Toward a feminist conception of self-respect'. Other feminists, however, have attempted to derive a notion of autonomy which is compatible with a feminist reading (e.g. Diana Myers in *Self, Society and Personal Choice*). I am more sympathetic to the second camp; my own aim is to suggest the basis for a 'woman-friendly' model of property.

14 For example, Lynne Segal, *Is the Future Female? Troubled Thoughts on Contemporary Feminism*.

15 Renée Hirschon, 'Introduction: property, power and gender relations', p. 1.

16 See, for example, Kathleen Jones, *Compassionate Authority: Democracy and the Representation of Women*; Gisela Bock and Susan James (eds), *Beyond Equality and Difference: Citizenship, Feminist Politics and Female Subjectivity*; and Nancy Hirschmann, *Rethinking Obligation: A Feminist Method for Political Theory*.

17 Irigaray's work has implications for the social contract but not for legal contract, property, poverty, or the other issues of social policy, jurisprudence and applied political theory which I consider.

18 Luce Irigaray, *This Sex which Is Not One*, p. 193. Margaret Whitford, in *Luce Irigaray: Philosophy in the Feminine*, p. 186, suggests that this is not a literal utopia, but an account of the idealized female symbolic.

19 William Shakespeare, Sonnet 94, 'They that have power to hurt', line 7.

20 Carole Pateman, *The Sexual Contract*, p. x.

21 Lenore Weitzman, *The Divorce Revolution: The Unexpected Social and Economic Consequences for Women and Children in America*.

22 Mavis MacLean, *Surviving Divorce: Women's Resources after Separation*.

23 Jan Pahl, *Money and Marriage*.

24 Charles Reich, 'The new property' (1964).

25 Alan Ryan, *Property*, p. 4.

26 Rose, *Property and Persuasion*. pp. 1–2, discussing respectively Wesley Newcomb Hohfeld (to whom I return in chapter 1) and Proudhon and Marx.

27 Ibid.

28 Catharine A. MacKinnon, 'The sexual politics of the First Amendment', in *Feminism Unmodified: Discourses on Life and Law*.

29 At this stage I do not want to limit the impact of this argument by defining at length who the dispossessed are. Obviously I have begun with a hypothesis that many women are dispossessed and propertyless – but not that *all* women are, or that *no* men are. The specifics of privilege should become clearer from the examples which form a large portion of the book.

30 Le Dœuff, *Hipparchia's Choice*, pp. 288–9.

31 Ibid., p. 165.

32 The emphasis on relationship begins, of course, with Carol Gilligan's *In a Different Voice*.

33 Alasdair MacIntyre, *After Virtue*; Martha Craven Nussbaum, *The Fragility of Goodness: Luck and Ethics in Greek Tragedy and Philosophy*; J. Budziszewski, *The Resurrection of Nature: Political Theory and the Human Character*; and James D. Wallace, *Virtues and Vices*.

34 Donna Dickenson, *Moral Luck in Medical Ethics and Practical Politics*, p. 21.
35 Anne Marie Goetz, 'Feminism and the claim to know: contradictions in feminist approaches to women in development'.
36 I am grateful to Jean Grimshaw for suggesting the deconstruction/reconstruction contrast.
37 Luce Irigaray, *Speculum of the Other Woman*, p. 133, cited in Karen Green, *The Woman of Reason: Feminism, Humanism and Political Thought*, p. 133.
38 Christine Sylvester, *Feminist Theory and International Relations in a Postmodern Era*.
39 Here I follow the very telling argument put forward by Michèle le Dœuff in *Hipparchia's Choice*.
40 The first strategy is followed by Stephen Munzer in *A Theory of Property*, the second by Jeremy Waldron in *The Right to Private Property*.
41 Le Dœuff, *Hipparchia's Choice*, p. 7.
42 Ibid., p. 13.
43 Ibid., p. 14.
44 Ibid.

Chapter 1 Property, Particularism and Moral Persons

1 Stephen R. Munzer, *A Theory of Property*.
2 Historical accounts detailing the political philosophy of property include, among others, Richard Schlatter, *Private Property: The History of an Idea*; Alan Ryan, *Property and Political Theory*; Alan Carter, *The Philosophical Foundations of Property Rights*; Andrew Reeve, *Property*; and Jeremy Waldron, *The Right to Private Property*.
3 Munzer, *Theory of Property*, p. ix: 'I also hope that, to the extent that the views argued for here are sound, they will serve as a basis for action to make institutions of property better than they now are. At a time when, in most of the countries of the world, a few have great material wealth and others are struggling for the scantiest material resources, making the case for better property institutions is not an optional intellectual endeavour but a practical imperative.' Here I am entirely in sympathy with Munzer, and he should in turn be sympathetic to the need to remedy theories of property to make them relevant to the majority of the world's poor, women.
4 Ibid., p. 5.
5 Ibid., p. 228.
6 Carol M. Rose, ' "Takings" and the practices of property: property as wealth, property as "propriety" ', ch. 3 in *Property and Persuasion: Essays on the History, Theory and Rhetoric of Ownership*.
7 Munzer, *Theory of Property*, p. 219.
8 Norman Frohlich and Joe A. Oppenheimer, in *Choosing Justice: An Experimental Approach to Ethical Theory*, showed that American, Canadian and Polish university students all tended to converge on a distribution satisfying Munzer's second principle, a minimum floor of income with a restricted spread above the floor.
9 Munzer, *Theory of Property*, pp. 9–12.
10 See Richard W. Miller, *Moral Differences: Truth, Justice and Conscience in a World of Conflict*, pp. 10ff.
11 Munzer, *Theory of Property*, p. 6.

12 Ibid., p. 209.
13 For a more extended argument against over-reliance on hypotheticals, see Kathy Wilkes, *Real People: Philosophy without Thought Experiments*.
14 Seyla Benhabib, 'On Hegel, women and irony', p. 131.
15 Munzer, *Theory of Property*, pp. 15–16.
16 Thomas Hobbes, *Leviathan*, part 1, ch. 13, pp. 64–5.
17 Munzer, *Theory of Property*, p. 79.
18 Ibid., p. 209.
19 Elizabeth Cady Stanton, *Eighty Years and More: Reminiscences 1815–1897*, pp. 31–2.
20 Munzer, *Theory of Property*, p. 141.
21 Ryan, *Property and Political Theory*, p. 7.
22 Sandra Burman, 'Divorce and the disadvantaged: African women in urban South Africa', p. 122.
23 One such society, on Mafia Island in Tanzania, is described by Patricia Caplan, in 'Cognatic descent, Islamic law and women's property on the East African coast', p. 25. Caplan notes that an ironic effect of socialism in Tanzania under Nyerere's government (1961–85) was to lessen women's property rights in land through the process of 'villagization' and the construction of more permanent houses, which were deeded to the husband – replacing the self-built housing which women could put up at will, for example on divorce.
24 Marilyn Strathern, 'Subject or object? Women and the circulation of valuables in Highlands New Guinea'.
25 Ibid.; see also Renée Hirschon, 'Introduction: property, power and gender relations' in the same volume, p. 3.
26 Munzer, *Theory of Property*, p. 75. The distinction between production and reproduction will be examined more critically in chapter 5.
27 Virginia Held, *Feminist Morality: Transforming Culture, Society and Politics*, p. 24.
28 See Ann Whitehead, 'I'm hungry, Mum: the politics of domestic budgeting'.
29 Heidi Hartmann, 'The family as the locus of gender, class and political struggle: the example of housework'.
30 Jan Pahl, in *Money and Marriage*, confirms earlier findings that working wives tend to use their wages to augment the family housekeeping, whereas men typically keep something by from their pay for personal spending. See also L. Morris and S. Ruane, *Household Finances Management and Labour Market Behaviour*.
31 Henrietta L. Moore, *A Passion for Difference: Essays in Anthropology and Gender*, p. 87.
32 Ursula Sharma, 'Dowry in North India: its consequences for women'.
33 Elizabeth Croll, 'The exchange of women and property: marriage in post-revolutionary China', p. 59.
34 Mari J. Matsuda, 'Liberal jurisprudence and abstracted visions of human nature: a feminist critique of Rawls' theory of justice', p. 478.
35 Ibid.
36 Patricia J. Williams, 'On being the object of property'.
37 For example, this position is taken by Annette Baier in *Postures of the Mind: Essays on Mind and Morals*. This 'anti-theory' movement is not unique to feminism: see, for example, Bernard Williams, *Ethics and the Limits of Philosophy*. A critique of, and rejoinder to, the anti-theory movement in ethics is offered by Robert B. Louden in *Morality and Moral Theory: A Reappraisal and Reaffirmation*, esp. ch. 5.

38 Kathy E. Ferguson, *The Man Question: Visions of Subjectivity in Feminist Theory*, p. 4.
39 V. Held, *Feminist Morality*, pp. 12ff.
40 Ibid., p. 37.
41 Munzer, *Theory of Property*, p. 105.
42 The Canadian philosopher Susan Sherwin, along with many other recent writers, refuses to call maternal or cultural 'feminisms' feminist at all. She prefers to term the ethic of care 'feminine', on the grounds that it conforms to and reinforces stereotypes about femininity and fails to recognize women's oppression as political – the basic condition of a feminist theory, she asserts ('Ethics, "feminine" ethics, and feminist ethics', ch. 2 in *No Longer Patient: Feminist Ethics and Health Care*). It is useful to make the distinction offered by Karen Green in *The Woman of Reason: Feminism, Humanism and Political Thought*, pp. 150–1: 'by itself an ethic of care is not necessarily feminist, but it becomes feminist when incorporated into a theory of the good of society which attempts to bring about the good of women as well as the good of men.'
43 For example, Nel Noddings, *Caring: A Feminine Approach to Ethics and Moral Education*; Sara Ruddick, *Maternal Thinking: Towards a Politics of Peace*; Robin West, 'Jurisprudence and gender'; and V. Held, *Feminist Morality*. One need not argue that the 'caring' virtues are unique to women, of course: Jeffrey Blustein, in *Care and Commitment: Taking the Personal Point of View*, presents a view of *human* motivation in which caring is more central than controlling. Nor need one separate an ethics of care from an ethics of justice, argues Jean Grimshaw (*Philosophy and Feminist Thinking*); justice can subsume care.
44 See, for example, Martha Minow, 'Feminist reason: getting it and losing it', and Patricia A. Cain, 'Feminist jurisprudence: grounding the theories'; Nancy Hewitt, 'Beyond the search for sisterhood: American women's history in the 1980s'; and Elizabeth Spelman, *Inessential Woman: Problems of Exclusion in Feminist Thought*.
45 Carol Gilligan, *In a Different Voice: Psychological Theory and Women's Development*. See Gilligan's 'Letter to Readers, 1993' in the second edition: 'When I hear my work being cast in terms of whether women and men are really (essentially) different or who is better than whom, I know that I have lost my voice, because these are not my questions' (p. xiii).
46 V. Held, *Feminist Morality*, p. 8.
47 Munzer, *Theory of Property*, p. 105.
48 Adam Smith, *An Inquiry into the Nature and Causes of the Wealth of Nations* (1776). Although this is the model commonly associated with Smith, there is also room for public provision and private benevolence in his work, especially in *The Theory of Moral Sentiments* (1759).
49 Jennifer Nedelsky, 'Law, boundaries and the bounded self'.
50 Sherwin, *No Longer Patient*, p. 50.
51 Minow, 'Feminist reason', p. 341.
52 Susan Phinney Conrad, *Perish the Thought: Intellectual Women in Romantic America 1830–1860*, p. 12; Donna Dickenson, *Margaret Fuller: Writing a Woman's Life*, p. 61.
53 Robin West, 'The difference in women's hedonic lives: a phenomenological critique of feminist legal theory', *3 Wisconsin Women's Law Journal* 81 (1987), cited in Angela P. Harris, 'Race and essentialism in feminist legal theory', p. 352.

54 Catharine A. MacKinnon, *Toward a Feminist Theory of the State*, p. 51.
55 Naomi Wolf, *Fire with Fire: The New Female Power and How It Will Change the 21st Century*.
56 Moore, *Passion for Difference*, ch. 5: 'Social identities and the politics of reproduction', p. 93.
57 James Mill, 'Article on Government' (1820), summarized by Richard Pankhurst in his introduction to William Thompson, *Appeal of one Half the Human Race, Women, Against the Pretensions of the Other Half, Men, To Retain Them in Political, and Thence in Civil and Domestic Slavery*, p. ix. Thompson's *Appeal* was largely moved by outrage at Mill's complacency about the needs and interests of women.
58 Nancy Fraser, *Unruly Practices: Power, Discourse and Gender in Contemporary Social Theory*, p. 166.
59 Thomas C. Grey, 'The disintegration of property', cited in Munzer, *Theory of Property*, pp. 31ff.
60 Munzer, *Theory of Property*, pp. 16–17.
61 Wesley Newcomb Hohfeld, *Fundamental Legal Conceptions as Applied in Judicial Reasoning*, cited in Munzer, *Theory of Property*, p. 21. Later, however, Munzer backtracks somewhat: intangibles such as copyrights and patents are property, but the most essential forms of property are material, he says (pp. 73ff.). In this 'the popular conception, which views property as things, is not, as some philosophers and lawyers might think, wholly misguided' (p. 74).
62 Munzer, *Theory of Property*, p. 79.
63 Ibid.
64 Martha Craven Nussbaum, *The Fragility of Goodness: Luck and Ethics in Greek Tragedy and Philosophy*, p. 2.
65 Munzer, *Theory of Property*, p. 79.
66 Donna Dickenson, *Moral Luck in Medical Ethics and Practical Politics*.
67 See V. Held, *Feminist Morality*, pp. 35ff. Rationality will be discussed at greater length in chapter 6.
68 Munzer, *Theory of Property*, pp. 81–2.
69 Ibid., p. 85.
70 Ibid., p. 92.
71 Ibid., p. 87.
72 See, for example, *Theory of Property*, p. 93, in which he praises property ownership as providing the privacy which 'protects owners in the recesses of their homes and workplaces. They can do things that they regard as intimate, shameful, embarrassing, or just silly.' It is inconceivable that anyone with an awareness of the issues surrounding domestic violence or child sexual abuse could regard the privacy of the home so sanguinely.
73 Munzer, *Theory of Property*, p. 120, citing Lawrence C. Becker, *Property Rights: Philosophic Foundations*, pp. 81–7.
74 Plato, *The Republic*; Henry David Thoreau, *Walden*; Karl Marx, *The Economic and Political Manuscripts of 1844* and *Capital*; Pierre-Joseph Proudhon, *Selected Writings*. In his later writings Proudhon became more conservative, coming to view *moderate* property-holding, especially by the peasantry, as a civic virtue in so far as it kept the state in check and protected liberty.
75 Smith, *Theory of Moral Sentiments*, cited in Munzer, *Theory of Property*, p. 134.
76 Albert Fried and Richard Elman (eds), *Charles Booth's London: A Portrait of the Poor at the Turn of the Century, Drawn from his 'Life and Labour of the People in London'*.

77 Waldron, *Right to Private Property*, p. 23.
78 Nel Noddings, for example, argues (in *Caring*) that whereas abstract rules of justice are insensitive to the quality of relationships, it may be permissible to favour those with whom we have the closest relationships.
79 Sherwin, *No Longer Patient*, pp. 47–8.
80 See the discussion in Hannah Fenichel Pitkin, *Fortune is a Woman: Gender and Politics in the Thought of Niccolò Machiavelli*, esp. pp. 109–37.
81 I owe this insight to Fiona Williams.
82 Mary Wollstonecraft, *A Vindication of the Rights of Woman*.
83 George Eliot, 'Margaret Fuller and Mary Wollstonecraft' (1855), repr. in Thomas Pinney (ed.), *The Essays of George Eliot*, p. 203.
84 For the United Kingdom in the 1980s and 1990s, see Caroline Glendinning and Jane Millar (eds), *Women and Poverty in Britain: The 1990s*; Ruth Lister, *Women's Economic Dependency and Social Security*.

Chapter 2 Origins, Narratives and Households

1 The most obvious example is Alasdair MacIntyre's standard for a well-lived life: having narrative unity. See MacIntyre, *After Virtue: A Study in Moral Theory*; and Gregory L. Jones, 'Alasdair MacIntyre on narrative, community and the moral life'. A related development is the growing interest in actual narratives, life experiences and first-person accounts as sources to rival or replace hypotheticals. See, for example, Kathy Wilkes, *Real People: Philosophy without Thought Experiments*.
2 Carol M. Rose, *Property and Persuasion: Essays on the History, Theory and Rhetoric of Ownership*.
3 Carol M. Rose, 'Possession as the origin of property', ch. 1 in Rose, *Property and Persuasion*, p. 18.
4 Simone de Beauvoir, *The Second Sex*, p. 19.
5 Carol M. Rose, 'Property as storytelling: perspectives from game theory, narrative theory, feminist theory', ch. 2 in Rose, *Property and Persuasion*, p. 25.
6 Ibid., p. 27.
7 Ibid., p. 39.
8 Ibid., p. 37.
9 Ibid., p. 39.
10 Karen Green, *The Woman of Reason: Feminism, Humanism and Political Thought*, p. 135.
11 Michèle le Dœuff, *Hipparchia's Choice: An Essay Concerning Women, Philosophy, etc.*, p. 221.
12 Ibid.
13 See also Donna Haraway, 'Situated knowledges: the science question in feminism and the privilege of partial perspective', p. 146: 'Relativism is a way of saying nothing while claiming to be everywhere equally.' Goetz agrees that particularly in development questions, cultural feminism is expressed in practice as a weak pluralism which condones endless excuses from uncooperative governments and international agencies. Chandra Talpade Mohanty ('Feminist encounters: locating the politics of experience') also asserts that the shift towards questions of subjectivity has generated an apolitical, individualized identity politics which questions both race and gender as meaningful categories and leaves the entire notion of exploitation or oppression seeming

out of date.

14 Aristotle, *The Generation of Animals*, 731b30.
15 Aristotle, *Politics*, 1252b1.
16 Ibid., 1252b12.
17 For example, G. E. M. de Ste Croix, *The Class Struggle in the Ancient Greek World: From the Archaic Age to the Arab Conquests.*
18 Aristotle, *Politics*, 1259a39.
19 Ibid., 1260a12. Arlene Saxonhouse ('On Aristotle', p. 36) points out that this leaves unsettled the question of whether women's lack of authority, their deliberative faculty's state of being *akuron*, is itself merely conventional, in a patriarchal society, or internal to women's souls.
20 Aristotle, *Politics*, 1252b5.
21 Ibid., 1253b17, 1254a18.
22 Ibid., 1255a4.
23 Alan Ryan, in *Property*, p. 8, distinguishes Greek debt slavery of this sort from the Roman version, in which the debtor's body actually became the property of his creditor. The Greek practice was abolished by Solon (638–558 BC), who forbade men to borrow money on the security of their persons.
24 Aristotle, *Politics*, 1275a8ff.
25 Ibid., 1275a23.
26 De Beauvoir, *Le deuxième sexe*, vol. 2, pp. 95–6, cited in le Dœuff, *Hipparchia's Choice*, p. 113.
27 Le Dœuff, *Hipparchia's Choice*, p. 113.
28 Donna Dickenson, 'Counting women in: redefining democratic politics'. The concept of the feminization of citizenship draws on the terminology used by Ann Douglas in *The Feminization of American Culture*.
29 See, for example, Martin Shaw, 'Post-military democracy'.
30 Aristotle, *Politics*, 1278a7.
31 Ibid., 1335a11. Here I take the opposite point of view from Saxonhouse, who optimistically maintains that 'Aristotle recognizes the importance of the female in the political life of Greece' because he mentions that the Spartan women were insufficiently controlled by their menfolk.
32 Both Susan Moller Okin and to a lesser extent Arlene Saxonhouse trace women's inequality to their reproductive role. Although Saxonhouse initially criticizes Okin for this view, preferring to attribute women's subordination in Aristotle to their less authoritative deliberative faculty, she concedes that 'so long as there continue to be females to keep the race in existence, there will be, for Aristotle, hierarchy, authority and inequality – the family' (Saxonhouse, 'On Aristotle', p. 43).
33 Sarah Pomeroy, *Goddesses, Whores, Wives and Slaves: Women in Classical Antiquity.*
34 Aristotle, *Politics*, 1329a19.
35 Ibid., 1328b40.
36 Ibid., 1336b1. Saxonhouse ignores this passage in romanticizing women's realm in Aristotle: 'a realm in which she not only gives birth but also gives stability, preserves and educates the young of the city' ('On Aristotle', p. 51).
37 Saxonhouse, 'On Aristotle', p. 44.
38 Susan Moller Okin, *Women in Western Political Thought*, p. 34.
39 Aristotle, *Politics*, 1255b19.
40 Ibid., 1259a39.
41 Ibid., 1254b12.
42 Ibid., 1257a21.

43 Ryan, *Property,* p. 10, citing A. Zimmern, *The Greek Commonwealth* (1935).
44 Aristotle, *Politics,* 1256a4.
45 Ibid., 1256a10.
46 Ibid., 1277b25.
47 Ibid., 1270a16, 22.
48 Here I follow Ste Croix's argument in his *Class Struggle in the Ancient Greek World.*
49 Bonnie S. Anderson and Judith P. Zinsser, *A History of Their Own: Women in Europe from Prehistory to the Present,* vol. 1, p. 400.
50 For example, N. R. E. Fisher, *Slavery in Classical Greece,* p. 15.
51 Mogens Herman Hansen, *The Athenian Democracy in the Age of Demosthenes: Structures, Principles and Ideology,* p. 318.
52 Nicole Loraux, *Tragic Ways of Killing a Woman.*
53 Saxonhouse, 'On Aristotle', p. 50. Most of Saxonhouse's essay is taken up with refuting this charge.
54 A sceptical account of Plato's motivations is given by Okin in *Women in Western Political Thought,* chs 1, 2, 3.
55 Plato, *Laws,* 807b.
56 Plato, *Republic,* 451c and 453d.
57 Aristotle, *Politics,* 1266a34.
58 For a comprehensive review, see Natalie Harris Bluestone, *Women and the Ideal Society: Plato's Republic and Modern Myths of Gender.*
59 Xenophon, *Oekonomikos,* VII, 7–10, reproduced in Mary F. Lefkowitz and Maureen Fant (eds), *Women in Greece and Rome,* pp. 74–84, at p. 76.
60 Ibid., p. 82.
61 Ibid.
62 From Diogenes Laertius, *Lives of Eminent Philosophers,* V. 11–16, reproduced in Lefkowitz and Fant, *Women in Greece and Rome,* pp. 19–21.
63 Okin, *Women in Western Political Thought,* p. 34.
64 Here I follow David M. Schaps, *Economic Rights of Women in Ancient Greece.*
65 Ibid., p. 48.
66 Ibid., p. 8.
67 Elizabeth Croll, 'The exchange of women and property: marriage in post-revolutionary China', p. 47.
68 Schaps, *Economic Rights of Women in Ancient Greece,* p. 17.
69 Violaine Vanoyeke, *La Prostitution en Grèce et à Rome.*
70 The courtesan Neaira (see note 84 below) had such an arrangement with her two 'protectors', Stephanos and Phrynion.
71 *Lex Gortyn,* II, 46–54, cited at p. 86 of Schaps, *Economic Rights of Women in Ancient Greece.*
72 For an iconoclastic argument in favour of generalized Egyptian influence on Greek bureaucratic structures and law, see Martin Bernal, *Black Athena: The Afroasiatic Roots of Classical Civilization,* vol. 1: *The Fabrication of Ancient Greece 1785–1985.*
73 Gay Robins, *Women in Ancient Egypt,* p. 127. An aroura equals about two-thirds of an acre.
74 R. B. Parkinson, *Voices from Ancient Egypt: An Anthology of Middle Kingdom Writings* (1991), cited in Robins, *Women in Ancient Egypt,* p. 127.
75 Demosthenes, *Against Makartos,* 51, 54, reproduced in Lefkowitz and Fant, *Women in Greece and Rome,* pp. 21–2.
76 Robins, *Women in Ancient Egypt,* p. 132.
77 Cited ibid., p. 133.

78 Ibid., p. 128.
79 Papyrus SBX 10756, Oxyrhynchus, reproduced in Lefkowitz and Fant, *Women in Greece and Rome*.
80 Ibid., pp. 127ff.
81 Robins, *Women in Ancient Egypt*, p. 112.
82 Moira Gatens, *Feminism and Philosophy: Perspectives on Difference and Equality*, p. 45.
83 Hannah Arendt, *The Human Condition*, pp. 29–30.
84 Demosthenes (attributed to), *Kata Neairas*, c.340 BC.
85 At p. 101 of *A Theory of Property* Munzer does consider the situation of a hypothetical urban American single mother living in rented accommodation and earning a minimal wage. This concrete discussion demonstrates graphically how the woman's lack of property entails loss of privacy and control, both legally and informally. For example, at the informal level she finds it difficult to keep her few personal possessions separate from those of her children, or to conduct intimate acts free from the attention of her family and neighbours. Even in formal legal terms her control and privacy are lessened by her landlord's right to inspect her apartment, and, one might add, by the duty of social services to monitor the well-being of her children.
86 MacIntyre, *After Virtue*.
87 De Beauvoir, *Le deuxième sexe*, vol. 1, p. 21, cited in le Dœuff, *Hipparchia's Choice*, p. 100.
88 Aristotle, *Politics*, 1263b9.
89 For example, Jeremy Waldron, *The Right to Private Property*, p. 23.

Chapter 3   Contract, Marriage and Property in the Person

1 Bonnie S. Anderson and Judith P. Zinsser, *A History of Their Own*, vol. 2, pp. 143, 148.
2 Other feminist critics of Lockean liberalism, in addition to Pateman, include Jean Bethke Elshtain, *Public Man, Private Woman: Women in Social and Political Thought*, pp. 108–46; Moira Gatens, *Feminism and Philosophy: Perspectives on Difference and Equality*; Zillah Eisenstein, *The Radical Future of Liberal Feminism*; Susan Moller Okin, *Women in Western Political Thought*, pp. 200–1; Nancy J. Hirschmann, *Rethinking Obligation: A Feminist Method for Political Theory*, pp. 55ff.; and Joan Cocks, *The Oppositional Imagination: Feminism, Critique and Political Theory*, pp. 128–35. A more favourable reading of Locke is given by Melissa A. Butler in 'Early liberal roots of feminism: John Locke and the attack on patriarchy'. Marxist and materialist feminisms, with their own critique of liberalism, are considered in chapter 5.
3 In the United States this aversion to the traditional subjects of contract and property was particularly marked in the proliferating ranks of women who entered law school in the early 1970s (introduction to D. Kelly Weisberg (ed.), *Feminist Legal Theory: Foundations*, p. xvi). In pressing for the inclusion of law on discrimination, sexual assault, and reproduction in the curriculum, these women were calling for more attention to be paid to women's experience. But it is unfortunate that property and contract should have come to be regarded, by implication, as foreign to women's experience. A powerful statement of the contradictions felt by an African-American woman teaching contract law is given by Patricia J. Williams in 'On being the object of property', in the same

volume.

4 Kathleen B. Jones, *Compassionate Authority: Democracy and the Representation of Women*, p. 89.

5 Hirschmann, *Rethinking Obligation*, p. 27.

6 John Dunn, for example, takes this position in 'Consent in the political theory of John Locke'.

7 For example, Alan Ryan in his otherwise clear analysis, 'Locke, labour and the purposes of God', ch. 1 in *Property and Political Theory*.

8 Harriet Taylor Mill, *The Enfranchisement of Women* (first published anonymously 1851); John Stuart Mill, *The Subjection of Women* (1869).

9 In separating out 'liberal' from 'contractarian', I exclude Rousseau (whom I regard as contractarian but not liberal). An excellent source to make good my omission is Gatens, *Feminism and Philosophy*, ch. 1.

10 Jeremy Waldron, *The Right to Private Property*, pp. 159ff.

11 Carole Pateman, *The Sexual Contract*, p. 182.

12 Ibid., p. 168. Pateman does not distinguish between property in the person and property in the body. I would say that the argument here concerns property in the body.

13 By agreeing to the original marriage contract, according to traditional English legal formulations, women ceded their right to control the sexual use of their bodies by their husbands for the duration of the marriage. Not until 1991 did the English Court of Appeal overturn the old common-law presumption that a man could not be convicted of raping his wife. The older doctrine, enunciated by Chief Justice Matthew Hale in the seventeenth century, was that by accepting the marriage contract, the wife 'hath given up her body to her husband', 'which she cannot retract'. In US jurisdictions where rape in marriage is recognized as an offence, it may attract a different tariff from 'real' rape. For example, in Pennsylvania wife rape is a second-degree felony with a five- to ten-year maximum sentence; non-spousal rape is a first-degree felony, punishable by ten to twenty years of imprisonment. For the property origins of the law on rape, see J. Schwendinger and H. Schwendinger, *Rape and Inequality*.

14 Pateman, *The Sexual Contract*, p. 166.

15 Virginia Held, *Feminist Morality: Transforming Culture, Society and Politics*, p. 169.

16 Williams, 'On being the object of property', p. 598.

17 The distinction between general and special rights originates in H. L. A. Hart's paper 'Are there any natural rights?' It is further analysed in Waldron, *Right to Private Property*, pp. 20, 106–24.

18 Nancy C. M. Hartsock, *Money, Sex and Power: Toward a Feminist Historical Materialism*.

19 Catharine A. MacKinnon, *Toward a Feminist Theory of the State*.

20 Hirschmann, *Rethinking Obligation*, p. 56.

21 Hirschmann develops the argument made by Mary O'Brien in *The Politics of Reproduction* to the effect that men's superfluity in reproduction gives them a tormenting sense of 'historical discontinuity'. They can only be assured of passing on their identity through the mechanisms of inheritance, to other men.

22 This association is epitomized by the notion of *Property as a Guarantor of Liberty*, a recent pamphlet by James M. Buchanan.

23 See also Carole Pateman, 'God hath ordained to man a helper: Hobbes, patriarchy and conjugal right'.

24 Robert Nozick, *Anarchy, State and Utopia*.

25 Waldron, *Right to Private Property*, p. 133.

26 David Held, *Models of Democracy*, pp. 54–5.
27 Pateman, *The Sexual Contract*, p. 55, referring to C. B. Macpherson, *The Political Theory of Possessive Individualism: Hobbes to Locke*.
28 John Locke, *The Second Treatise on Civil Government*, s. 27.
29 John Rawls, *A Theory of Justice*, p. 467. There have been numerous feminist critiques of Rawls: one of the most influential is Susan Moller Okin, 'Reason and feeling in thinking about justice'.
30 In recent years Rawls has modified his position somewhat in response to feminist critiques; my discussion, however, pertains to *A Theory of Justice* in its original form.
31 Thomas Hobbes, *Leviathan*, p. 48.
32 Locke, *Second Treatise*, s. 27.
33 Pateman, *The Sexual Contract*, p. 2.
34 Ibid., p. 8.
35 Cocks, *The Oppositional Imagination*, pp. 129–30.
36 Pateman, *The Sexual Contract*, p. 11.
37 Ibid., p. 41.
38 Ibid., p. 181.
39 See also Pateman, 'God hath ordained to man a helper'.
40 Pateman, *The Sexual Contract*, p. 102.
41 William Blackstone, *Commentaries on the Laws of England*, cited in Marylynn Salmon, *Women and the Law of Property in Early America*, p. 41.
42 Melissa Butler offers some counterexamples to illustrate Locke's favourable view of women, but does not tackle the question of his overall acceptance of the doctrine of coverture, to which Pateman rightly draws our attention.
43 Thomas Hobbes, *De Cive*, quoted in David Held, 'Introduction: central perspectives on the modern state', p. 5.
44 Pateman, *The Sexual Contract*, p. 60.
45 Waldron, *Right to Private Property*, pp. 177ff.
46 Ibid., p. 180.
47 James Tully, *A Discourse on Property: John Locke and his Adversaries*.
48 John Locke, *An Essay concerning Human Understanding*, book 2, ch. 27, s. 16, quoted in Waldron, *Right to Private Property*, p. 179.
49 Waldron, *Right to Private Property*, p. 179.
50 Locke, *Second Treatise*, s. 173.
51 Ibid., s. 123.
52 Ibid., s. 173.
53 W. Paschal Larkin, *Property in the Eighteenth Century: with Special Reference to England and Locke*, p. 53.
54 Thomas Overton, *An Arrow against All Tyrants* (12 Oct. 1646), quoted in Macpherson, *Possessive Individualism*, p. 140.
55 See Carol M. Rose, ' "Takings" and the practices of property: property as wealth, property as "propriety" ', in Rose, *Property and Persuasion*, pp. 58–9.
56 Locke, *Second Treatise*, s. 102.
57 Ibid., s. 103.
58 Ibid., ss. 36, 102.
59 Held, *Models of Democracy*, p. 48.
60 Seyla Benhabib, 'The generalized and the concrete other', pp. 83–4.
61 Jean-Jacques Rousseau, *Discourse on the Origin and Foundations of Inequality (Second Discourse)*, pp. 146–7.
62 Locke, *Second Treatise*, s. 34.
63 Larkin, *Property in the Eighteenth Century*, p. 77.

64 Arlene Saxonhouse, 'On Aristotle', p. 35.
65 *The Lawes Resolutions of Woman's Rights* (1632), cited in Antonia Fraser, *The Weaker Vessel*, pp. 10–11.
66 Norma Basch, *In the Eyes of the Law: Women, Marriage and Property in Nineteenth-Century New York*, p. 17.
67 Blackstone, *Commentaries*, cited in Basch, *Eyes of the Law*, pp. 48–9.
68 Ibid., p. 50.
69 The Connecticut jurist Tapping Reeve stated the ancient principles in his compilation, *The Law of Baron and Feme, of Parent and Child, of Guardian and Ward, of Master and Servant, and of the Powers of Courts of Chancery*, quoted in Salmon, *Women and the Law of Property*, p. 42.
70 Blackstone, *Commentaries*, cited in Basch, *Eyes of the Law*, p. 52.
71 In the US as of 1980, common-law property systems obtained in forty-two states and community of property in eight. See Lenore J. Weitzman, *The Marriage Contract*.
72 Basch, *Eyes of the Law*, p. 18.
73 Quoted in Salmon, *Women and the Law of Property*, p. 55.
74 *Lawes Resolutions*, cited in Eleanor Flexner, *Century of Struggle: The Woman's Rights Movement in the United States*, pp. 7–8.
75 Fraser, *Weaker Vessel*, p. 5.
76 Lawrence Stone, *Road to Divorce: England 1530–1987*.
77 Basch, *Eyes of the Law*, p. 27.
78 Stone, *Road to Divorce*, p. 67.
79 Scotland retained the witnessed verbal contract as a valid form of marriage until the nineteenth century, and at the same time allowed women comparatively full property rights in civil law. This suggests that contract, properly interpreted, goes hand in hand with female property rights; it is coverture which is inimical to them. Ironically, the Scottish judges bemoaned this property regime as uncivilized: 'What was the law of all Europe, while Europe was barbarous, is now the law of Scotland only, when Europe has become civilized' (Lord Hailes, 1772, quoted in Stone, *Road to Divorce*, p. 171).
80 Salmon, *Women and the Law of Property*.
81 Ruth Barnes Moynihan, Cynthia Russett and Laurie Crumpacker (eds), *Second to None: A Documentary History of American Women*, pp. 33–4. This analysis is also borne out by Margaret Fuller's report on Chippewa marriage customs in her *Summer on the Lakes in 1843* (excerpted in Margaret Fuller, *Woman in the Nineteenth Century*, pp. 150–203).
82 Moynihan, Russett and Crumpacker, *Second to None*, p. 34.
83 William Wood, *New England's Prospect*, reproduced in Moynihan, Russett and Crumpacker, *Second to None*, pp. 35–8, at p. 38.
84 William Thompson, *Appeal of One Half the Human Race, Women, Against the pretensions of the other half, Men, To Retain Them in Political, and Thence in Civil and Domestic, Slavery*, pp. 55–6, original emphasis. Pateman rightly notes, 'Thompson makes the very important point that no husband can divest himself of the power he obtains through marriage. I have found in discussing this subject that confusion easily arises because we all know of marriages where the husband does not use, and would not dream of using, his remaining powers, and it thus seems that feminist criticism is (today, at least) very wide of the mark. But this is to confuse particular examples of married couples with the *institution* of marriage. Thompson carefully draws a distinction between the actions of any one husband and the power embodied in the structure of the relation between "husband" and "wife" ' (*The Sexual Contract*, p. 158, original emphasis). Yet

Pateman seems to miss the implication of Thompson's 'audacious falsehood' – that the marriage contract is not properly a contract at all.

85 Waldron, *Right to Private Property*, p. 4.

86 G. W. F. Hegel, *The Philosophy of Right*, s. 49A, p. 237, cited in Waldron, *Right to Private Property*, p. 130.

87 For a further elaboration of this argument, see Nadine Taub and Elizabeth M. Schneider, 'Women's subordination and the role of the law', in Weisberg, *Feminist Legal Theory*, pp. 9–21.

Chapter 4   Property and Moral Self-Development

1 I owe this distinction to Alan Ryan's *Property and Political Theory*. Ryan sites the instrumental tradition primarily in Locke, but finds its reverberations continuing up to and including John Stuart Mill. The self-developmental tradition, he asserts, begins in Rousseau, moves on through Hegel, and ends in Marx. The tension between the two viewpoints is not absolute: Locke contains elements of the *developmental* model in so far as his theistic assumptions predispose him towards seeing property as *instrumental* in enabling humanity to flourish according to God's plan.

2 William E. Connolly notes how central the idea of being at home is to Hegel, echoing a similar remark by Nietzsche: 'German philosophy as a whole – Leibniz, Kant, Hegel, Schopenhauer, to name the greatest – is the most fundamental form of romanticism and homesickness there ever has been . . . One is no longer at home anywhere: at last one longs back for that place in which alone one can be at home: the *Greek* world' (Connolly, *Political Theory and Modernity*, p. 135, quoting Friedrich Nietzsche, *The Will to Power*).

3 Connolly, *Political Theory and Modernity*, p. 174.

4 G. W. F. Hegel, *Hegel's Philosophy of Right*, 164A. In Hegel scholarship the convention 'A' (occasionally 'Z', for *Zusatz*) denotes the additions at the end of the *Philosophy of Right*, of more doubtful authenticity than the body of the text. The symbol 'R' after a section number denotes the remarks following the section in the main text. Further quotations from the *Philosophy of Right* will be cited in the main body of my text according to these conventions, for example, *PR*, 164A.

5 For anti-Hegelian feminist critiques, see, for example, Carole Pateman, *The Sexual Contract*, pp. 173–84; Susan Moller Okin, *Women in Western Political Thought*, pp. 282–5; and Jean Bethke Elshtain, *Public Man, Private Woman*, pp. 170–83. A more ambivalent attitude towards Hegel is found in Genevieve Lloyd, *The Man of Reason: 'Male' and 'Female' in Western Philosophy*, pp. 70–93.

6 Susan M. Easton, 'Hegel and feminism', p. 34.

7 Lloyd, *Man of Reason*, p. 93.

8 Christine di Stefano, *Configurations of Masculinity: A Feminist Perspective on Modern Political Theory*. A similarly psychoanalytical, non-literal, and apolitical approach to the 'instructive fiction' of the master–servant analogy is taken by Judith Butler in *Subjects of Desire: Hegelian Reflections in Twentieth-Century France*, pp. 43ff. Lloyd (in *Man of Reason*, pp. 91ff.) likewise interprets the master–servant struggle psychologically, as being about developing (male) self–consciousness, the transcendence of the servant's immersion in life and fear of death. Beauvoir follows Sartre in conceiving the struggle as being

about who shall play the role of the looker, who the object. Easton does also make a brief mention of one political factor – the centrality of ideology – which can be extracted from the master–servant relationship ('Hegel and feminism', p. 42). She also touches on the problem of political obligation in her discussion of the slave's apparent consent to his own victimization, and the countervailing argument that 'precisely because Hegel attributes slavery to the will of an individual or people, he opens up the possibility of a dramatic change in social relationships through the power of rational reflection' (p. 46).

9 The most informed and extensive 'mainstream' discussion of Hegel and feminism is found in Harry Brod, *Hegel's Philosophy of Politics: Idealism, Identity, and Modernity*, pp. 174–9. At p. 175 Brod distinguishes between 'feminist Hegelianism', the growing body of writing on Hegel from feminist perspectives, and 'Hegelian feminism', the sympathetic application of the Hegelian framework to feminist concerns, which is closer to my own project. There are subsections on divorce and the family in Michael Hardimon's *Hegel's Social Philosophy: The Project of Reconciliation*, and one on 'man and woman' in Allen W. Wood's *Hegel's Ethical Thought*. Connolly's two chapters on Hegel in his *Political Theory and Modernity* contain an interesting theoretical discussion of gender difference as a fundamental expression of the ontology of Spirit, but nothing on applied questions such as property. Gender is conspicuous by its absence in the treatments of Hegel and property by Ryan, *Property and Political Theory*, and Jeremy Waldron, *The Right to Private Property*.

10 Connolly, *Political Theory and Modernity*, p. 117.

11 This criticism is made particularly forcefully by Elshtain.

12 *Philosophy of Right*, 163A, 176A. See also Hegel's *Vorlesungen über Rechtsphilosophie*, vol. 4, p. 434. These transcriptions of Hegel's lectures leave a more sympathetic and rounded impression of Hegel than does the frequently obscure style of the better-known texts, as is also true with Kant's lectures. As Allen Wood says of Hegel, 'all his major writings after 1817 were merely outlines to be lectured upon' (*Hegel's Ethical Thought*, p. xiv). This includes *The Philosophy of Right* (1821).

13 Wood makes a similar point (*Hegel's Ethical Thought*, p. 245), likening Hegel's view of women's 'separate moral voice' to that of Nancy Chodorow and Carol Gilligan. However, on p. 246 he wrongly implies that Gilligan accepts the idea that the separate voice is only and always found in women. Wood is right, however, to note that although Hegel privileges reflection, he locates reflection in a context of 'feelings, dispositions and personal relationships' (p. 246).

14 Brod, *Hegel's Philosophy of Politics*, pp. 31ff.

15 Hegel, *Philosophy of Right*, preface, p. 2: 'the whole, like the formation of its parts, rests on the logical spirit. It is also from this point of view above all that I should like my book to be taken and judged. What we have to do with is philosophical *science*, and in such science content is essentially bound up with form. We may of course hear from those who seem to be taking a profound view that the form is something external and indifferent to the subject-matter, that the latter alone is important . . .'

16 Kathy E. Ferguson, *The Man Question: Visions of Subjectivity in Feminist Theory*, p. 41. Ferguson explicitly identifies the Hegelian subject as male, but she also remarks that Hegel 'frames the central issues of modern subjectivity with and against which feminism works' (p. 40).

17 Wood, *Hegel's Ethical Thought*, p. 23. I have simplified somewhat in this sentence by collapsing personality and subjectivity. In *PR*, 35A Hegel distinguishes between the two in these terms: '"Person" is essentially different from

"subject", since "subject" is only the possibility of personality; every living thing of any sort is a subject. A person, then, is a subject aware of this subjectivity, since in personality it is of myself alone that I am aware.'

18 Thomas Hobbes, *De Cive*, quoted in David Held, 'Introduction: central perspectives on the modern state', p. 5.

19 I owe this insight to Jeremy Waldron's similar point on p. 302 of *The Right to Private Property*.

20 Hegel, *Vorlesungen*, p. 608. It is a tempting piece of speculation to identify this 'rich rabble' attitude with current American right-wing anger at everything to do with government.

21 Thomas Hill Green, 'Liberal legislation and freedom of contract', cited in Waldron, *Right to Private Property*, p. 316.

22 See Waldron, *Right to Private Property*, p. 351, for further elaboration of this point.

23 Ibid., p. 356.

24 G. W. F. Hegel, *Nurnberger Propadeutik* (1808–11), cited in Wood, *Hegel's Ethical Thought*, p. 87.

25 G. W. F. Hegel, *Phenomenology of Spirit*, 192–3, cited in Wood, *Hegel's Ethical Thought*, p. 88.

26 Connolly, *Political Theory and Modernity*, p. 96.

27 Pateman, *The Sexual Contract*, p. 178.

28 Lloyd, *Man of Reason*, pp. 91–2.

29 Waldron, *Right to Private Property*, pp. 312–13. The first sentence is slightly confusing, implying that Locke believes the property I have worked on literally contains my physical substance. That would give credence to the common view that I mix my physical substance with the object of my property claim, which Waldron is at pains to refute elsewhere. What Waldron means here, I think, is that the material on which I have worked comes to embody my personhood in the shape of my aims and intentions.

30 Pateman, *The Sexual Contract*, pp. 122–3.

31 Julia Kristeva, *Revolution in Poetic Language*.

32 'For government is an expedient by which men would fain succeed in letting one another alone; and, as has been said, when it is most expedient, the governed are most let alone by it' (Henry David Thoreau, 'Essay on civil disobedience' (1849), p. 110).

33 Waldron, *Right to Private Property*, p. 358.

34 Connolly, *Political Theory and Modernity*, p. 117.

35 The epitome of 'real' contract is exchange; Hegel differentiates it from 'formal' contract such as gift, 'where only one of the parties acquires property or surrenders it' (*PR*, 76A).

36 Pateman, *The Sexual Contract*, p. 179.

37 Ibid., p. 173.

38 Ibid., p. 181.

39 G. W. F. Hegel, 'Love', cited in Seyla Benhabib, 'On Hegel, women and irony', p. 137.

40 Pateman, *The Sexual Contract*, p. 175.

41 Ibid., p. 177.

42 For example, Wood, *Hegel's Ethical Thought*, p. 245.

43 Easton takes a different, non-literal view: 'Antigone . . . in burying her brother, protects him from death and dishonour and rescues him from subjectivity' ('Hegel and feminism', p. 38).

44 George Lukács, *The Young Hegel*, p. 121.

45 Hegel, *Phenomenology of Spirit*, 475.
46 Ibid., 457.
47 Ibid., 276.
48 Wood, *Hegel's Ethical Thought*, p. 98.
49 Benhabib, 'On Hegel, women and irony', at p. 133, mentions as evidence the remarks scattered throughout the *Lectures on the Philosophy of History* about Chinese concubinage, Egyptian sexual divisions of labour, and other matters of custom concerning women in various cultures. Easton, 'Hegel and feminism', pp. 40–1, likewise cites the mention in the *Lectures* of female rulers in the Congo and woman soldiers in Dahomey.
50 Here I summarize what is a highly complex and heated debate in Hegelian scholarship. My conclusions are similar to those Waldron draws on pp. 344–6 of *The Right to Private Property*. Other scholars see Hegel as more concerned to justify existing institutions; some see him as a frank apologist for Prussian bureaucratic rule.
51 Ryan, *Property and Political Theory*, p. 2.
52 Hegel, *Vorlesungen*, cited in Wood, *Hegel's Ethical Thought*, p. 251.
53 Benhabib, 'On Hegel, women and irony', p. 134.
54 Hardimon, *Hegel's Social Philosophy*, p. 2.
55 Ibid., p. 186.
56 Ibid., p. 250, citing *PR*, 238A.
57 Ibid., p. 189.
58 Benhabib, 'On Hegel, women and irony', pp. 132–3.
59 Brod, *Hegel's Philosophy of Politics*, p. 107.
60 G. W. F. Hegel, *Phenomenology of Spirit*, 478.
61 There is a rather ambiguous reference to provision for divorced women through community of property in the original marriage settlement in *PR*, 172R, but none to maintenance.
62 See Susan Phinney Conrad, *Perish the Thought: Intellectual Women in Romantic America 1830–1860*; Barbara Welter, *Dimity Convictions: The American Woman in the Nineteenth Century*; Ann Douglas, *The Feminization of American Culture*; and Donna Dickenson, *Margaret Fuller: Writing a Woman's Life*.
63 I realize that it is somewhat anachronistic to use the term 'feminist' for a period when such concerns were more often referred to as 'the Woman Question', but, as many other feminist writers have remarked, the alternatives seem too cumbersome for comfort.
64 Maire Cross and Tim Gray, *The Feminism of Flora Tristan*, p. 51. In this respect, too, Tristan makes an interesting adjunct to Hegel, whose political philosophy is so often presented in terms of lessons learned from the French Revolution.
65 Michael Ryan, *Prostitution in London, with a Comparative View of that of Paris and New York . . . with an Account of the Nature and Treatment of the Various Diseases* (London, 1839).
66 Lynda Nead, *Myths of Sexuality: Representations of Women in Victorian Britain*, pp. 110–11.
67 Flora Tristan, *Promenades dans Londres* (1842), pp. 81–2.
68 Cross and Gray, *Feminism of Flora Tristan*, p. 51, original emphasis.
69 Tristan, *Promenades dans Londres*, p. 82.
70 Bram Dijkstra, *Idols of Perversity: Fantasies of Feminine Evil in Fin-de-Siècle Culture*, p. 3.
71 See, for example, John D'Emilio and Estelle B. Freedman, *Intimate Matters: A History of Sexuality in America*, pp. 41ff.; Dickenson, *Margaret Fuller*,

pp. 151ff.; Nancy F. Cott, 'Passionlessness: an interpretation of Victorian sexual ideology, 1790–1850'; and Peter Gay, *The Bourgeois Experience: Victoria to Freud*, vol. 1: *Education of the Senses*.
72 Margaret Fuller, *Woman in the Nineteenth Century*, p. 99.
73 Waldron, *Right to Private Property*, p. 389.

Chapter 5 Labour, Alienation and Reproduction

1 See also James Grunebaum, *Private Ownership*.
2 Similarly, Western feminists have been criticized for exporting the assumption that paid work is liberating to the Third World (see, for example, Jessie Bernard, *The Female World from a Global Perspective*). I shall go on to show that this assumption is not necessarily feminist as such, but more typical of Engels – or Hegel, perhaps. Indeed, it has taken a feminist analysis to show why paid work has not necessarily liberated *First* World women.
3 The best account of early nineteenth-century utopian socialism and feminism remains that by Barbara Taylor in *Eve and the New Jerusalem: Socialism and Feminism in the Nineteenth Century*.
4 One reason why this distinction is rough is that Hegel and Marx conceptualize property differently. Generally Marx operates with quite a narrow focus on private property of the means of production – excluding non-productive wealth (which would include household goods, if reproduction is distinguished from production).
5 I use the term entitlements very broadly here; 'rights' would be inappropriate in the Marxist context, but it can be argued that there is an underlying moral position about labour and desert in Marx. (On the question of Marx's ethical presuppositions, see Stephen Lukes, *Marxism and Morality*.) For the time being I accept the distinction introduced by Waldron in relation to Locke, between property in the body and property in the person, and generally confine my discussion to the latter (though see note 46). I will return to the distinction in chapter 7.
6 Partha Dasgupta, *An Inquiry into Well-Being and Destitution*.
7 'Assetless' refers primarily to lack of assets in *productive* property. What women often own instead is jewellery, Dasgupta points out (ibid., p. 241); as men will only part with land in extreme crisis, so women with their jewellery – to which they probably have an attachment as an heirloom or wedding present, as men do to plots of land that they have tilled since boyhood. But jewellery cannot produce further wealth; nor do men labour on it without hope of making it their property, as women do with land.
8 Anne Marie Goetz, 'Feminism and the claim to know: contradictions in feminist approaches to women in development'.
9 See, for example, Sandra L. Bartky, 'On psychological oppression', and Ann Foreman, *Femininity as Alienation: Women and the Family in Marxism and Psychoanalysis*. Michèle Barrett, in *Women's Oppression Today*, also foregrounds psychological factors as well as traditional Marxist concepts. Ann Ferguson considers whether contemporary high-technology childbirth is a form of 'alienated labour' (in *Sexual Democracy: Women, Oppression, and Revolution*).
10 Carole Pateman, *The Sexual Contract*, ch. 5.
11 Karl Marx, *Early Writings*, p. 156n, cited in Alison M. Jaggar, *Feminist Politics and Human Nature*, p. 221.

12 Karl Marx and Friedrich Engels, 'Manifesto of the Communist Party', p. 50.
13 Karl Marx and Friedrich Engels, *The German Ideology*, part 1, p. 52. As Jaggar points out (*Feminist Politics and Human Nature*, p. 218), all that is consistent in Marx and Engels's terminology of husband–wife relations is that the relation is one of dominance and subordination. Alternatively, the wife is presented as the proletarian and the husband as the bourgeois in a metaphor 'borrowed' from Flora Tristan. The anthropological links between wife and slave are discussed in Gerda Lerner, *The Creation of Patriarchy*, and in Deborah Fahy Bryceson, 'African women hoe cultivators', in Bryceson (ed.), *Women Wielding the Hoe: Lessons from Rural Africa for Feminist Theory and Development*, p. 15.
14 Friedrich Engels, *The Origin of the Family, Private Property and the State*, pp. 137–8.
15 Besides Jaggar, see also Bonnie Fox (ed.), *Hidden in the Household: Women's Domestic Labour under Capitalism*, and Ellen Malos, *The Politics of Housework*. Engels is less vulnerable to this criticism in that he advocated a system of public provision of care and education for children in *Origin of the Family*.
16 Engels, *Origin of the Family*, p. 121.
17 For example, the usual conditions under which contracts may be broken are invalid; nor may any payment take place. As Jaggar points out, courts have overturned contracts by husbands to pay wives for their domestic services (Jaggar, *Feminist Politics and Human Nature*, p. 217, citing Muriel Nazzari, 'The significance of present-day changes in the institution of marriage', *Review of Political Economics* 12:2 (1980), pp. 63–75; Nazzari in turn refers to 'Marriage contracts for support and services', *NYU Law Review* (Dec. 1974), p. 1166).
18 Christine Delphy, *Close to Home: A Materialist Analysis of Women's Oppression*.
19 Dasgupta, *Inquiry into Well-Being and Destitution*, p. 242.
20 See Bridget O'Laughlin, 'Myth of the African family in the world of development', p. 70.
21 See, for example, Vina Mazumdar and Kumud Sharma, 'Sexual division of labor and the subordination of women: a reappraisal from India'; Maria Mies, *Lacemakers in Narsapur: Indian Housewives Produce for the World Market*, and *Patriarchy and Accumulation on a World Scale: Women in the International Division of Labor*. Although Mies is a Marxist feminist, she sees domestic labour as creating a surplus for the capitalist (who need not bear the full costs of workers' reproduction) and for male workers (who retain the pay packet while women only retain responsibility for allocating food). Particularly where women are secluded, they cannot be formally integrated into the 'productive' sphere because they cannot take part in market transactions.
22 Carol M. Rose, *Property and Persuasion: Essays on the History, Theory and Rhetoric of Ownership*, p. 19.
23 Although Ester Boserup (*Women's Role in Economic Development*) presents this situation as general throughout sub-Saharan Africa, other more recent writers have pointed out that it does not apply to some countries, Ghana for example (see Takyiwaa Manuh, 'Ghana: women in the public and informal sectors under the economic recovery programme'). Ghanaian customary law recognizes women's exclusive right to separate property and supports their right to work; the man is expected to contribute to his wives' and children's upkeep, but until the Intestate Succession Act of 1985 a wife had no claim on her husband's resources after his death.

24 Jaggar, *Feminist Politics and Human Nature*, p. 216.
25 Chandra Talpade Mohanty, 'Introduction: cartographies of struggle: Third World women and the politics of feminism', in Mohanty, Ann Russo and Lourdes Torres (eds), *Third World Women and the Politics of Feminism*.
26 Donna J. Haraway, *Simians, Cyborgs and Women: The Reinvention of Nature*, pp. 192–3, citing Mohanty, Russo and Torres, *Third World Women and the Politics of Feminism*.
27 Goetz, 'Feminism and the claim to know', p. 141.
28 Monica Lazreg, 'Feminism and difference: the perils of writing as a woman on women in Algeria'.
29 Michael J. Trebilcock, *The Limits of Freedom of Contract*, p. 28.
30 The first position is taken by Carmel Shalev in *Birth Power: The Case for Surrogacy*, and by Martha A. Field in *Surrogate Motherhood: The Legal and Human Issues*; the second by Christine Overall in *Human Reproduction: Principles, Practice, Policies*, and by Elizabeth Anderson in 'Is women's labor a commodity?' I return to contract motherhood in chapter 7, where I discuss property in the body in more detail.
31 Karl Marx, *Grundrisse: Foundations of the Critique of Political Economy*, p. 611.
32 I do not mean that all feminist writers have made this claim: it would have been eschewed by 'domestic feminists' such as Catharine Beecher, for example. But it is a powerful argument in Mary Wollstonecraft, Margaret Fuller and innumerable others.
33 Karl Marx, *Capital*, p. 351.
34 Pateman, *The Sexual Contract*, p. 134.
35 Ibid., p. 142, original emphasis.
36 Marx, *Early Writings*, p. 125.
37 Marx and Engels, *German Ideology*, part 1, p. 52.
38 Trebilcock, *Limits of Freedom of Contract*, p. 24. Margaret Radin, in 'Market inalienability', expands on this argument, illustrating how the internal and subjective can be infiltrated by the external and objective in a manner which undermines both liberal and Hegelian theory.
39 Marx and Engels, *German Ideology*, part 2, p. 117.
40 Ibid., p. 102.
41 Jaggar, *Feminist Politics and Human Nature*, p. 216.
42 Karl Marx, *The Economic and Philosophic Manuscripts of 1844*, quoted in Nancy C. M. Hartsock, *Money, Sex and Power: Toward a Feminist Historical Materialism*, p. 5.
43 Christopher J. Berry, *The Idea of a Democratic Community*, p. 23.
44 I do not mean to imply that this elementary insight has not been noticed by other feminists. Shulamith Firestone called for 'a dialectic of sex' as far back as 1970 (*The Dialectic of Sex: The Case for Feminist Revolution*). But Firestone's biological determinism deflected her inquiry down a path which later feminists regarded as unproductive and which may even have discredited the entire notion of a 'dialectic of sex'. As Michèle Barrett wrote in 1988, 'In some ways, the intellectual project of reconciling a feminist and a Marxist understanding of the social world could be said to have been shelved – it was abandoned rather than resolved' (introduction to 1988 edn of *Women's Oppression Today*). This, along with the lure of postmodernism, may help to explain why so many feminist theorists of Marxist sympathies abandoned conventional Marxist terrain for 'cultural materialism': see Donna Landry and Gerald Maclean, *Materialist Feminisms*, pp. 64ff., on the 1980s substitution of values in

signifiers and discourse for the 1970s concern with value in domestic labour. This 'cultural materialism' still saw itself as materialist because language is material, but it seems a long way from the concerns of the present book. A systematic attempt to revive a more strictly economic historical materialism and to incorporate the notion that male dominance is historically specific rather than universal can be found in Ferguson, *Sexual Democracy*.

45 Catharine A. MacKinnon, *Toward a Feminist Theory of the State*, p. 3.
46 In MacKinnon's materialist context, I think 'property in the body' rather than 'person' is the right terminology.
47 MacKinnon, *Feminist Theory of the State*, p. 11. MacKinnon concedes that 'Engels, by contrast, considered women's status a social phenomenon that needed explanation. He just failed to explain it' (ibid.). She also contends that 'beneath Engels' veneer of dialectical dynamism lies a static, positivistic materialism that reifies woman socially to such an extent that her status might as well have been considered naturally determined' (ibid.).
48 Ibid., p. 15.
49 Ibid., p. 122.
50 Ibid., p. 124.
51 Ibid., p. 131.
52 Preface by Diana Leonard to Delphy, *Close to Home*, p. 10.
53 Hartsock, *Money, Sex and Power*, p. 10.
54 See Ferguson, *Sexual Democracy*, p. 32, for further elaboration of this inconsistency.
55 In addition to Delphy, MacKinnon also cites Juliet Mitchell, *Woman's Estate*; Lise Vogel, 'The earthly family', p. 28; and Eli Zaretsky, 'Socialism and feminism III: socialist politics and the family'.
56 MacKinnon, *Feminist Theory of the State*, p. 65.
57 Christine Delphy, 'The main enemy', ch. 4 in *Close to Home*.
58 Lerner, *Creation of Patriarchy*; Mies, *Patriarchy and Accumulation*.
59 H. J. J. Reynders, 'The geographical income of the Bantu areas in South Africa'.
60 A recent UK Budget afforded tax relief for workplace nurseries but not for any other form of paid childcare.
61 Leonore Davidoff, 'The rationalization of housework', p. 83.
62 Delphy, *Close to Home*, p. 60.
63 Delphy, 'Introduction to the collection', in *Close to Home*, p. 18.
64 Christine Delphy, 'The main enemy', p. 63.
65 *Shariah*, Islamic religious law, does not require continued maintenance of a divorced wife, beyond the requirement for three months' support during the *iddah* waiting period to see if the woman is carrying her ex-husband's child. This is because marriage is a contract, and divorce terminates any contractual obligation. However, the divorcing husband is required to return his wife's dowry. See Peter J. Awn, 'Indian Islam: The Shah Bono affair'. For the Jewish marriage contract, see David Davidovitch, *The Ketuba: Jewish Marriage Contracts through the Ages*.
66 Boserup, *Women's Role in Economic Development*, p. 41.
67 See the essays in the volume edited by Deborah Fahy Bryceson, *Women Wielding the Hoe*.
68 An exception is Daisy Dwyer and Judith Bryce (eds), *A Home Divided: Women and Income in the Third World*.
69 See also Mazumdar and Sharma, 'Sexual division'; Simi Afonja, 'Changing patterns of gender stratification in West Africa'.

70 Ester Boserup, 'Economic change and the roles of women', p. 14. The situation is complicated, however, in countries such as South Africa, where tribal systems coexist with civil law. Sandra Burman points out that the effect of women's entry into paid labour is usually to deprive the wife of the protections of customary law but to leave the husband with control of her business transactions ('Divorce and the disadvantaged: African women in urban South Africa', p. 124).

71 See, for example, Maria Sagrario Floro, 'The dynamics of economic change and gender roles: export cropping in the Philippines'. Women have been greatly affected throughout the South in recent years by Structural Adjustment Programmes (SAPs) comprising a laissez-faire 'free market' ideology, less government intervention, production for export rather than local consumption, higher interest rates, and/or wage restraint. The most empowering effect on women of SAPs in the Philippines is the new chance of cash income, but while women now do less unpaid farmwork and more labour for wages, this has not always translated to more paid work and a better bargaining position within the family. Indeed, where SAPs have also spelled a shift to piecework rates for male agricultural labourers, men rely on their wives' extra 'help' to bring their pay up to prior levels, but husbands still regard the wages as theirs to control.

72 Delphy, 'The main enemy', p. 68.

73 Ibid., p. 69.

74 See also Susan Moller Okin, *Justice, Gender and the Family*, and Lenore J. Weitzman, *The Divorce Revolution: The Unexpected Social and Economic Consequences for Women and Children in America*. Okin points out that 'By far the most important property acquired in the average marriage is its career assets, or human capital, the vast majority of which is likely to be invested in the husband . . . It takes the average divorced man only about *ten months* to earn as much as the couple's entire net worth' (p. 163, citing Weitzman, pp. 53 and 60). However, Carol Brown hypothesizes that men have lost interest in supporting children because children now represent a net loss rather than an economic asset ('Mothers, fathers and children: from private to public patriarchy').

75 S. Jayaweera, 'Structural adjustment policies, industrial development and women in Sri Lanka'.

76 Charlotte Bunch and Roxanna Carrillo, 'Feminist perspectives on women in development'.

77 Judith Tendler, *What Happened to Poverty Alleviation?*

78 Irene Tinker, 'The making of a field: advocates, practitioners and scholars', ch. 3 in Tinker (ed.), *Persistent Inequalities: Women and World Development*, p. 53, citing Helen I. Safa, 'Women and change in Latin America'.

79 This line of argument is suggested by Hartsock, *Money, Sex and Power*, p. 232.

Chapter 6   Another Sort of Subject?

1 Ann Ferguson, *Sexual Democracy: Women, Oppression, and Revolution*, esp. ch. 5, 'A feminist aspect theory of the self', pp. 14ff.

2 Adrienne Rich, *Of Women Born*.

3 Kathy E. Ferguson, *The Man Question: Visions of Subjectivity in Feminist Theory*, p. 53.

4 Judith Butler, *Subjects of Desire: Hegelian Reflections in Twentieth-Century France*, p. 45.
5 Ibid., p. 44.
6 Ferguson, *Man Question*, pp. 40–1.
7 Luce Irigaray, 'L'invisible de la chair' (Invisible of the flesh), lecture on Maurice Merleau-Ponty, *Le visible et l'invisible*, in Irigaray, *Éthique de la différence sexuelle*, p. 143, translation mine.
8 Some deconstructionist analyses, such as Derrida's, also question the category 'woman', although many commentators would be unwilling to call Derridean deconstructionism feminist. Derrida himself has denounced feminism as reifying the category of woman and entrapping theory in discredited 'objective' and ironically dualist formulations. Although many commentators stress Irigaray's debt to Derrida, this disagreement over how genuine sexual difference really is appears to be a crucial dissimilarity between their interpretations.
9 Ferguson, *Man Question*, p. 14.
10 Ibid., p. 37.
11 For the criticism that Irigaray is essentialist, see, for example, Janet Sayers, *Biological Politics: Feminist and Anti-feminist Perspectives*, and *Sexual Contradictions: Psychology, Psychoanalysis and Feminism*; Toril Moi, *Sexual/Textual Politics: Feminist Literary Theory*; and Lynne Segal, *Is the Future Female? Troubled Thoughts on Contemporary Feminism*.
12 Irigaray, 'L'invisible de la chair', p. 165, translation mine.
13 Luce Irigaray, 'L'universel comme médiation' (The universal as mediation), in Irigaray, *Sexes et parentés*, p. 152, translation mine.
14 Ibid.
15 Ibid., p. 154.
16 Margaret Whitford, *Luce Irigaray: Philosophy in the Feminine*, p. 33.
17 Ibid., p. 53.
18 Ibid., p. 58.
19 Margaret Fuller, *Woman in the Nineteenth Century*, pp. 75–6.
20 Whitford, *Luce Irigaray*, p. 50.
21 For Hegel, see Peter Singer, *Hegel*; for Irigaray, Whitford, *Luce Irigaray*, p. 16.
22 Ferguson, *Man Question*, p. 5.
23 William E. Connolly, *Political Theory and Modernity*, p. 123.
24 Luce Irigaray, *Le Temps de la différence: pour une révolution pacifique*.
25 See, among other instances in which Irigaray returns to the symbol of Antigone as the 'antiwoman', 'La nécessité de droits sexués' (The necessity of gendered rights), in *Sexes et parentés*, p. 14.
26 Irigaray, *Éthique de la différence sexuelle*, p. 133.
27 Whitford, *Luce Irigaray*, p. 104, original emphasis.
28 Luce Irigaray, 'L'amour de l'autre' (The love of the other), in *Éthique de la différence sexuelle*, p. 133, translation mine.
29 See, for example, 'L'amour de l'autre', p. 134: 'And if man nourishes himself, takes advantage of the maternal-feminine, consciously or unconsciously, in order to live, survive, inhabit, work, he forgets the other and his own proper becoming . . . So it is with the *tool of money* which he uses to inhabit and judge the other. But money doesn't exchange for life. It may be necessary, but it is not a substitute' (translation mine, original emphasis).
30 Irigaray, preface to *Sexes et parentés*, p. 8, translation mine.
31 Whitford, *Luce Irigaray*, p. 83, emphasis added.
32 Ibid., p. 237.
33 In addition to the *écriture feminine* school and the maternal feminists,

whom I have already mentioned, see also Carol McMillan, *Women, Reason and Nature: Some Philosophical Problems with Feminism*; and Louise Anthony and Charlotte Witt (eds), *A Mind of Her Own*. A counterblast against the denigration of reason by some feminists is offered by Martha Nussbaum in 'Feminists and philosophy', in turn critiqued by Naomi Scheman and Vance Cope-Kasten in an exchange with Nussbaum, 'Feminism and philosophy: an exchange', and by Joanna Kerr in 'Martha Nussbaum and unreasonable philosophy'.

34 Genevieve Lloyd, *The Man of Reason: 'Male' and 'Female' in Western Philosophy*, p. ix.

35 Jeremy Waldron, *The Right to Private Property*, p. 145.

36 G. W. F. Hegel, *The Phenomenology of Mind*, cited by Moira Gatens in *Feminism and Philosophy: Perspectives on Difference and Equality*, p. 7.

37 Carole Pateman, *The Sexual Contract*, p. ix.

38 As is done by Sara Ruddick in 'Remarks on the sexual politics of reason'.

39 See, among many others, David Collard, *Altruism and Economy: A Study in Non-Selfish Economics*; David Gauthier, *Moral Dealing: Contract, Ethics and Reason*; Jonathan Dancy, *Moral Reasons*; Susan L. Hurley, *Natural Reasons: Personality and Polity*; Lawrence A. Blum, *Friendship, Altruism and Morality*; and Alan Gibbard, *Wise Choices, Apt Feelings: A Theory of Normative Judgment*. A far-reaching critique of Enlightenment rationalism is offered by Alasdair MacIntyre in *After Virtue* and its sequel, *Whose Justice? Which Rationality?*; the dilemmas introduced by MacIntyre's work are considered in Jeffrey Stout, *Ethics after Babel: The Languages of Morals and Their Discontents*.

In my writings on medical ethics, I have also suggested an alternative model of rationality, one linked with personal identity. See, for example, Donna Dickenson, 'Children's informed consent to treatment: is the law an ass?', and (with David Jones), 'True wishes: philosophical and clinical approaches to children's informed consent'.

40 This alliance is discussed very ably by Karen Green in *The Woman of Reason: Feminism, Humanism and Political Thought*, at pp. 18ff. She notes that Jacques Derrida in fact describes deconstruction as a new rationalism.

41 Mary Wollstonecraft, *A Vindication of the Rights of Woman*. For a distinction between 'rationalist' and 'romantic' feminisms, see Ursula Vogel, 'Rationalism and romanticism: two strategies for women's liberation'.

42 Gatens, *Feminism and Philosophy*, p. 21. A more sympathetic portrayal of Wollstonecraft, which sees her emphasizing not only rationality but also imagination and emotion, appears in ch. 5 of Karen Green's *Woman of Reason*. It is not Wollstonecraft's notion of reason which is the Achilles' heel of her work, Green alleges, but her failure to provide for women's economic independence – her weakness on issues of property and income, one might say.

43 Lloyd, *Man of Reason*, p. xi.

44 Ibid., pp. xix, 104.

45 Ibid., p. 105.

46 Ibid.

47 Green, *Woman of Reason*, pp. 154–5.

48 Michèle le Dœuff, *Hipparchia's Choice: An Essay Concerning Women, Philosophy, etc.*, pp. 208ff.

49 Carol M. Rose, 'Women and property: gaining and losing ground', ch. 8 in *Property and Persuasion: Essays on the History, Theory and Rhetoric of Ownership*.

50　Ibid., p. 255.
51　Ferguson, *Man Question*, p. 61.
52　Stephen R. Munzer, *A Theory of Property*, p. 16.

Chapter 7　Reconstructing Property

1　Lewis Hyde, *The Gift: Imagination and the Erotic Life of Property*, ch. 6, 'A female property'.
2　Moira Gatens, 'Power, bodies and difference', p. 135.
3　Anne Phillips, 'Universal pretensions in political thought', p. 11.
4　HFEA Day Conference on Payment for Donors, St Anne's College, Oxford, 1 June 1995.
5　When I raised this point at the conference, I was told by one gynaecologist that infertile *wives* felt particularly proprietorial about their husbands' sperm, and that they would never accept free donation by their husbands to the infertile husbands of fertile women. This emotional sense of ownership may be understandable, but it is difficult to see why these wives should feel that payment of £15 a time overcomes their objections.
6　Sale of oocytes is more common in the United States; in 1991 the going rate was between $900 and $1,200 per cycle. Putting this in context, the rate for contract motherhood at that time was about $10,000 (L. R. Schover et al., 'Psychological follow-up of women evaluated as oocyte donors'; Barbara Berg, 'Listening to the voices of the infertile'). A newspaper article written in 1992 estimated average payment to oocyte donors at $1,500 to $3,000 (Paula Monarez, 'Halfway there', *Chicago Tribune*, 2 Feb., sec. 6, cited in Mary B. Mahowald, 'As if there were fetuses without women: a remedial essay', p. 209).
7　Donald Evans, 'Procuring gametes for research and therapy'; John Harris, *Wonderwoman and Superman: The Ethics of Human Biotechnology*, pp. 118–39; Gillian Lockwood, 'Donating life: The practical and ethical problems of gamete donation'. Lockwood's objections to gamete donation are twofold: that the risks of oocyte donation are so considerable that we should not allow anyone to be so altruistic, and that abuses of the altruistic system for eggs already occur. It is hard to see why selling gametes gets round the risk question; indeed, it opens up the possibility of rank exploitation if clinics are effectively paying gamete providers to shoulder risks which are known to be unacceptably high. The second issue is more troubling, and Lockwood does offer some examples of real abuse from her own clinical experience, such as the pressure put on one woman to donate eggs to the wife of a business partner in repayment of her husband's debt. But again, if the clinic pays the woman for her eggs, that does not eliminate the abuse; rather, the clinic is effectively paying the husband's business debts.
8　Ken Daniels, 'Assisted human reproduction: a review of the ministerial advisory committee report'.
9　Richard Titmuss, *The Gift Relationship: From Human Blood to Social Policy*.
10　Rachel Cook and Susan Golombok, 'A survey of semen donation: phase II – the view of the donors'.
11　Ian Cooke, 'Practical considerations and implications of paying gamete providers'.
12　Françoise Shenfield and S. J. Steele, 'Why gamete donors should not be paid', p. 253. See also M. J. Radin, 'Market inalienability', Glover Report, *Fertility*

and the Family; and M. A. Ryan, 'The argument for unlimited procreative liberty: a feminist critique'.

13 Lockwood, 'Donating life'.

14 Hyde, *The Gift*, pp. 101ff.

15 It is interesting that New Zealand has opted not only for non-commercialized gamete donation, but also for identifiable semen donors. See Daniels, 'Assisted human reproduction'.

16 William Blackstone, *Commentaries on the Laws of England* (1766), p. 2 in 1979 edn.

17 The better-known term 'surrogacy' has fallen out of favour because it prejudices the matter by implying that the woman who carries and gives birth to the baby (the gestational mother) is not the real mother unless she is also the genetic mother. However, 'contract motherhood' has disadvantages, too, if the arrangement is not a conventional contract: for example, a sister bearing a child for love, not money. Many recent writers prefer the term 'gestational mother', but I have chosen 'contract motherhood' to highlight the applications of my discussion of contract elsewhere in the book.

18 The wife or partner of the contracting father should also be considered, of course, although many state laws prohibit her from being a party to the contract. This is itself illuminating, particularly in jurisdictions where husbands are required to give consent to their wives' artificial insemination by donor. It implies that men own their sperm unequivocally – as we have seen in the case study on gamete provision – and that in addition to these property rights, they also have a sort of property interest in their wives' use of another man's sperm. In addition, the surrogate mother's husband, if any, *is* often required to be a party to the contract, agreeing not to form any parent-child bond with the expected infant and to facilitate the child's transfer to the genetic father. This may imply *his* property in his wife's labour.

19 *In the Matter of Baby M*, 217 N.J. Supr. 313 (1987), affirmed in part and reversed in part, 109 N.J. 396 (1988). In this case the gestational mother was also the genetic mother. Another ruling, *Anna J. v. Mark C.* (286 Cal. Rptr. 369 [1991]), concerned a gestational mother, Anna Johnson, who wanted to keep the baby she had borne for the genetic parents, Mark and Crispina Calvert; the court ruled that the genetic progenitors were the legal parents. In a perverse display of liberal reasoning taken to the extreme, the judge asserted that it would actually be sex discrimination to deny the contracting mother the right (possessed by the genetic father) to establish her parenthood through blood testing. Because the birth mother was not the genetic mother, she was of course unable to establish genetic parenthood through blood testing. In both cases the effect was to give the baby to the genetic father; but where the gestational mother is also the genetic mother, and yet she is denied custody of the child, women's propertylessness in their own genes is the more blatant.

20 Carole Pateman, *The Sexual Contract*, pp. 209ff.

21 Elizabeth Anderson, 'Is woman's labor a commodity?', p. 177.

22 See, for example, Ruth Macklin, 'Is there anything wrong with surrogate motherhood? An ethical analysis'; and Lori Andrews, 'Surrogate motherhood: the challenge for feminists'; see also note 30 to ch. 5 above for further sources in the contract motherhood debate.

23 Rosemarie Tong has shifted from advocating that commercial surrogacy should be banned, but that non-commercial surrogacy should be allowed and its procedures amalgamated with those of adoption, to arguing that *all* forms of gestational motherhood can be dealt with under modified adoption laws. For

the earlier position, see 'The overdue death of a feminist chameleon: taking a stand on surrogacy arrangements'; for the later one, 'Feminist perspectives and gestational motherhood: the search for a unified legal focus'.

24 Joan Mahoney, 'An essay on surrogacy and feminist thought'.

25 Joan Mahoney, 'Adoption as a feminist alternative to reproductive technology'.

26 See note 19 above.

27 A similar argument is made by Lori B. Andrews in 'Alternative modes of reproduction'.

28 Here I accept John Harris's argument in *Wonderwoman and Superman*, although I disagree with Harris's assumption that gametes are unequivocally ours in the way that labour is clearly the woman's.

29 Pateman, *The Sexual Contract*, pp. 212–13.

30 See, for example, Berg, 'Listening to the voices of the infertile'.

31 Anderson, 'Is woman's labor a commodity?', pp. 168 and 175.

32 If paid surrogacy is criminalized, she has even fewer protections if she does enter into such an arrangement, even if it is only the agency making the arrangement which pays the penalty (as under the UK Surrogacy Arrangements Act of 1985).

33 Anderson, 'Is woman's labor a commodity?', p. 189.

34 See, for example, Philip Parker, 'Motivation of surrogate mothers: initial findings'. This argument is similar to that made by Carol M. Rose (discussed in ch. 6 above) in 'Women and property: gaining and losing ground', ch. 8 in *Property and Persuasion: Essays on the History, Theory and Rhetoric of Ownership*.

35 Anderson, 'Is women's labor a commodity?', p. 180.

36 However, we need to take into account how unlikely it is that contract mothers will present their motivation as purely economic, whatever the truth of the matter.

37 For example, Mahoney, 'Adoption as a feminist alternative'.

38 I use the term 'pregnant woman' rather than 'mother' throughout, in order to avoid prejudging the issue. My thanks to Frances Kamm for pointing out this caution in relation to an earlier version of this paper given at the Oxford–Mt Sinai conference, Oxford, March 1996.

39 This is the point of the famous 'violinist' hypothetical in Judith Jarvis Thomson, 'A defense of abortion'.

40 Among many possible examples, see Frank A. Chervenak, Laurence B. McCullough and Stuart Campbell, 'Is third trimester abortion justified?', p. 434.

41 I qualify this statement with 'competent' because organ donations by people with severe learning difficulties have been tentatively approved in both US and UK law, particularly when the recipient is also the donor's caretaker. For the US, see *Strunk v. Strunk*, 455 SW2d 145, 35 ALR3d 683 (Ky, 1969).

42 A much-maligned exception, reversed on appeal, was the Angela Carder enforced Caesarean case (*In re A.C.*, D.C. App. No. 87–609, April 26, 1991). Here the judge ruled that a dying woman's rights of bodily integrity were of less weight than the survival of her fetus, whose continued existence was thus presumed more certain than hers. In the event both mother and fetus died after the Caesarean. However, other cases of coerced medical treatment of pregnant women have been allowed to stand in the United States, and in Britain the Carder judgment was actually used as a favourable precedent in the *S* case, in which a woman was forced to undergo a Caesarean against her will: *In re S (Adult: Refusal of Treatment)* [1993] Fam. 123. See Cynthia R. Daniels, *At Women's Expense: State Power and the Politics of Fetal Rights*.

43 Exceptions include the child's right to sue the mother for negligent driving causing injury to it while *in utero*, and the *T* case in England – *In re T (Adult: Refusal of Treatment)* [1993] Fam. 95 – which established that the mother's right to refuse a procedure was limited if it led to the death of a viable fetus. However, in *Re F (in utero)* ([1988] Fam. 122, [1988] 2 All ER193), the court refused to ward a fetus *in utero*. In Scotland it has been suggested that the fetus might theoretically be able to petition through its 'tutor' – i.e. its father – for an injunction against threatened harm. See J. K. Mason and R. A. McCall Smith, *Law and Medical Ethics*, p. 140.

44 Mary Ann Warren, 'The moral significance of birth'.

45 This pattern was common in propaganda exchanges between the United States and the Sovet Union at the height of the Cold War: for example, the US depicted the USSR as governed by dictatorial one-party rule, and the USSR presented the US as ruled by equally undemocratic financial and military elites.

46 Although the upper limit for most terminations was brought down from twenty-eight weeks to twenty-four weeks by the Human Fertilisation and Embryology Act of 1990, revising the terms of the 1967 Abortion Act, there was concern about physicians' inability to diagnose some abnormalities until late in the second trimester or early in the third. Pregnancy may thus be lawfully terminated in England, Wales and Scoland at any gestation period if the fetus is at serious risk of grave abnormality. In 1992 a total of over 1,800 abortions were performed at twenty or more weeks, including sixty at twenty-five or more weeks. See Royal College of Obstetricians and Gynaecologists, *Termination of Pregnancy for Fetal Abnormality in England, Wales and Scotland*, p. 5.

47 *Natanson v. Kline* (Kansas 1960).

48 Stephen R. Munzer, *A Theory of Property*, p. 18.

49 Donna Dickenson and Susan Bewley, 'Abortion, relationship and property in labour: a case study'.

50 Titmuss, *Gift Relationship*.

51 The case study in Dickenson and Bewley, 'Abortion, relationship and property in labour', illustrates such a case, in which a woman pregnant with a fetus diagnosed with microencephaly in the third trimester elects to give birth because the father insists that everything will turn out all right.

52 This is the term used by Chervenak, McCullough and Campbell in 'Is third trimester abortion justified?'

53 Daniels, *At Women's Expense*.

54 Mahowald, 'As if there were fetuses', p. 203.

55 For example, Lori B. Andrews, 'My body, my property'.

56 Dorothy E. Vawter et al., *The Use of Human Fetal Tissue: Scientific, Ethical and Policy Concerns*.

57 Mahowald, 'As if there were fetuses', p. 214.

58 Recent feminist theory has taken an interest in the notion of the body as socially constructed, rather than as an object. This is to see the sex–gender divide as an ironically Cartesian dualism, thereby viewing sex and gender as indistinguishable in so far as *both* are socially constructed. Besides Irigaray, see Gatens, 'Power, bodies and difference'; R. Diprose and R. Ferrel (eds), *Cartographies: The Mapping of Bodies and Spaces*; and Gill Jaggar, 'Beyond essentialism and construction: subjectivity, corporeality and sexual difference'. This approach extends to women the sort of analysis undertaken by Michel Foucault in his *History of Sexuality*. However, the common usage of property in the body does not generally take this line of reasoning into account.

59 Jeremy Waldron, *The Right to Private Property*, p. 179, drawing on James

Tully, *A Discourse on Property: John Locke and his Adversaries*, pp. 106–8.

60 John Locke, *The Second Treatise on Civil Government*, s. 44.

61 Lenore Weitzman, *The Divorce Revolution: The Unexpected Social and Economic Consequences for Women and Children in America.*

62 Lenore Weitzman, *The Marriage Contract*, p. xv; note also Weber's concept of the 'status contract', in *Max Weber on Law in Economy and Society*, p. 105.

63 Pateman does also examine position 3 in her chapter on 'Wives, slaves and wage slaves', but concludes that no other comparison, such as slaves or workers, fully captures women's subordination (*The Sexual Contract,* p. 117).

64 James Gordley, 'Equality in exchange', cited in Rose, *Property and Persuasion,* pp. 215–16. Gordley concludes that market-based exchanges benefit most from this tendency; but of course under the domestic mode of production there is little or no market-based exchange.

65 William Thompson (with Anna Wheeler), *Appeal of One Half the Human Race, Women, Against the Pretensions of the Other Half, Men, To Retain Them in Political, and Thence in Civil and Domestic, Slavery*, pp. 55–6.

66 John Stuart Mill (with Harriet Taylor Mill), *The Subjection of Women.*

67 Margaret Fuller, *Woman in the Nineteenth Century*, p. 17.

68 Charles Brockden Brown, *Alcuin: A Dialogue.*

69 See Peter J. Awn, 'Indian Islam: the Shah Bono affair'.

70 Mary Ann Glendon, 'Marriage and the state: the withering away of marriage'.

71 Here I use the classic distinction made by Sir Henry Maine in *Ancient Law* (1931), p. 141, between status, the prevalent concept in pre-industrial society, and contract as the hallmark of more modern systems.

72 Michael J. Trebilcock, *The Limits of Freedom of Contract*, p. 44.

73 Ibid., p. 45.

74 Some US and UK jurisdictions are beginning to weight pension rights into divorce settlements, generally through an actuarial estimate at the time of divorce rather than ongoing entitlements to the husband's income after his retirement. The latter course sullies the 'clean break' principle, penalizes the ex-wife who is older than her ex-husband, and risks leaving the wife with nothing if the ex-husband dies before retirement (unless she retains some claim on his death in service benefits or life insurance).

75 Trebilcock, *Limits of Freedom of Contract*, p. 47.

76 David Davidovitch, *The Ketuba: Jewish Marriage Contracts through the Ages*, p. 112. See also Shiloh, 'Marriage and divorce in Israel', cited in Weitzman, *Marriage Contract*, p. 139; and Margaret Sokolov, 'Marriage contracts for support and services: constitutionality begins at home'.

77 *Wener v. Wener*, 59 Misc. 2d 957, 301 NYS 2d 237 (Sup Ct 1969), affirmed 35 App. Div. 2d 50, 312 NYS 2d 815 (2d Dept. 1970).

78 Émile Durkheim, *The Division of Labor in Society*, p. 1135.

79 Rose, *Property and Persuasion*, p. 35.

80 Carol M. Rose, 'Crystals and mud in property law', ch. 7 in *Property and Persuasion*, pp. 199–232.

81 For example, Catharine A. MacKinnon, *Toward a Feminist Theory of the State*; Nancy J. Hirschmann, *Rethinking Obligation: A Feminist Method for Political Theory*; Anne Phillips, *Engendering Democracy*; and Kathleen B. Jones, *Compassionate Authority: Democracy and the Representation of Women.* Whereas earlier second-wave feminism typically rejected canonical political concepts as implacably oppressive to women, there is now much more optimism about reconstructing them so as to make them work for us. In this, Pateman's rejection of contract and my reconstruction of it are quite typical,

except that property and contract are still not considered to be concepts worth reconstructing. See also Nancy Hirschmann and Christine Di Stefano (eds), *Revisioning the Political: Feminist Reconstructions of Traditional Concepts in Western Political Theory*, and Mary Lyndon Shanley and Uma Narayan, *Reconstructing Political Theory: Feminist Perspectives*. The reworking of these concepts by women of colour is also important: see, for example, Toni Morrison (ed.), *Race-ing Justice, En-Gendering Power*; Sneja Gunew and Anna Yeatman (eds), *Feminism and the Politics of Difference*; Angela Davis, *Women, Culture and Politics*; and Patricia Hill Collins, *Black Feminist Thought*.

82 Elizabeth Kiss, 'Alchemy or fool's gold? Assessing feminist doubts about rights'.

83 Karen Green, *The Woman of Reason: Feminism, Humanism and Political Thought*, p. 134. The next sentence goes on to identify a similar discouraging tendency in Irigaray.

84 This is similar to the argument made by Marilyn Strathern in 'Subject or object? Women and the circulation of valuables in Highlands New Guinea'. It is surprising how easily even the most iconoclastic feminists have accepted the identification of women with the objects of exchange. Karen Green, in *Woman of Reason*, pp. 136ff., views this as the legacy of Beauvoir, who, like Pateman and Irigaray, reads Lévi-Strauss too uncritically. See, for example, Carol M. Rose, ' "Takings" and the practices of property: property as wealth, property as "propriety" ', in Rose, *Property and Persuasion*, which seems to accept the huge generalization made by the medieval historian Howard Bloch that females simply *were* money, 'the kind of property which circulates between men' (quoting unpublished MS by Bloch). The contravening view holds that women had *more* autonomy of person and *greater* property rights in the Middle Ages, particularly during the days before monasteries succeeded in depriving nunneries of their landed property rights. See Bonnie S. Anderson and Judith P. Zinsser, *A History of Their Own: Women in Europe from Prehistory to the Present*, vol. 1; Régine Pernoud, *La Femme au temps des cathédrales* and *La Femme au temps des croisades*.

85 For a similar point about grand theory in general, see the introduction by Shanley and Narayan to *Reconstructing Political Theory*. None the less, they surmise that feminist theory has come of age in so far as it no longer reflects merely an undifferentiated critique of the mainstream.

86 Audre Lorde, 'The master's tools will never dismantle the master's house'.

Bibliography

Afonja, Simi, 'Changing patterns of gender stratification in West Africa', in Irene Tinker (ed.), *Persistent Inequalities: Women and World Development* (Oxford: Oxford University Press, 1990), pp. 198–209.

Allmark, Peter, 'Can there be an ethics of care?', *Journal of Medical Ethics* 21: 1 (Feb. 1995), pp. 19–24.

Anderson, Bonnie S. and Zinsser, Judith P., *A History of Their Own: Women in Europe from Prehistory to the Present* (2 vols, New York: Harper and Row, 1988).

Anderson, Elizabeth, 'Is women's labor a commodity?', in Anderson, *Value in Ethics and Economics* (Cambridge: Harvard University Press, 1993), pp. 168–89; rev. version of 'Is women's labor a commodity?', *Philosophy and Public Affairs* 19 (1990), pp. 71–92.

Andrews, Lori B., 'Alternative modes of reproduction', in Sherrill Cohen and Nadine Taub (eds), *Reproductive Laws for the 1990s* (Clifton, N.J.: Humana Press, 1989), pp. 380–8.

—— 'My body, my property', *Hastings Center Report* 16:5 (Oct. 1986), pp. 28–38.

—— 'Surrogate motherhood: the challenge for feminists', in Larry Gostin (ed.), *Surrogate Motherhood: Politics and Privacy* (Bloomington: Indiana University Press, 1990), pp. 167–82.

Anna J. v. Mark C., 286 Cal. Rptr. 369 (1991).

Anthony, Louise and Witt, Charlotte (eds), *A Mind of Her Own* (Boulder: Westview Press, 1992).

Arendt, Hannah, *The Human Condition* (Chicago: University of Chicago Press, 1958).

Aristotle, *The Generation of Animals*, tr. William Ogle. In *The Basic Works of Aristotle*, ed. and introd. Richard McKeon (New York: Random House, 1941).

—— *Politics*, tr. Benjamin Jowett. In *The Basic Works of Aristotle*, ed. and introd. Richard McKeon (New York: Random House, 1941).

Ashworth, Georgina, 'International linkages in the women's movement', in Peter Willetts (ed.), *Pressure Groups in the Global System: The Transnational*

Relations of Issue-Orientated Non-Governmental Organizations (London: Frances Pinter, 1982), pp. 125–47.

Awn, Peter J., 'Indian Islam: the Shah Bono affair', in John Stratton Hawley (ed.), *Fundamentalism and Gender* (Oxford: Oxford University Press, 1994), pp. 63–78.

Baier, Annette, *Postures of the Mind: Essays on Mind and Morals* (Minneapolis: University of Minnesota Press, 1985).

—— 'What do women want in a moral theory?', in Mary Jeanne Larrabee (ed.), *An Ethic of Care* (New York and London: Routledge, 1993), pp. 19–32.

Barrett, Michèle, *Women's Oppression Today: Problems in Marxist Feminist Analysis* (London: Verso, 1980); reprinted, with new introd., as *Women's Oppression Today: The Marxist Feminist Encounter* (1988).

Bartky, Sandra L., 'On psychological oppression', in Sharon Bishop and Marjorie Weinzweig (eds), *Philosophy and Women* (Belmont, Calif.: Wadsworth, 1979), pp. 33–41.

Basch, Norma, *In the Eyes of the Law: Women, Marriage and Property in Nineteenth-Century New York* (Ithaca: Cornell University Press, 1982).

Becker, Lawrence C., *Property Rights: Philosophic Foundations* (London and Boston: Routledge and Kegan Paul, 1977).

Benhabib, Seyla, 'The generalized and the concrete Other: the Kohlberg–Gilligan controversy and feminist theory', in Benhabib and Drucilla Cornell (eds), *Feminism as Critique: Essays on the Politics of Gender in Late-Capitalist Societies* (Cambridge: Polity Press, 1987), pp. 77–95.

—— 'On Hegel, women and irony', in Mary Lyndon Shanley and Carole Pateman (eds), *Feminist Interpretations and Political Theory* (Cambridge: Polity Press, 1991), pp. 129–45.

Berg, Barbara, 'Listening to the voices of the infertile', in Joan C. Callahan (ed.), *Reproduction, Ethics and the Law* (Bloomington: Indiana University Press, 1995), pp. 80–108.

Bernal, Martin, *Black Athena: The Afroasiatic Roots of Classical Civilization*, vol. 1: *The Fabrication of Ancient Greece 1785–1985* (New Brunswick: Rutgers University Press, 1987).

Bernard, Jessie, *The Female World from a Global Perspective* (Bloomington and Indianapolis: Indiana University Press, 1987).

Berry, Christopher J., *The Idea of a Democratic Community* (Brighton: Harvester, 1989).

Blackstone, William, *Commentaries on the Laws of England,* facsimile ed. (Chicago: Chicago University Press, 1979).

Bluestone, Natalie Harris, *Women and the Ideal Society: Plato's Republic and Modern Myths of Gender* (Oxford: Berg, 1987).

Blum, Lawrence A., *Friendship, Altruism and Morality* (London: Routledge and Kegan Paul, 1980).

—— 'Gilligan and Kohlberg: implications for moral theory', *Ethics* 98:3 (Apr. 1988), pp. 772–91.

Blustein, Jeffrey, *Care and Commitment: Taking the Personal Point of View* (Oxford and New York: Oxford University Press, 1991).

Bock, Gisela and James, Susan (eds), *Beyond Equality and Difference: Citizenship, Feminist Politics, and Female Subjectivity* (London: Routledge, 1992).

Boserup, Ester, 'Economic change and the roles of women', in Irene Tinker, *Persistent Inequalities: Women and World Development* (Oxford: Oxford University Press, 1990), pp. 14–26.

—— *Women's Role in Economic Development*, 2nd edn (1970; London: Earthscan, 1989).

Bradshaw, Ann, 'Yes, there is an ethics of care!', reply to Peter Allmark, *Journal of Medical Ethics* 22:1 (Feb. 1996).

Brod, Harry, *Hegel's Philosophy of Politics: Idealism, Identity, and Modernity* (Boulder and Oxford: Westview Press, 1992).

Brown, Carol, 'Mothers, fathers and children: from private to public patriarchy', in Lydia Sargent (ed.), *Women and Revolution* (Boston: South End Press, 1981), pp. 239–68.

Brown, Charles Brockden, *Alcuin: A Dialogue*, ed. Lee R. Edwards (New York, 1970).

Bryceson, Deborah Fahy (ed.), *Women Wielding the Hoe: Lessons from Rural Africa for Feminist Theory and Development* (Oxford: Berg, 1995).

Buchanan, James M., *Property as a Guarantor of Liberty* (Aldershot: Shaftesbury Papers, 1993).

Budziszewski, J., *The Resurrection of Nature: Political Theory and the Human Character* (Ithaca and London: Cornell University Press, 1986).

Bunch, Charlotte and Carrillo, Roxanna, 'Feminist perspectives on women in development', in Irene Tinker (ed.), *Persistent Inequalities: Women and World Development* (Oxford: Oxford University Press, 1990), ch. 5.

Burman, Sandra, 'Divorce and the disadvantaged: African women in urban South Africa', in Renée Hirschon (ed.), *Women and Property – Women as Property* (London: Croom Helm, 1984), pp. 117–39.

Butler, Judith, *Subjects of Desire: Hegelian Reflections in Twentieth-Century France* (New York: Columbia University Press, 1987).

Butler, Melissa A., 'Early liberal roots of feminism: John Locke and the attack on patriarchy', in Mary Lyndon Shanley and Carole Pateman (eds), *Feminist Interpretations and Political Theory* (Cambridge: Polity Press, 1991), pp. 74–94.

Cain, Patricia A., 'Feminist jurisprudence: grounding the theories', in D. Kelly Weisberg (ed.), *Feminist Legal Theory: Foundations* (Philadelphia: Temple University Press, 1993), pp. 359–70.

Caplan, Patricia, 'Cognatic descent, Islamic law and women's property on the East African coast', in Renée Hirschon (ed.), *Women and Property – Women as Property* (London: Croom Helm, 1984), pp. 23–43.

Carter, Alan, *The Philosophical Foundations of Property Rights* (Brighton: Harvester Wheatsheaf, 1989).

Chervenak, Frank A., McCullough, Laurence B. and Campbell, Stuart, 'Is third trimester abortion justified?', *British Journal of Obstetrics and Gynaecology*, 102 (June 1995), pp. 434–5.

Chodorow, Nancy, *The Reproduction of Mothering* (Berkeley: University of California Press, 1978).

Christman, John, *The Myth of Property: Towards an Egalitarian Theory of Ownership* (Oxford: Oxford University Press, 1994).

Cocks, Joan, *The Oppositional Imagination: Feminism, Critique and Political Theory* (London and New York: Routledge, 1989).

Collard, David, *Altruism and Economy: A Study in Non-Selfish Economics* (Oxford: Martin Robertson, 1978).

Collins, Patricia Hill, *Black Feminist Thought* (Boston: Unwin Hyman, 1990).

Connolly, William E., *Political Theory and Modernity* (Oxford: Blackwell, 1988).

Conrad, Susan Phinney, *Perish the Thought: Intellectual Women in Romantic America 1830–1860* (New York: Oxford University Press, 1976).

Cook, Rachel and Golombok, Susan, 'A survey of semen donation: phase II – the view of the donors', *Human Reproduction* 10:4 (1995).

Cooke, Ian, 'Practical considerations and implications of paying gamete providers', paper given at Human Fertilisation and Embryology Authority Day Conference on Payment for Donors, St Anne's College, Oxford, 1 June 1995.

Cott, Nancy F., 'Passionlessness: an interpretation of Victorian sexual ideology, 1790–1850', in Nancy F. Cott and Elizabeth H. Pleck (eds), *A Heritage of Her Own* (New York: Simon and Schuster, 1979).

Croll, Elizabeth, 'The exchange of women and property: marriage in post-revolutionary China', in Renée Hirschon (ed.), *Women and Property – Women as Property* (London: Croom Helm, 1984), pp. 44–61.

Cross, Maire and Gray, Tim, *The Feminism of Flora Tristan* (Oxford and Providence: Berg, 1992).

Dancy, Jonathan, *Moral Reasons* (Oxford: Blackwell, 1993).

Daniels, Cynthia R., *At Women's Expense: State Power and the Politics of Fetal Rights* (Cambridge: Harvard University Press, 1993).

Daniels, Ken, 'Assisted human reproduction: a review of the ministerial advisory committee report', *Otago Bioethics Report* 3:3 (Oct. 1994), p. 4.

Dasgupta, Partha, *An Inquiry into Well-Being and Destitution* (Oxford: Clarendon Press, 1993).

Davidoff, Leonore, 'The rationalization of housework', in Davidoff, *Worlds Between: Historical Perspectives on Gender and Class* (Cambridge: Polity Press, 1995).

Davidovitch, David, *The Ketuba: Jewish Marriage Contracts through the Ages*, with foreword by Cecil Roth (Tel Aviv: E. Lewin-Epstein, 1979).

Davis, Angela, *Women, Culture and Politics* (New York: Vintage, 1990).

De Beauvoir, Simone, *The Second Sex*, tr. and ed. H. M. Parshley (New York: Knopf, 1957).

Delphy, Christine, *Close to Home: A Materialist Analysis of Women's Oppression*, tr. and ed. Diana Leonard (London: Hutchinson, in assoc. with the Explorations in Feminism Collective, 1984).

D'Emilio, John and Freedman, Estelle B., *Intimate Matters: A History of Sexuality in America* (New York: Harper and Row, 1988).

Demosthenes (attributed to), *Kata Neairas* (*The Prosecution of Neaira*) (340 BCE); extracts in Peter Jones et al., *Reading Greek: Text* (Cambridge: Cambridge University Press, 1978).

Devereux, J. A., Jones, D. P. H. and Dickenson, D. L. 'Can children withhold consent to treatment?', *British Medical Journal* 306 (29 May 1993), pp. 1459–61.

Dickenson, Donna, 'Children's informed consent to treatment: is the law an ass?', guest editorial, *Journal of Medical Ethics* 20:4 (1994), pp. 205–6, 222.

—— 'Counting women in: redefining democratic politics', in Anthony McGrew (ed.), *The Transformation of Democracy? Globalization and the Post-Westphalian World Order* (Cambridge: Polity Press, 1997).

—— *George Sand: A Brave Man, the Most Womanly Woman* (Oxford: Berg, 1988).

—— *Margaret Fuller: Writing a Woman's Life* (Basingstoke: Macmillan, 1993).

—— *Moral Luck in Medical Ethics and Practical Politics* (Aldershot: Gower, 1991).

—— 'Property, particularism and moral persons', in Morwenna Griffiths and Margaret Whitford (eds), *Women Review Philosophy: New Writing by Women in Philosophy* (Nottingham: Nottingham University Press, 1996).

Dickenson, Donna and Bewley, Susan, 'Abortion, relationship and property in

214   *Bibliography*

labour: a case study', in K. W. M. Fulford, Donna Dickenson and Thomas Murray (eds), *The Blackwell Reader in Healthcare Ethics and Human Values* (Oxford: Blackwell, forthcoming).

Dickenson, Donna and Jones, David, 'True wishes: philosophical and clinical approaches to children's informed consent', *Philosophy, Psychiatry and Psychology* 2:4 (1995).

Dijkstra, Bram, *Idols of Perversity: Fantasies of Feminine Evil in Fin-de-Siècle Culture* (Oxford: Oxford University Press, 1986).

Dillon, Robin S., 'Toward a feminist conception of self-respect', *Hypatia* 7:1 (winter 1992), pp. 52–69.

Diprose, R. and Ferrel, R. (eds), *Cartographies: The Mapping of Bodies and Spaces* (Sydney: Allen and Unwin, 1991).

Di Stefano, Christine, *Configurations of Masculinity: A Feminist Perspective on Modern Political Theory* (Ithaca and London: Cornell University Press, 1991).

Douglas, Ann, *The Feminization of American Culture* (New York: Knopf, 1977).

Dunn, John, 'Consent in the political theory of John Locke', in Dunn, *Political Obligation in its Historical Context* (Oxford: Oxford University Press, 1980).

Durkheim, Émile, *The Division of Labor in Society*, tr. George Simpson (New York: Free Press, 1960).

Dwyer, Daisy and Bryce, Judith (eds), *A Home Divided: Women and Income in the Third World* (Palo Alto: Stanford University Press, 1988).

Easton, Susan M., 'Hegel and feminism', in David Lamb (ed.), *Hegel and Modern Philosophy* (London: Croom Helm, 1987).

—— *The Problem of Pornography: Regulation and the Right to Free Speech* (London and New York: Routledge, 1994).

Economic Commission for Africa, *United Nations Handbook on Women in Africa* (1975), cited in Toril Brekke et al., *Women: A World Report* (London: Methuen, 1985).

Eisenstein, Zillah, *The Radical Future of Liberal Feminism* (New York: Longman, 1981).

Eliot, George, 'Margaret Fuller and Mary Wollstonecraft', *Leader* 6 (13 Oct. 1855), pp. 988–9; repr. in Thomas Pinney (ed.), *The Essays of George Eliot* (London: Routledge and Kegan Paul, 1983), pp. 199–206.

Elshtain, Jean Bethke, *Public Man, Private Woman: Women in Social and Political Thought* (Oxford: Martin Robertson, 1984).

Engels, Friedrich, *The Origin of the Family, Private Property and the State* (New York: International, 1972).

Epstein, Richard, 'Possession as the root of title', *Georgia Law Review* 13 (1979), pp. 1221–8.

Evans, Donald, Procuring gametes for research and therapy', guest editorial, *Journal of Medical Ethics* 21:5 (Oct. 1995), pp. 261–4.

Ferguson, Ann, *Sexual Democracy: Women, Oppression, and Revolution* (Boulder and Oxford: Westview Press, 1991).

Ferguson, Kathy E., *The Man Question: Visions of Subjectivity in Feminist Theory* (Berkeley and Oxford: University of California Press, 1993).

Field, Martha A., *Surrogate Motherhood: The Legal and Human Issues* (Cambridge: Harvard University Press, 1988).

Firestone, Shulamith, *The Dialectic of Sex: The Case for Feminist Revolution* (New York: Bantam, 1970).

Fisher, R. E., *Slavery in Classical Greece* (London: Duckworth, 1993).

Flexner, Eleanor, *Century of Struggle: The Woman's Rights Movement in the United States*, rev. edn (Cambridge: Belknap Press, 1975).

Floro, Maria Sagrario, 'The dynamics of economic change and gender roles: export cropping in the Philippines', in Pamela Sparr (ed.), *Mortgaging Women's Lives: Feminist Critiques of Structural Adjustment* (London: Zed Books, 1994), pp. 116–33.

Foreman, Ann, *Femininity as Alienation: Women and the Family in Marxism and Psychoanalysis* (London: Pluto Press, 1977).

Foucault, Michel, *History of Sexuality* (London: Allen Lane, 1978).

Fox, Bonnie (ed.), *Hidden in the Household: Women's Domestic Labour under Capitalism* (Toronto: Women's Press, 1980).

Fraser, Antonia, *The Weaker Vessel: Women's Lot in Seventeenth–Century England* (1984; London: Mandarin Paperbacks, 1989).

Fraser, Nancy, *Unruly Practices: Power, Discourse and Gender in Contemporary Social Theory* (Cambridge: Polity Press, 1989).

Fried, Albert and Elman, Richard (eds), *Charles Booth's London: A Portrait of the Poor at the Turn of the Century, Drawn from his Life and Labour of the People in London*, with foreword by Raymond Williams (Harmondsworth: Penguin, 1971).

Frohlich, Norman and Oppenheimer, Joe A., *Choosing Justice: An Experimental Approach to Ethical Theory* (Berkeley: University of California Press, 1992).

Fromm, Erich, *To Have and To Be* (London: Jonathan Cape, 1978).

Fuller, Margaret, *Woman in the Nineteenth Century*, ed. Donna Dickenson (Oxford: Oxford World's Classics, 1994).

Gatens, Moira, *Feminism and Philosophy: Perspectives on Difference and Equality* (Cambridge: Polity Press, 1991).

—— 'The oppressed state of my sex: Wollstonecraft on reason, feeling and equality', in Mary Lyndon Shanley and Carole Pateman (eds), *Feminist Interpretations and Political Theory* (Cambridge: Polity Press, 1991), pp. 112–28.

—— 'Power, bodies and difference', in Michèle Barrett and Anne Phillips (eds), *Destabilizing Theory* (Cambridge: Polity Press, 1992), pp. 120–37.

Gauthier, David, *Moral Dealing: Contract, Ethics and Reason* (Ithaca and London: Cornell University Press, 1990).

Gay, Peter, *The Bourgeois Experience: Victoria to Freud*, vol. 1: *Education of the Senses* (Oxford: Oxford University Press, 1984).

Gibbard, Alan, *Wise Choices, Apt Feelings: A Theory of Normative Judgment* (Oxford: Clarendon, 1990).

Gilligan, Carol, *In a Different Voice: Psychological Theory and Women's Development* (Cambridge: Harvard University Press, 1982).

—— 'Letter to readers, 1993', in *In a Different Voice: Psychological Theory and Women's Development*, 2nd edn (Cambridge: Harvard University Press, 1993).

Glendinning, Caroline and Millar, Jane (eds), *Women and Poverty in Britain: The 1990s* (Hemel Hempstead: Harvester Wheatsheaf, 1992).

Glendon, Mary Ann, 'Marriage and the state: the withering away of marriage', *Virginia Law Review* 62:4 (May 1976), pp. 663–720.

Glover Report: *Fertility and the Family* (London: Fourth Estate, 1989).

Goetz, Anne Marie, 'Feminism and the claim to know: contradictions in feminist approaches to women in development', in Rebecca Grant and Kathleen Newland (eds), *Gender and International Relations* (Milton Keynes: Open University Press, 1991), pp. 133–57.

Gordley, James, 'Equality in exchange', *California Law Review* 69 (1981).

Green, Karen, *The Woman of Reason: Feminism, Humanism and Political Thought* (Cambridge: Polity Press, 1995).

Greeno, Catherine G. and Maccoby, Eleanor E., 'How different is the different voice?', in Mary Jeanne Larrabee (ed.), *An Ethic of Care: Feminist and Interdisciplinary Perspectives* (New York and London: Routledge, 1993), pp. 193–8.

Grey, Thomas C., 'The disintegration of property', in J. Roland Pennock and John W. Chapman (eds), *NOMOS XXII: Property* (New York: New York University Press, 1980), pp. 69–85.

Griffiths, Morwenna, *Feminisms and the Self: The Web of Identity* (London: Routledge, 1996).

Grimshaw, Jean, 'Feminism, philosophy and universalism', paper presented to the 'Issues in Feminism' seminar series, University of Oxford, 15 May 1995.

—— *Philosophy and Feminist Thinking* (Brighton: Harvester Wheatsheaf, 1986).

Grunebaum, James, *Private Ownership* (London: Routledge and Kegan Paul, 1987).

Gunew, Sneja and Yeatman, Anna (eds), *Feminism and the Politics of Difference* (Boulder: Westview Press, 1993).

Hansen, Mogens Herman, *The Athenian Democracy in the Age of Demosthenes: Structures, Principles, Ideology* (Oxford: Blackwell, 1991).

Haraway, Donna J., *Simians, Cyborgs and Women: The Reinvention of Nature* (New York: Routledge, 1991).

—— 'Situated knowledges: the science question in feminism and the privilege of partial perspective', *Feminist Studies* 14:3 (fall 1988).

Hardimon, Michael O., *Hegel's Social Philosophy: The Project of Reconciliation* (Cambridge: Cambridge University Press, 1994).

Harding, Sandra, 'Is gender a variable in conceptions of rationality? A survey of issues', in Carol C. Gould (ed.), *Beyond Domination: New Perspectives on Feminism and Philosophy* (Totowa, N.J.: Rowman and Allanheld, 1984), pp. 43–63.

Harris, Angela P., 'Race and essentialism in feminist legal theory', in D. Kelly Weisberg (ed.), *Feminist Legal Theory: Foundations* (Philadelphia: Temple University Press, 1993), pp, 348–58.

Harris, John, *Wonderwoman and Superman: The Ethics of Human Biotechnology* (Oxford: Oxford University Press, 1992).

Hart, H. L. A., 'Are there any natural rights?', in Jeremy Waldron (ed.), *Theories of Rights* (Oxford: Oxford University Press, 1984), pp. 83–8.

Hartmann, Heidi, 'The family as the locus of gender, class and political struggle: the example of housework', *Signs* 6:3, pp. 366–94.

Hartsock, Nancy C. M., *Money, Sex and Power: Toward a Feminist Historical Materialism* (Boston: Northeastern University Press, 1983).

Hegel, G. W. F., *Phenomenology of Spirit*, tr. A. V. Miller (Oxford: Oxford University Press, 1977).

—— *Hegel's Philosophy of Right*, tr. T. M. Knox (Oxford: Oxford University Press, 1967).

—— *Vorlesungen über Rechtsphilosophie*, vol. 4, ed. K. H. Ilting (Stuttgart: Fromman, 1974).

Held, David, 'Introduction: central perspectives on the modern state', in Held et al. (eds), *States and Societies* (Oxford: Martin Robertson, in assoc. with the Open University, 1983).

—— *Models of Democracy*, 2nd edn (1987; Cambridge: Polity Press, 1996).

Held, Virginia, *Feminist Morality: Transforming Culture, Society and Politics* (Chicago and London: University of Chicago Press, 1993).

—— *Rights and Goods: Justifying Social Action* (New York: Free Press, 1984).

Hewitt, Nancy, 'Beyond the search for sisterhood: American women's history in the 1980s', *Social History* 10 (1985), p. 299.

Hewlett, Sylvia Ann, *A Lesser Life: The Myth of Women's Liberation* (London: Michael Joseph, 1987).

Hirschmann, Nancy J., *Rethinking Obligation: A Feminist Method for Political Theory* (Ithaca and London: Cornell University Press, 1992).

Hirschmann, Nancy and Di Stefano, Christine (eds), *Revisioning the Political: Feminist Reconstructions of Traditional Concepts in Western Political Theory* (Boulder: Westview Press, 1996).

Hirschon, Renée, 'Introduction: property, power and gender relations', in Hirschon (ed.), *Women and Property – Women as Property* (London: Croom Helm, 1984), pp. 1–22.

Hobbes, Thomas, *Leviathan*, with an introd. by A. D. Lindsay (London: Dent, 1962).

Hohfeld, Wesley Newcomb, *Fundamental Legal Conceptions as Applied in Judicial Reasoning*, ed. Walter W. Cook, with foreword by Arthur L. Corbin (1919; Westport, Conn.: Greenwood Press, 1978).

Honoré, A. M., 'Ownership', in A. G. Guest (ed.) *Oxford Essays in Jurisprudence* (Oxford: Oxford University Press, 1961).

Hurley, Susan L., *Natural Reasons: Personality and Polity* (Oxford: Oxford University Press, 1989).

Hyde, Lewis, *The Gift: Imagination and the Erotic Life of Property* (New York: Random House, 1979).

In re S (Adult: Refusal of Treatment) [1993] Fam. 123.

In re T (Adult: Refusal of Treatment) [1993] Fam. 95.

In the matter of Baby M, 217 N.J. Supr. 313 (1987), 109 N.J. 396 (1988).

Irigaray, Luce, *Éthique de la différence sexuelle* (Paris: Minuit, 1984).

—— *Sexes et parentés* (Paris: Minuit, 1987).

——*Speculum of the Other Woman*, tr. Gillian C. Gill (Ithaca: Cornell University Press, 1985).

—— *Le Temps de la différence: pour une révolution pacifique* (Paris: Livre de Poche, 1989).

—— *This Sex Which Is Not One*, tr. Catherine Porter with Caroline Burke (Ithaca: Cornell University Press, 1985).

Jaggar, Alison M., *Feminist Politics and Human Nature* (Totowa, N.J.: Rowman and Allanheld, 1983).

Jaggar, Gill, 'Beyond essentialism and construction: subjectivity, corporeality and sexual difference', in Morwenna Griffiths and Margaret Whitford (eds), *Women Review Philosophy: New Writing by Women in Philosophy* (Nottingham: Nottingham University Press, 1996), pp. 142–60.

Jayaweera, S., 'Structural adjustment policies, industrial development and women in Sri Lanka', in Pamela Sparr (ed.), *Mortgaging Women's Lives: Feminist Critiques of Structural Adjustment* (London: Zed Books, 1994), pp. 96–115.

Jones, Gregory L., 'Alasdair MacIntyre on narrative, community and the moral life', *Modern Theology* 4:1 (1987), pp. 53–69.

Jones, Kathleen B., *Compassionate Authority: Democracy and the Representation of Women* (London: Routledge, 1993).

Kerr, Joanna, 'Martha Nussbaum and unreasonable philosophy', in Morwenna Griffiths and Margaret Whitford (eds), *Women Review Philosophy: New Writing by Women in Philosophy* (Nottingham: Nottingham University Press, 1996), pp. 85–101.

Kiss, Elizabeth, 'Alchemy or fool's gold? Assessing feminist doubts about rights', in Mary Lyndon Shanley and Uma Narayan (eds), *Reconstructing Political Theory: Feminist Perspectives* (Cambridge: Polity Press, 1997).

Kristeva, Julia, *Revolution in Poetic Language*, tr. Margaret Walker (New York: Columbia University Press, 1984).

Land, Hilary, 'Review of Patricia Hewitt, *About Time: The Revolution in Work and Family Life* ', *Journal of Social Policy* (Oct. 1993), part 4, p. 22.

Landry, Donna and MacLean, Gerald, *Materialist Feminisms* (Oxford: Blackwell, 1993).

Larkin, W. Paschal, *Property in the Eighteenth Century: With Special Reference to England and Locke* (Dublin and Cork: Cork University Press, 1930).

Lazreg, Monica, 'Feminism and difference: the perils of writing as a woman on women in Algeria', *Feminist Studies* 14:1 (spring 1988).

Le Dœuff, Michèle, 'Ants and women, or philosophy without borders', in A. Phillips Griffiths (ed.), *Contemporary French Philosophy* (Cambridge: Cambridge University Press, 1987).

—— *Hipparchia's Choice: An Essay Concerning Women, Philosophy, etc.*, tr. Trista Selous (Oxford: Blackwell, 1991); originally *L'Étude et le Rouet* (1989).

—— *The Philosophical Imaginary* (London: Athlone Press, 1989).

Lefkowitz, Mary F. and Fant, Maureen (eds), *Women in Greece and Rome* (Sarasota, Fla.: Samuel Stevens, 1977).

Lerner, Gerda, *The Creation of Patriarchy* (Oxford: Oxford University Press, 1976).

Lister, Ruth, *Women's Economic Dependency and Social Security* (Manchester: Equal Opportunities Commission, 1992).

Lloyd, Genevieve, *The Man of Reason: 'Male' and 'Female' in Western Philosophy*, 2nd edn (London: Routledge, 1993).

Locke, John, *The Second Treatise on Civil Government* (1689), in Howard R. Penniman (ed.), *On Politics and Education* (New York: D. Van Nostrand, 1947).

Lockwood, Gillian, 'Donating life: the practical and ethical problems of gamete donation', paper presented at the Oxford–Mt Sinai conference, Oriel College, Oxford, March 1996.

Loraux, Nicole, *Tragic Ways of Killing a Woman*, tr. Anthony Foster (Cambridge: Harvard University Press, 1987).

Lorde, Audre, 'The master's tools will never dismantle the master's house', in Cherrie Moraga and Gloria Anzaldua (eds), *The Bridge Called My Back* (New York: Kitchen Table, 1983), pp. 98–101.

Louden, Robert B., *Morality and Moral Theory: A Reappraisal and Reaffirmation* (Oxford: Oxford University Press, 1992).

Lukács, George, *The Young Hegel* (London: Merlin Press, 1975).

Lukes, Stephen, *Marxism and Morality* (Oxford: Oxford University Press, 1987).

Machan, Tibor R., 'A defence of property rights and capitalism', in Brenda Almond (ed.), *Introducing Applied Ethics* (Oxford: Blackwell, 1995), pp. 260–71.

MacIntyre, Alasdair, *After Virtue* (London: Duckworth, 1981).

—— *Whose Justice? Which Rationality?* (Notre Dame: University of Notre Dame Press, 1988).

MacKinnon, Catharine A., *Feminism Unmodified: Discourses on Life and Law* (Cambridge: Harvard University Press, 1987).

—— *Toward a Feminist Theory of the State* (Cambridge: Harvard University Press, 1989).

Macklin, Ruth, 'Is there anything wrong with surrogate motherhood? An ethical analysis', in Larry Gostin (ed.), *Surrogate Motherhood: Politics and Privacy* (Bloomington: Indiana University Press, 1990), pp. 136–150.

MacLean, Mavis, *Surviving Divorce: Women's Resources after Separation* (London: Macmillan, 1991).

McMillan, Carol, *Women, Reason and Nature: Some Philosophical Problems with Feminism* (Oxford: Blackwell, 1982).

Macpherson, C. B., *The Political Theory of Possessive Individualism: Hobbes to Locke* (Oxford and New York: Oxford University Press, 1962).

Mahoney, Joan, 'Adoption as a feminist alternative to reproductive technology', in Joan C. Callahan (ed.), *Reproduction, Ethics and the Law* (Bloomington: Indiana University Press, 1995), pp. 35–54.

—— 'An essay on surrogacy and feminist thought', in Larry Gostin (ed.), *Surrogate Motherhood: Politics and Privacy* (Bloomington: Indiana University Press, 1990), pp. 183–97.

Mahowald, Mary B., 'As if there were fetuses without women: a remedial essay', in Joan C. Callahan (ed.), *Reproduction, Ethics and the Law: Feminist Perspectives* (Bloomington: Indiana University Press, 1995), pp. 199–218.

Maitre, Henry, *Ancient Law* (Oxford: Oxford University Press, 1931).

Malos, Ellen, *The Politics of Housework* (London: Allison and Busby, 1980).

Manuh, Takyiwaa, 'Ghana: women in the public and informal sectors under the economic recovery programme', in Rebecca Grant and Kathleen Newland (eds), *Gender and International Relations* (Milton Keynes: Open University Press, 1991), pp. 61–77.

Marx, Karl, *Capital*, ed. Friedrich Engels, tr. Samuel Moore and Edward Aveling (New York: International, 1967).

—— *Early Writings*, tr. and ed. T. B. Bottomore (New York: McGraw-Hill, 1963).

—— *The Economic and Philosophic Manuscripts of 1844*, ed. Dirk J. Struik (New York: International, 1964).

—— *Grundrisse: Foundations of the Critique of Political Economy*, tr. with foreword by Martin Nicolas (New York: Vintage Books, 1973).

Marx, Karl and Engels, Friedrich, *The German Ideology*, ed. and introd. C. J. Arthur (London: Lawrence and Wishart, 1970).

—— 'Manifesto of the Communist Party', in *Selected Works* (New York: International, 1968).

Mason, J. K. and McCall Smith, R. A., *Law and Medical Ethics*, 3rd edn (London: Butterworth, 1991).

Matsuda, Mari J., 'Liberal jurisprudence and abstracted visions of human nature: a feminist critique of Rawls' theory of justice', in D. Kelly Weisberg (ed.), *Feminist Legal Theory: Foundations* (Philadelphia: Temple University Press, 1993), pp. 476–84.

Mazumdar, V. and Sharma, K., 'Sexual division of labor and the subordination of women: a reappraisal from India', in Irene Tinker (ed.), *Persistent Inequalities: Women and World Development* (Oxford: Oxford University Press, 1994), pp. 185–97.

Menefee, Samuel Pyeatt, *Wives for Sale: An Ethnographic Study of British Popular Divorce* (Oxford: Blackwell, 1981).

Meyers, Diana, *Self, Society and Personal Choice* (New York: Columbia University Press, 1988).

Mies, Maria, *Lacemakers in Narsapur: Indian Housewives Produce for the World Market* (London: Zed Press, 1982).

—— *Patriarchy and Accumulation on a World Scale: Women in the International Division of Labor* (London: Zed Press, 1986).

Mill, Harriet Taylor, *The Enfranchisement of Women* (London: Virago, 1983), first published anonymously in *Westminster Review*, 1851.

Mill, James, 'Article on Government' (1820), published in the 1824 supplement to the *Encyclopaedia Britannica*.

Mill, John Stuart (with Harriet Taylor Mill), *The Subjection of Women* (1869; London: Virago, 1983).

Miller, Richard W., *Moral Differences: Truth, Justice and Conscience in a World of Conflict* (Princeton: Princeton University Press, 1992).

Minow, Martha, 'Feminist reason: getting it and losing it', in D. Kelly Weisberg (ed.), *Feminist Legal Theory: Foundations* (Philadelphia: Temple University Press, 1993), pp. 339–47.

Mitchell, Juliet, *Women's Estate* (New York: Random House, 1971).

Mohanty, Chandra Talpade, 'Feminist encounters: locating the politics of experience', in Michèle Barrett and Anne Phillips (eds), *Destabilizing Theory: Contemporary Feminist Debates* (Cambridge: Polity Press, 1992).

—— , Russo, Ann and Torres, Lourdes (eds), *Third World Women and the Politics of Feminism* (Bloomington and Indianapolis: Indiana University Press, 1991).

Moi, Toril, *Sexual/Textual Politics: Feminist Literary Theory* (London: Methuen, 1985).

Moore, Henrietta L., *A Passion for Difference: Essays in Anthropology and Gender* (Cambridge: Polity Press, 1994).

Morris, L. and Ruane, S., *Household Finances Management and Labour Market Behaviour* (Durham: Work and Employment Research Unit, University of Durham, 1986).

Morrison, Toni (ed.), *Race-ing Justice, En-Gendering Power* (New York: Pantheon, 1992).

Moser, Caroline O. N., 'Gender planning in the Third World', in Rebecca Grant and Kathleen Newland (eds), *Gender and International Relations* (Milton Keynes: Open University Press, 1991).

Mount, Ferdinand, *The Subversive Family: An Alternative History of Love and Marriage* (New York: Free Press, 1982).

Moynihan, Ruth Barnes, Russett, Cynthia and Crumpacker, Laurie (eds), *Second to None: A Documentary History of American Women* (Lincoln and London: University of Nebraska Press, 1993), vol. 1.

Munzer, Stephen R., *A Theory of Property* (Cambridge: Cambridge University Press, 1990).

Myers, Diana, *Self, Society and Personal Choice* (New York: Columbia University Press, 1988).

Nead, Lynda, *Myths of Sexuality: Representations of Women in Victorian Britain* (Oxford: Blackwell, 1988).

Nedelsky, Jennifer, 'Law, boundaries and the bounded self', *Representations* 30 (spring 1990), pp. 169–81.

Newland, Kathleen, 'From transnational relationships to international relations: women in development and the international decade for women', in Rebecca Grant and Kathleen Newland (eds), *Gender and International Relations* (Milton Keynes: Open University Press, 1991), pp. 122–32.

Noddings, Nel, *Caring: A Feminine Approach to Ethics and Moral Education* (Berkeley: University of California Press, 1984).

Nozick, Robert, *Anarchy, State and Utopia* (New York: Basic Books, 1974).

Nunner-Winkler, Gertrud, 'Two moralities? A critical discussion of an ethic of care and responsibility versus an ethic of rights and justice', in Mary Jeanne Larrabee (ed.), *An Ethic of Care: Feminist and Interdisciplinary Perspectives* (New York and London: Routledge, 1993), pp. 143–56.

Nussbaum, Martha Craven, 'Feminists and philosophy', *New York Review of Books* 41:17 (1994), pp. 59–63.

—— *The Fragility of Goodness: Luck and Ethics in Greek Tragedy and Philosophy* (Cambridge: Cambridge University Press, 1986).

O'Brien, Mary, *The Politics of Reproduction* (London: Routledge and Kegan Paul, 1981).

Okin, Susan Moller, *Justice, Gender and the Family* (New York: Basic Books, 1989).

—— 'Reason and feeling in thinking about justice', *Ethics* 99:2 (Jan. 1989).

—— *Women in Western Political Thought* (1979; London: Virago, 1980).

O'Laughlin, Bridget, 'Myth of the African family in the world of development', in Deborah Fahy Bryceson (ed.), *Women Wielding the Hoe: Lessons from Rural Africa for Feminist Theory and Development* (Oxford: Berg, 1995), pp. 63–91.

Overall, Christine, *Human Reproduction: Principles, Practice, Policies*, 2nd edn (Toronto: Oxford University Press, 1993).

Pahl, Jan, *Money and Marriage* (London: Macmillan, 1989).

Parker, Philip, 'Motivation of surrogate mothers: initial findings', *American Journal of Psychiatry* 140 (1983), pp. 117–18.

Pateman, Carole, 'God hath ordained to man a helper: Hobbes, patriarchy and conjugal right', in Mary Lyndon Shanley and Carole Pateman (eds), *Feminist Interpretations and Political Theory* (Cambridge: Polity Press, 1991), pp. 53–73.

—— *The Sexual Contract* (Cambridge: Polity Press, 1988).

Pernoud, Régine, *La Femme au temps des cathédrales* (Paris: Stock, 1980).

—— *La Femme au temps des croisades* (Paris: Stock/Laurence Pernoud, 1990).

Peterson, V. Spike and Runyan, Anne Sisson, *Global Gender Issues* (Boulder: Westview Press, 1993).

Phillips, Anne, *Engendering Democracy* (Cambridge: Polity Press, 1991).

—— 'Universal pretensions in political thought', in Michèle Barrett and Anne Phillips (eds), *Destabilizing Theory* (Cambridge: Polity Press, 1992), pp. 10–30.

Pitkin, Hannah Fenichel, *Fortune Is a Woman: Gender and Politics in the Thought of Niccolò Machiavelli* (Berkeley and London: University of California Press, 1984).

Plato, *The Republic*, tr. Paul Shorey. In *The Collected Dialogues of Plato including the Letters*, ed. Edith Hamilton and Huntington Cairns (New York: Pantheon Books, 1961), pp. 845–919.

Pomeroy, Sarah, *Goddesses, Whores, Wives and Slaves: Women in Classical Antiquity* (New York: Schocken, 1975).

Proudhon, Pierre-Joseph, *Selected Writings*, ed. and introd. by Stewart Edwards, tr. Elizabeth Fraser (New York: Anchor Books, 1969).

Radin, Margaret J., 'Market inalienability', *Harvard Law Review* 100 (1989), pp. 1849ff.; reproduced in K. D. Alpern (ed.), *The Ethics of Reproductive Technology* (Oxford: Oxford University Press, 1992).

Rawls, John, *A Theory of Justice* (Cambridge: Harvard University Press, 1971).

Re F (in utero) [1988] Fam. 122, [1988] 2 All ER193.

Reeve, Andrew, *Property* (London: Macmillan, 1986).

Reich, Charles, 'The new property', *Yale Law Review* 73 (1964), pp. 733–86.

Reynders, H. J. J., 'The geographical income of the Bantu areas in South Africa', in L. H. Samuels (ed.), *African Studies in Income and Wealth* (London, 1963).

Rich, Adrienne, *Of Woman Born* (New York: Harper and Row, 1976).

Robins, Gay, *Women in Ancient Egypt* (Cambridge: Harvard University Press, 1993).

Rose, Carol M., *Property and Persuasion: Essays on the History, Theory and Rhetoric of Ownership* (Boulder: Westview Press, 1994).

Rousseau, Jean-Jacques, *Discourse on the Origin and Foundations of Inequality (Second Discourse)*, ed. Roger D. Masters, tr. Roger D. Masters and Judith R. Masters (New York: St Martin's, 1964).

Royal College of Obstetricians and Gynaecologists, *Termination of Pregnancy for Fetal Abnormality in England, Wales and Scotland* (London, 1996).

Rubin, Gayle, 'The traffic in women: notes on the "political economy" of sex', in Rayna R. Reiter (ed.), *Toward an Anthropology of Women* (New York: Monthly Review Press, 1975), pp. 157–210.

Ruddick, Sara, *Maternal Thinking: Towards a Politics of Peace* (New York: Ballantine Books, 1989).

—— 'Remarks on the sexual politics of reason', in Eva Kittay and Diana Meyers (eds), *Women and Moral Theory* (Totowa, N.J.: Rowman and Littlefield, 1987), pp. 237–60.

Ryan, Alan, *Property* (Milton Keynes: Open University Press, 1987).

—— *Property and Political Theory* (Oxford: Blackwell, 1984).

Ryan, M. A., 'The argument for unlimited procreative liberty: a feminist critique', in C. S. Campbell (ed.), *What Price Parenthood? Ethics and Assisted Reproduction* (Briarcliff Manor, New York: Hastings Center, 1992).

Safa, Helen I., 'Women and change in Latin America', in Jack Hopkins (ed.), *Latin America: Perspectives on a Region* (New York: Holmes and Meier, 1987).

Ste Croix, G. E. M. de, *The Class Struggle in the Ancient Greek World: From the Archaic Age to the Arab Conquests* (London: Duckworth, 1981).

Salmon, Marylynn, *Women and the Law of Property in Early America* (Chapel Hill and London: University of North Carolina Press, 1986).

Sandford, Stella, 'Feminist philosophy and the fate of Hegel's Antigone', in Morwenna Griffiths and Margaret Whitford (eds), *Women Review Philosophy: New Writing by Women in Philosophy* (Nottingham: Nottingham University Press, 1996).

Saxonhouse, Arlene, 'On Aristotle', in Mary Lyndon Shanley and Carole Pateman (eds), *Feminist Interpretations and Political Theory* (Cambridge: Polity Press, 1991), pp. 32–52.

Sayers, Janet, *Biological Politics: Feminist and Anti-feminist Perspectives* (London: Tavistock, 1982).

—— *Sexual Contradictions: Psychology, Psychoanalysis and Feminism* (London: Tavistock, 1986).

Schaps, David M., *Economic Rights of Women in Ancient Greece* (Edinburgh: Edinburgh University Press, 1979).

Scheman, Naomi, Cope-Kasten, Vance and Nussbaum, Martha Craven, 'Feminism and philosophy: an exchange', *New York Review of Books* 42:6 (1995), pp. 48–9.

Schlatter, Richard, *Private Property: The History of an Idea* (London: Allen and Unwin, 1951).

Schover, L. R. et al., 'Psychological follow-up of women evaluated as oocyte donors', *Human Reproduction* 6 (1991), pp. 1487–91.

Schwendinger, J. and Schwendinger, H., *Rape and Inequality* (Beverly Hills: Sage, 1983).

Segal, Lynne, *Is the Future Female? Troubled Thoughts on Contemporary Feminism* (London: Virago, 1988).

Shalev, Carmel, *Birth Power: The Case for Surrogacy* (New Haven: Yale University Press, 1989).

Shanley, Mary Lyndon and Narayan, Uma, *Reconstructing Political Theory: Feminist Perspectives* (Cambridge: Polity Press, 1997).

Sharma, Ursula, 'Dowry in North India: The consequences for women', in Renée Hirschon (ed.), *Women and Property – Women as Property* (London: Croom Helm, 1984), pp. 62–74.

Shaw, Martin, 'Post-military democracy', in Anthony McGrew (ed.), *The Transformation of Democracy? Globalization and the Post-Westphalian World Order* (Cambridge: Polity Press, 1997).

Shenfield, Françoise and Steele, S. J.,'Why gamete donors should not be paid', *Human Reproduction* 10:2 (1995), pp. 253–5.

Sherwin, Susan, *No Longer Patient: Feminist Ethics and Health Care* (Philadelphia: Temple University Press, 1992).

Singer, Peter, *Hegel* (Oxford: Oxford Past Masters, 1983).

Smiley, Jane, *Moo* (New York: HarperCollins, 1995).

Smith, Adam, *An Inquiry into the Nature and Causes of the Wealth of Nations*, ed. Edwin Cannon (1776; Chicago: University of Chicago Press, 1976).

—— *The Theory of Moral Sentiments*, ed. Dugald Stewart (1759; London: George Bell and Sons, 1892).

Sokolov, Margaret, 'Marriage contracts for support and services: constitutionality begins at home', *New York University Law Review* 49 (Dec. 1974), pp. 1195ff.

Spelman, E., *Inessential Woman: Problems of Exclusion in Feminist Thought* (Boston: Beacon Press, 1988).

Stanton, Elizabeth Cady, *Eighty Years and More: Reminiscences 1815–1897* (New York: Schocken, 1971), reprint of T. Fisher Unwin edn of 1898).

Stone, Lawrence, *Road to Divorce: England 1530–1987* (Oxford: Oxford University Press, 1990).

Stout, Jeffrey, *Ethics after Babel: The Languages of Morals and their Discontents* (Boston: Beacon Press, 1988).

Strathern, Marilyn, 'Subject or object? Women and the circulation of valuables in Highlands New Guinea', in Renée Hirschon (ed.), *Women and Property – Women as Property* (London: Croom Helm, 1984), pp. 158–75.

Strunk v. Strunk, 455 SW2d 145, 35 ALR3d 683 (ky, 1969).

Sylvester, Christine, *Feminist Theory and International Relations in a Postmodern Era* (Cambridge: Cambridge University Press, 1994).

Taylor, Barbara, *Eve and the New Jerusalem: Socialism and Feminism in the Nineteenth Century* (London: Virago, 1983).

Tendler, Judith, *What Happened to Poverty Alleviation?* (New York: Ford Foundation, 1987).

Thahn Dam, T., 'The dynamics of sex tourism: the case of South East Asia', *Development and Change* 14 (1983), pp. 533–53.

Thompson, William (with Anna Wheeler), *Appeal of One Half the Human Race, Women, Against the Pretensions of the Other Half, Men, To Retain Them in Political, and Thence in Civil and Domestic, Slavery*, introd. Richard Pankhurst (1825; London: Virago, 1983).

Thomson, Judith Jarvis, 'A defense of abortion', *Philosophy and Public Affairs* 1:1 (1971), pp. 47–66.

Thoreau, Henry David, 'Essay on civil disobedience', in *The Portable Thoreau*, ed. Carl Bode (1849; New York: Viking, 1961), pp. 109–38.

—— *Walden*, in *The Portable Thoreau*, ed. Carl Bode (1854; New York: Viking, 1961), pp. 258–572.

Tinker, Irene (ed.), *Persistent Inequalities: Women and World Development* (Oxford: Oxford University Press, 1994).

Titmuss, Richard, *The Gift Relationship: From Human Blood to Social Policy* (London: Allen and Unwin, 1971).

Tong, Rosemarie, 'Feminist perspectives and gestational motherhood: the search for a unified legal focus', in Joan C. Callahan (ed.), *Reproduction, Ethics and the Law* (Bloomington: Indiana University Press, 1995), pp. 55–79.

—— 'The overdue death of a feminist chameleon: taking a stand on surrogacy arrangements', *Journal of Social Philosophy* 2:3 (fall/winter 1990), pp. 40–56.

Trebilcock, Michael J., *The Limits of Freedom of Contract* (Cambridge: Harvard University Press, 1993).

Tristan, Flora, *Promenades dans Londres* (1842), tr. Jean Hawkes as *The London Journal of Flora Tristan 1842, or, The Aristocracy and the Working Class of England* (London: Virago, 1982).

Tully, James, *A Discourse on Property: John Locke and his Adversaries* (Cambridge: Cambridge University Press, 1980).

Van Hooft, Stan, 'Bioethics and caring', *Journal of Medical Ethics* 22:2 (Apr. 1996), pp. 83–9.

Vanoyèke, Violaine, *La Prostitution en Grèce et à Rome* (Paris: Belles Lettres, 1990).

Vawter, Dorothy E. et al., *The Use of Human Fetal Tissue: Scientific, Ethical and Policy Concerns* (Minneapolis: University of Minnesota Press, 1990).

Vogel, Lise, 'The earthly family', *Radical America* 7 (July–Oct. 1973).

Vogel, Ursula, 'Rationalism and romanticism: two strategies for women's liberation', in Judith Evans et al., *Feminism and Political Theory* (London: Sage, 1986), pp. 17–46.

Vogler, C. and Pahl, J., 'Social and economic change and the organisation of money within marriage', *Work, Employment and Society* 7:1, pp. 71–95.

Waldron, Jeremy, *The Right to Private Property* (Oxford: Clarendon Press, 1988).

Wallace, James D., *Virtues and Vices* (Ithaca and London: Cornell University Press, 1978).

Waring, Marilyn, *If Women Counted: A New Feminist Economics*, introd. Gloria Steinem (London: Macmillan, 1989).

Warren, Mary Ann, 'The moral significance of birth', *Hypatia* 4:3 (fall 1989).

Weber, Max, *Max Weber on Law in Economy and Society*, ed. M. Rheinstein (Cambridge: Harvard University Press, 1954).

Weisberg, D. Kelly (ed.), *Feminist Legal Theory: Foundations* (Philadelphia: Temple University Press, 1993).

Weitzman, Lenore, *The Divorce Revolution: The Unexpected Social and Economic Consequences for Women and Children in America* (New York: Free Press, 1985).

—— *The Marriage Contract* (New York: Free Press, 1981).

—— 'No-fault divorce in California', unpublished MS, Center for the Study of Law and Society, Berkeley, 1980.

Welter, Barbara, *Dimity Convictions: The American Woman in the Nineteenth Century* (Athens, Ohio: Ohio University Press, 1976).

Wener v. Wener, 59 Misc. 2d 957, 301 NYS 2d 237 (Sup Ct 1969), affirmed 35 App. Div. 2d 50, 312 NYS 2d 815 (2d Dept. 1970).

West, Robin, 'Jurisprudence and gender', in D. Kelly Weisberg (ed.), *Feminist Legal Theory: Foundations* (Philadelphia: Temple University Press, 1993), pp. 75–98.

Whitehead, Ann, 'I'm hungry, Mum: the politics of domestic budgeting', in Kate

Young, Carol Wolkowitz and Roslyn McCullagh (eds), *Of Marriage and the Market* (London: CSE Books, 1981), pp. 49–68.

Whitford, Margaret, *Luce Irigaray: Philosophy in the Feminine* (London and New York: Routledge, 1991).

Wilkes, Kathy, *Real People: Personal Identity without Thought Experiments* (Oxford: Oxford University Press, 1994).

Williams, Bernard, *Ethics and the Limits of Philosophy* (London: Fontana/Collins, 1985).

Williams, Patricia J., 'On being the object of property', in D. Kelly Weisberg (ed.), *Feminist Legal Theory: Foundations* (Philadelphia: Temple University Press, 1992), pp. 594–602.

Wolf, Naomi, *The Beauty Myth* (London: Chatto and Windus, 1990).

—— *Fire with Fire: The New Female Power and How It Will Change the 21st Century* (London: Chatto and Windus, 1993).

Wollstonecraft, Mary, *A Vindication of the Rights of Woman*, ed. M. Kramnick (Harmondsworth: Penguin, 1982).

Wood, Allen W., *Hegel's Ethical Thought* (Cambridge: Cambridge University Press, 1990).

Zaretsky, Eli, 'Socialism and feminism III: socialist politics and the family', *Socialist Revolution* 4 (Jan.–Mar. 1974), pp. 83–99.

Index